MYTH AND RITUAL IN CHRISTIANITY

MYTH AND RITUAL IN CHRISTIANITY

ALAN W. WATTS

BEACON PRESS   BOSTON

First published as a Beacon Paperback in 1968
by arrangement with Vanguard Press

All rights reserved

Beacon Press books are published under the auspices
of the Unitarian Universalist Association

Printed in the United States of America

International Standard Book Number: 0-8070-1375-7

9   8   7

AD

A A T · R H P · R C A

SACERDOTES IN ECCLESIA DEI

*

MEMENTOTE MOMENTUM

IMMEMORABILE

CONTENTS

ILLUSTRATIONS

Line Drawings and Woodcuts

ILLUSTRATIONS

Halftone Illustrations

Note

All the drawings in this book were executed by the author.

*

Acknowledgements

Thanks are due to the following sources for supplying photographic material: Alinari, Florence (2 and 5); British Museum, London (3); Albertina Collection, Vienna (6); W. F. Mansell, London (7); Kunstmuseum, Basel (8). Plate 4, from *The Celebration of Mass* by Father J. B. O'Connell, is reproduced by permission of Messrs. Burns, Oates and Washbourne, and the Abbot of Prinknash Abbey.

MYTH AND RITUAL IN
CHRISTIANITY

PREFACE

ONE of the special delights of my childhood was to go and see the cases of illuminated manuscripts in the British Museum, and to walk, as every child can, right into their pages—losing myself in an enchanted world of gold, vermilion and cobalt arabesques, of palaces, gardens, landscapes and skies whose colours were indwelt with light as if their sun shone not above but in them. Most marvelous of all were the many manuscripts mysteriously entitled "Books of Hours", since I did not know how one kept hours in a book. Their title-pages and richly ornamented initials showed scenes of times and seasons— ploughing in springtime, formal gardens bright in summer with heraldic roses, autumn harvesting, and logging in winter snow under clear, cold skies seen through a filigree screen of black trees. I could only assume that these books were some ancient device for marking the passage of time, and they associated themselves in my mind with sundials in old court-yards upon hot afternoons, with the whirring and booming of clocks in towers, with astrolabes engraved with the mysterious signs of the Zodiac, and—above all—with the slow, cyclic sweep of the sun, moon and stars over my head.

I could see that these books were somehow connected with the wonderful recurrence of interesting seasons with strange names—Advent, Christmas, Epiphany, Lent, Easter, Whit-sun, Trinity, Michaelmas—names which marked the rotation of the calendar, and lent a kind of form and music to the simple succession of days. Under all this was a fascination with time itself, with the fact that the seasons and the heavenly bodies went on and yet round, and that men observed their changes with a ceremony of signs and numbers and bells. I had no sense of the passage of time as a running out of life wherein everything gets later and later, until too late. I had no

I

feeling of it as a going on and on in an ever upward flight to some ultimate consummation. I simply marveled at the way in which it went round, again and again for ever, so that the marking of time seemed to be the proper and wholly absorbing ritual with which one watched over eternity.

Of course the "Books of Hours" contained, not the mysterious hours of time themselves, but the so-called Day Hours of the Breviary, the seasonal ritual of the Work of God whereby, day after day and year after year, the Catholic Church relives the life of Time's redeemer and creator. And this cyclic re-enactment is the surest sign that the Christ-story is not primarily an event which happened some two thousand years ago, but something perennial, both in all time and beyond all time. As the changing miracle of the seasons brightens the mere march of days, so Time itself is delivered from mere inanity by being lived *sub specie aeternitatis*, under the shape of eternity.

In so far, then, as the inner life of Christianity—the contemplation of God—is not just the reverent remembering of a past history, but the recurrent celebration and reliving of a timeless truth, it is possible for us to discuss the Christian story as something much more profound than mere facts which once happened, to give it not only the status of history but also the tremendous dignity of myth, which is "once upon a time" in the sense that it is behind all time.

Yet, in a relatively short book, such a discussion presents a formidable problem of selection, because it is a subject for which our materials and sources are almost too rich and too vast. Thus in the following approach to the Christian story, every reader will discover that important aspects of the theme have been left out or inadequately treated. For the problem is not merely that the materials are so multitudinous; it is also that many of them are so familiar. There is, for example, no point in retelling Bible stories which everyone knows already, or, at least, can easily refer to in the inimitable language of the

Bible itself. There is an immense quantity of material, such as the Graal legends and the miraculous lives of the saints, which might have been included in a book of this kind but which would have blurred the clear outline of the essential narrative upon which Christianity is founded.

In order to discuss that narrative in such a way as to present it clearly without merely rewriting the relevant parts of the Bible, and, at the same time, to bring out its profound mytho/logical significance, it seemed best to describe it in terms of liturgy rather than history. For the most part, then, this book will assume that the reader has a general knowledge of the Old and New Testament narratives, and, like a Missal or Book of Hours, will present Christianity as the ritual reliving of the Christ/story through the seasonal cycle of the ecclesi/astical year. This has the special advantage of being the form in which Christianity is actually lived, today as yesterday, enabling us to study it as a living organism rather than a dead fossil. Furthermore, it is the perfect form in which to discuss Christianity as a process for the "redemption of time", the dimension of life which is so strangely problematic for Western man.

Even with these limitations upon the material to be used, the subject is endless. It is not only that Christian liturgy and ritual have been so richly embellished through the centuries with art and architecture, poetry and symbolism. It is also that each single element, each symbol, each image, each figure of speech and action which the liturgy employs is connected with such a wealth of associations, of history, and of mythological parallels, that at every step one is tempted to go off on fascinating digressions which would interfere with the orderly unfolding of the main story. This accounts for a rather considerable use of footnotes in the following pages, and I trust that the reader will take them, not as an annoying apparatus of pedantry, but as hints of the marvelous complexity of branches, twigs, and leaves which spring from a peculiarly fertile Tree of Life.

Because my subject is not a museum piece but a living symbolism which lies at the roots of our present civilization, and is inseparably bound up with our whole philosophy of life, I cannot possibly treat its mythological aspects from a purely "folk-lorist" or anthropological point of view. "Christian mythology" cannot be studied without bringing in its many implications of a theological, metaphysical, and psychological character, so that I do not feel it necessary to apologize for the fact that a book devoted to a particular form of myth and ritual has also the aspect of a philosophical essay.

ALAN W. WATTS

American Academy of Asian Studies,
San Francisco, 1953

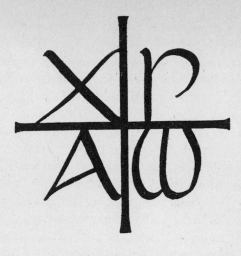

PROLOGUE

A BOOK on Christian Mythology has not, I believe, been written before. There are some sound reasons for this omission, for the subject is one of extreme delicacy and complexity, not because of the actual material, but because the whole problem is, in a very special way, "touchy". There are extreme differences of violently held opinion about Christianity itself—both as to what it is, and as to whether or not it is a "good thing". Similarly, there are rather wide differences as to the nature and value of Mythology, which has only quite recently become a subject of serious study. But when one takes the two together, one is doing something best expressed by the colloquialism "sticking one's neck out"—and sticking it out very far.

To begin with, what is Christianity? On this matter there is no common agreement. Does it consist of the teaching of Jesus, or of the teachings of the Church *about* Jesus, or of both, and, if so, whose versions of the teachings of Jesus, and which Church? There is simply no way of making a decision on these questions so as to please everyone. Furthermore, because all Western peoples are so closely involved with the Christian

5

tradition, it is quite impossible to be "scientifically objective" about it, for we do not stand at a convenient "cultural distance" from Christianity. If one attempts to be objective, one is automatically pigeon-holed with the "liberals" as distinct from the "orthodox", and thus gets into a rut in the very effort to get out of one.

Therefore, in order to get into the subject at all without volumes of preliminary argumentation, a decision must be made, and it will of necessity be somewhat arbitrary. This book starts, then, from the avowedly arbitrary position that "Christianity" is contained in the teachings and traditions of the Catholic Church, both Roman and Eastern Orthodox. Perhaps this decision is not *quite* arbitrary, for the author is neither a Christian nor a Catholic in any "party" sense of these words. The basis for the decision is twofold. On the one hand, the Catholic tradition is both the largest and the oldest Christian tradition, and seems to have had the greatest cultural influence. On the other hand, it is the richest in mythological content.

This brings us to the second problem: what is Mythology? To use this word in its popular sense, and to put it in the same phrase as the word "Christianity" is to invite immediate protest from almost every variety of Christian orthodoxy. For the majority of Catholics and Protestants will insist that everything really important in Christianity is not myth, but history and fact. The orthodoxies do, of course, debate a number of minor, and a smaller number of major, points of factual truth. Protestants, for example, do not agree that the Assumption of the Virgin Mary is an historical event, and Catholics will not insist on the historicity of all the legends about the Wood of the Cross. But debates of this nature will not concern us here, for in this book we are going to treat of the entire body of Catholic tradition without making any distinctions as between fact and fancy. In the sense of the word taken by this book, the whole tradition is "mythological".

For the word "myth" is not to be used here as meaning "untrue" or "unhistorical". Myth is to be defined as a complex of stories—some no doubt fact, and some fantasy—which, for various reasons, human beings regard as demonstrations of the inner meaning of the universe and of human life. Myth is quite different from philosophy in the sense of abstract concepts, for the form of myth is always concrete—consisting of vivid, sensually intelligible, narratives, images, rites, ceremonies, and symbols. A great deal of myth may therefore be based on historical events, but not all such events acquire the mythic character. No one has based any type of cult or religion upon the undoubted fact that Dr. Samuel Johnson drank immoderate quantities of tea. For this fact is regarded as unedifying and trivial, despite its actually infinite consequences, and despite the philosophical position that any and every fact embodies the entire mystery of the universe.

Alles Vergängliche
Ist nur ein Gleichnis.

Even such a momentous fact as the discovery of printing by Gutenberg has acquired no mythological significance, for it lacks those special qualities which fire the imagination, which demand of the human mind that it recognize a revelation of the meaning behind the world.

This definition of myth is probably clear enough, even though many specialists in mythology may not altogether agree with it. The problem is much less clear when we come to consider how and why certain events, legends, or symbols acquire the status of myth. Still deeper is the problem of what, if anything, these myths "really mean". I do not believe that we are anywhere near to a full understanding of the processes governing the formation of myth, of the *rationale* whereby the human mind selects some narratives as mythic in significance and others as simply historical or merely inconsequential. These processes are very largely unconscious. Only quite rarely do people, upon hearing or witnessing a narrative, say, "This is obviously mythical because it clearly symbolizes our philosophical views about the meaning of the universe." For many people who have myths have nothing very much in the way of philosophical views.

Moreover, many stories which become mythical bear no label which marks them as such. It is otherwise with the Christian stories, for the priests and prophets who first uttered them said, "Thus saith the Lord", and felt sincerely that they were not inventing idle tales but were in receipt of divine revelations—and there is no doubt that Jesus himself actually claimed some type of divine origin or affinity. But a great number of hero and fairy tales bear no such obvious stamp. In general, however, it would be safe to say that they are received as mythical because their events have a miraculous or "numinous" quality which marks them as special, queer, out of the ordinary, and therefore representative of the powers or Power behind the world.

But it is not at all easy to say why, at certain times, certain of these uncommon narratives, certain images and symbols, seem to embody the "world-feeling" of immense numbers of people and to exercise such a compulsive and moving quality that men have the sense that life itself depends on their repetition and re-enactment. Why, for instance, was the mind of Western man captured by the Christ-myth rather than the story of Mithras? How is it that myths lose their power, and that, after flourishing for centuries in Egypt and passing over into Roman civilization, the myth of Isis and Osiris did not live on in Western Europe? How is it, however, that the myth which becomes dominant retains some of the characteristics of the myth that wanes, that there are certain important resemblances between Osiris and Christ, Isis and the Virgin Mother?

This, of course, is inseparably bound up with the problem of what myths "really mean"—this is, if they *do* mean something and are not just "natural growths" like flowers and fish.

Perhaps myths come out of the human mind in the same way that hair comes out of the human head. Now there have been many fashions of opinion among those who claim to interpret myths scientifically. Anthropologists of the era and school of Sir James Frazer inclined to the view that the significance of myths was either astronomical, vegetative, or sexual—a view that still carries a great deal of weight. Myths were held to be naïve explanations of the behaviour of the heavenly bodies, of the mysterious forces governing the growth of plants, crops, and cattle, or of the entrancing powers behind sexual love and generation. With the development of more sophisticated theological and philosophical ideas, these explanations under⁄went transformations which frequently involved a change of the mystery being explained—as the mind of man conceived the powers in question to be more than the sun, the crops, and the feeling of love themselves. In other words, the actual stories remained, but their meanings as well as the names of their central characters were changed to fit more mature ways of thinking.

While this theory probably accounts for some myths, there are several ways in which it is unsatisfactory. The older generation of anthropologists were always apt to see "early" or "primitive" man in terms of the assumption that intelligence began with the Greeks and reached a fulfilment in Western Europe—in comparison with which all other cultures were in relative darkness and superstition. They therefore invented an idea of "primitive man" as a being whose total intelligence was supposed to consist in some rudimentary fumblings towards the kind of wisdom monopolized by Western civilization. Hardly dreaming that there are other—and highly developed—types of intelligence and wisdom, as well as different life⁄goals, than those contemplated by Western man, these anthropologists found only what their prejudices enabled them to see. Their premise was that their own culture as the "latest" in time represented the height of evolution. Earlier cultures must therefore be elementary forms of "modern" culture, and their degree of civilization and intelligence had to be estimated by the degree to which their values approximated to modern values.

Thus we still speak of certain peoples as "primitive" and "backward" because they do not care to rush about the earth at immense speeds, to accumulate more possessions than they can possibly enjoy, to annihilate all peace and silence of the mind with an incessant stream of verbiage from newspaper or radio, or to live like sardines in the din and the fumes of great cities. It seems to have escaped our imagination that evolution and progress have occurred in quite other directions than these. In short, these so-called early and primitive cultures were not so stupid as we like to think, and their mythologies may have had purposes quite other than attempts to solve the special problems in which our own science is interested.

We should therefore consider two other theories of myth, the first of which derives from the researches of the Swiss psychologist Carl Gustav Jung. Stated simply, his theory is that myth originates in dream and spontaneous fantasy, rather than in any deliberate attempt to explain anything. This is based on the discovery that the dreams and free fantasies of thousands of modern patients contain the same motifs, patterns, and images as ancient mythologies, and that very frequently they arise without any previous knowledge of these ancient materials. For this Jung has an explanation which is much more simple and direct than his terminology suggests at first acquaintance. His theory of the origination of myth in the Collective Unconscious sounds highly speculative and "mystical", for which reason it is unpopular among lovers of scientific objectivity.

For the Collective Unconscious is not some kind of trans-cendental ghost permeating all human beings. Consider the human body. At all times and in all places it assumes the same general shape and structure, and it does not surprise us in the least that men born today in New York have the same bone-formation as men born four thousand years ago in Mohenjo-daro. Furthermore, the bone-formation, as well as the complex structure of respiration, circulation, digestion, and the entire nervous-system, was not designed by us consciously. It just grows, and we have only the vaguest notions of *how* it grows. And the physical structure of a physio-chemist grows neither more nor less efficiently than that of an illiterate peasant. Thus the material form of man is collective in the sense of common to all men, since men—by definition—are creatures which have just this form. The process by which this form develops is unconscious—and thus the Collective Unconscious is simply a name for this process which is both unconscious and common to all men.

Extreme differences in the human form are largely the result of some conscious interference with this process, as when Ubangi women stretch their lips around wooden disks. But when one leaves the shaping of the body to the unconscious process, a body grown in Africa remains in all general respects just like a body grown in America. Assuming that thoughts, feelings, ideas, and images are either parts of the human body, or functions thereof, or at least activities shaped by the same process—one would expect to find the same collective or common character when thoughts and images are allowed to develop without conscious interference, as in dreams and spontaneous fantasy. This would give us an explanation both reasonable and simple for the fact that myths "dreamed up" five thousand years ago in Chaldea are in essential respects like those found three thousand years later in Mexico or today in London or Los Angeles.[1]

If Jung's theory is correct, does it tell us anything about the significance of myth? Jung believes that he has very strong

[1] One can account in the same way for the common character of logical thinking. It is evident to both a Greek philosopher and an Indian pandit that two and two make four because the structure of the brain is common to both.

evidence for the fact that dreams and fantasies are symptoms of the directions being taken by unconscious psychological processes. In other words, they enable a psychiatrist to diagnose a psychological condition of health or disease in the same way that feeling the pulse, making a blood-count, or taking a urinalysis enables a physician to test the general health of the body. From this comes a further idea of immense importance.

So far as bodily health is concerned, we estimate "health" by a collective or normal standard. That is to say, a man is healthy if his unconscious physical processes work without special interference, enabling him to survive without undue pain to the greatest age which seems attainable by any large number of human beings. Furthermore, the healing work of a physician is usually a matter of *helping* unconscious processes of the body to accomplish a resistance to disease in which they are *already* engaged—with immense ingenuity. Not unreasonably, Jung has transposed this into psychological terms. He believes that the psychiatrist heals most effectively when he helps mental processes which are similarly unconscious, formative, healing, and common to all men. This has led him to trust and respect the "wisdom" of the psychological Unconscious, just as physicians trust the ingenious wisdom of the body.

What is particularly interesting for our purposes, however, is his contention that the dreams and fantasies of psychologically healthy people tend to resemble the general form of those great collective myths which underlie the spiritual and religious traditions of the race. For example, he finds that in the final stages of psychological healing patients will dream or produce in fantasy the image of a quartered circle or *mandala* under an enormous variety of particular forms. Strangely enough, mythological traditions as widely different as the Christian and the Buddhist use types of this circle or *mandala* image to represent their different notions of fulfilment—famous instances of the Christian *mandala* being the rose-windows in Gothic cathedrals and the vision of God in Dante's *Paradiso*.

The general implication of Jung's theory is, then, that the great collective myths in some way represent the healing and formative work of man's unconscious psychological processes, which he must learn to trust, respect, and aid in his conscious thought and action. With a few changes in terminology, there is nothing in this theory which should be objectionable to a Christian of almost any variety. I have stated the theory in its most "physical" form, but since no one has now any very clear notions as to what physical or material things are, or whether such words mean anything at all, it would not be stretching things too far to equate the "wisdom" of the Unconscious with the inspiration of the Holy Spirit—always provided that we are not too cocksure as to what the Holy Spirit may have in mind. "For my thoughts are not your thoughts, neither are your ways my ways, saith the Lord. For as the heavens are higher than the earth, so are my ways higher than your ways, and my thoughts than your thoughts." (*Isa.* 55: 8–9.)

Jung's theory of myth is useful and highly suggestive so far as it goes, particularly in its explanation of the way in which myths are actually formed. Yet it leaves something to be desired in its actual interpretation of the symbols of myth, for the final "meaning" which emerges is a life-theory, a psychological philosophy, which is Jung's own personal hypothesis, despite the fact that it contains a number of universal and time-honoured elements. I feel that a still deeper light has been thrown upon the whole nature of myth by one of the most learned and universal-minded scholars of our time—the late Ananda Coomaraswamy, for many years curator of the Boston Museum of Fine Arts.

Coomaraswamy represented an increasingly growing school of mythological and anthropological thought which has outgrown the provincialism of the nineteenth century, and has ceased to equate wisdom, progress, and culture with the peculiar abnormalities and agitations of the modern West. Since *homo sapiens* has probably inhabited this earth for something like a million years, it is rather rash to suppose that culture is a relatively recent phenomenon. Ananda Coomaraswamy has ably shown that extremely sophisticated and profound cultures have existed quite apart from the special types of apparatus which we think essential—such as writing, building in brick or stone, or the employment of machinery. Obviously, such cultures will neither pursue nor attain the life-goals which *we* consider important, but will have other goals out of all relation to the peculiar desires and "goods" of modern man.[1]

Indeed, modern man confesses—in effect—that he has no life-goal. Progress, as he conceives it, is not towards anything save more progress, so that his life is dedicated to the ever more frantic pursuit of a "tomorrow which never comes". Coomaraswamy has pointed out that in this respect our culture is historically abnormal, and the greater part of his work was a vast documentation of the fact that in almost every other culture there has existed a unanimous, common, and perennial philosophy of man's nature and destiny—differing from place to place only in terminology and points of emphasis and technique. This was not philosophy in the current sense of "speculative theory"; it was the love of a wisdom which consisted, not in thoughts and words, but in a state of knowing and being. In such cultures this *philosophia perennis* occupied a central and honoured position, even when any deep interest in it was confined to a minority.[2]

Today we have come to identify philosophy with "thought" —that is, with a vast confusion of verbal opinions—to the extent that we mistake the traditional philosophies of other cultures for the same sort of speculations. Thus we are hardly

---

[1] See especially his *Am I My Brother's Keeper* (New York, 1947), published the same year in London with the title *The Bugbear of Literacy*.

[2] This is Coomaraswamy's view, which I would modify to the point of saying that the *philosophia perennis* certainly exists within our culture, in however an unhonoured position, but that we are not at a sufficient historical distance from our own time to determine its actual influence.

aware of the extreme peculiarity of our own position, and find it difficult to recognize the plain fact that there has otherwise been a single philosophical consensus of universal extent. It has been held by men who report the same insights and teach the same essential doctrine whether living today or six thousand years ago, whether from New Mexico in the Far West or from Japan in the Far East. To the degree that we realize its existence at all, we call it "metaphysics" or "mysticism", but both the insight on which it is founded and the doctrine or the symbols in which it is expressed are so generally misunderstood that "it would hardly be an exaggeration to say that a faithful account of it might well be given in the form of a categorical denial of most of the statements that have been made about it"[1] both by its contemporary critics and by many of its present-day enthusiasts. For amongst both the opinion prevails that "mysticism" is a retreat from the realities of life into a purely subjective frame of mind which is declared to be more real than the plain evidence of our senses.

By way of "categorical denial" I might begin by saying that a traditional "metaphysic" of this kind involves a far more acute awareness of the plain evidence of the senses than is usual, and that, so far from retreating into a subjective and private world of its own, its entire concern is to transcend subjectivity, so that man may "wake up" to the world which is concrete and actual, as distinct from that which is purely abstract and conceptual. Those who undertake this task unanimously report a vision of the world startlingly different from that of the average socially conditioned man—a vision in whose light the business of living and dying, working and eating, ceases to be a problem. It goes on, yes, but it ceases to be the frantic and frustrating pursuit of an ever-receding goal, because of the discovery that time—as ordinarily understood—is an illusion.

[1] I adapt some words which Coomaraswamy used with specific reference to Hinduism, in his *Hinduism and Buddhism* (New York, 1943), p. 8.

One is delivered from the mania of pursuing a future which one does not have.

Yet another consequence of this acute awareness of the real world is the discovery that what has been felt to be one's "self" or "ego" is also an abstraction without reality—a discovery in which the "mystic" oddly joins hands with the scientist who "has never been able to detect any organ called the soul". That which takes the place of the conventional world of time and space, oneself and others, is properly described by negations— "unborn, unoriginated, uncreated, unformed"—because its nature is neither verbal nor conceptual. In brief, the "seers" of this reality are the "disenchanted" and "disillusioned"—those who are able to employ thoughts, ideas, and words without being *spell*-bound and hypnotized by their magic.[1]

Before indicating the connexion of their doctrine with myth, I must briefly summarize its general principles, realizing, however, that the form in which they must for the moment be stated is not that best suited for their comprehension at the present day. The world of conventional, everyday experience appears as a multitude of separate things extended in space and succeeding one another in time. Their existence is always realized by contrast or opposition. That is to say, we realize or

[1] The doctrine of these "knowers of the real" constitutes the central core of three of the great historical religion-philosophies of Asia—Hinduism, Buddhism, and Taoism. In Islam it appears in a sectarian form as the teaching of the Sufis. In Judaism it is found chiefly as the Holy Kabala—a corpus of teaching contained in an early mediaeval work called the *Zohar*, descending, perhaps, from Philo Alexandraeus. In the traditions of Greece it appears, somewhat diluted and confused with other elements, in a line of doctrine which runs from the Orphic mysteries, through Plato, to the Neoplatonists of Alexandria—in particular Plotinus, Proclus, and the Christian Clement. In Christianity itself it exercised a far-reaching influence from the Syrian monk known as Dionysius the Areopagite in the sixth century, through John Scotus Erigena, St. Albert the Great, Meister Eckhart, and John of Ruysbroeck, to Nicolas of Cusa in the fifteenth century. In the Near East and the West, that is to say, in Judaism, Christianity, and Islam, the doctrine has almost always been "at odds" with an official orthodoxy bitterly opposed to its universalism, because of an immature compulsion to believe in the exclusive perfection of one's own "party-religion".

isolate the experience of light by contrast with darkness, pleasure with pain, life with death, good with evil, subject with object. Opposition, duality, is therefore the inevitable condition of this world, however much we may struggle to overcome it, to hold to the pleasant and the good and to reject the painful and the evil—an effort which is of necessity a vicious circle, since without pain pleasure is meaningless. However, this world of opposites is conventional and "seeming"; it is not the real world. For reality is neither multiple, temporal, spatial, nor dual. Figuratively speaking, it is the One rather than the Many. But it appears to be the Many by a process variously described as manifestation, creation by the Word, sacrificial dismemberment, art, play, or illusion—to name but a few of the terms by which the doctrine accounts for the existence of the conventional world.

In sum then, the manifold world of things proceeds from the One and returns to the One, though in actuality it is never at any time other than the One save in play, "art", or seeming. Its coming from and returning to the One, its Alpha and Omega, appears to be a temporal process because the "art" by which it is manifested involves the convention of time. So long as the human mind is enchanted by this "art", it takes the convention for the reality and, in consequence, becomes involved in the tormenting vicious circle of wrestling with the opposites, of the pursuit of pleasure and the flight from pain. But one may be liberated or saved from this everlasting (circular) torment by disenchantment, by seeing through the illusion.

Coomaraswamy has shown that this doctrine is communi-cated in two ways. One is by the more-or-less direct statement of its principles such as I have just given, and such as one finds in the explicit teachings of the "mystical" tradition. The other way is by figurative statement or myth. In some cases myth may have originated in parable or allegory, that is to say by the deliberate composition of "tales of instruction" by teachers of the traditional doctrine. But probably in many more cases the origination of myth is unconscious and spontaneous, in the manner suggested by Jung, but represents the same truth as the doctrine—because it springs from a submerged level of the mind which has never actually been "taken in" by the illusion of the conventional world. This may seem to be a fantastic hypothesis, but surely it is no less fantastic than the common psychoanalytic practice of healing neuroses by following the hints and directions contained in the "wisdom" of dreams. If, as Jung maintains, the dream is the symptom of unconscious but formative processes of the mind which work towards "wholeness" as certain bodily processes work towards health, it should not surprise us that myth "represents" what is also taught in the doctrine of disenchantment—for it could well be that freedom from illusion is the proper health of the mind. The human body is often wiser than the sophisticated doctor, and we might well expect the still more amazing organism of brain and nerves to be wiser than the conventional philosopher and theologian.[1]

Thus while Jung does not go quite so far as Coomaraswamy in equating the content of myth with that *philosophia perennis* which has had its honoured place in almost every culture save our own, his theory of the formation of mythical symbols provides us with a reasonable explanation of the process whereby a wisdom of this type could be divined by the unschooled and unsophisticated folk-mind from which those symbols emerge. Indeed, there are ways in which the symbols express their truth more adequately than the more formal and exact language of the doctrine, for the truth in question is not an idea but a reality-of-experience so fundamental and alive

[1] It is really the most astonishing *hybris* to suppose that the highest wisdom is constituted by the standpoint of conscious reason, for we hardly begin to under-stand the neural processes without which the very simplest act of reasoning is impossible. The entire possibility of logical and scientific thought rests upon a structure which was formed unconsciously, which we do not understand, and cannot manufacture. Should the finger accuse the hand of clumsiness?

that we cannot "pin it down" and know "about it" in exact terms.

An expression that stands for a known thing always remains merely a sign and is never a symbol. . . . Every psychic product, in so far as it is the best possible expression at the moment for a fact as yet unknown or only relatively known, may be regarded as a symbol, provided also that we are prepared to accept the expression as designating something that is only divined and not yet clearly conscious.[1]

Coomaraswamy makes the same point in a slightly different way:

It is one of the prime errors of historical and rational analysis to suppose that the "truth" and "original form" of a legend can be separated from its miraculous elements. It is in the marvels themselves that the truth inheres: "Wonder—for this is no other than the very beginning of philosophy," Plato, *Theatetus* 155O, and in the same way Aristotle, who adds, "So that the lover of myths, which are a compact of wonders, is by the same token a lover of wisdom" (*Metaphysics* 982 B). Myth embodies the nearest approach to absolute truth that can be stated in words.[2]

In this sense the "absolute truth" is not the end-result of rational speculation, but the most central and fundamental, and thus the most real, state of our own being, which is "only divined and not yet clearly conscious".

In a book devoted to a special mythology, as distinct from Mythology in general, there is not space to give any complete argument as to the merits of these two theories—for which the reader must resort to the works of Jung and Coomaraswamy

---

[1] Jung, *Psychological Types* (London and New York, 1933), p. 602.
[2] *Hinduism and Buddhism* (New York, 1943), p. 33, n. 21.

quoted in the course of this book.[1] The argument about the nature of Mythology must now be brought to the same rather arbitrary conclusion as the argument about the nature of Christianity—if this book is *ever* to begin. For it will be impossible in the field of so inexact a science either to please or to convince everybody, and, if pursued rigorously, the whole endeavour will resemble the race between Achilles and the tortoise. The Achilles of scientific scholarship will never catch up with the tortoise of the subject, because it must ever stop to split hairs, and to split split hairs *ad infinitum*.

An entirely different solution to the problem of this book would be to explain the Christian and Catholic mythology in the terms provided by the official doctrine of the Church. I am well aware that a strong argument can be made for this course, for the work of modern Catholic apologists such as von Hügel, Gilson, and Maritain is of the highest intellectual respectability. Yet this course has some overwhelming defects which, I think, will appear sufficiently in the course of this book so that at this point we need only summarize them.

The first is that the Church's official doctrine confuses its own position by trying to include within the myth, the dogma, statements which define the myth—as that the events described therein are historical or metaphysical facts, or that this myth is the only true myth. Now a statement which attempts to

[1] It is my great regret that at the time of writing this book I was unable to consult Jung's recent *magnum opus* on the symbolism of Christianity, the 384-page volume *Aion*, lately published in German. Neither have I been able to obtain access to nearly as many of the obscure writings of Coomaraswamy as I could have wished. Helen Ladd's marvelous bibliography of his works in *Ars Islamica*, vol. 9, 1942, lists no less than 494 books, articles, and reviews from his hand, excluding many more written in the few years before his death. But the problems which confront anyone wishing to make an exhaustive study of his researches are considerable, since he had a "squirrel-like" tendency to bury the best of his knowledge in elaborate footnotes in articles contributed to the most obscure journals—often published in far-off lands.

state something about itself is always a meaningless vicious circle—like trying to think about thought *A* while you are thinking thought *A*! It is thus that, on the authority of the Church or the Bible, one believes that this is the only true authority.

The second is that what I have called the *philosophia perennis* does not have this defect, since the authority of its exponents is always corroborated by others, who speak from the standpoints of entirely different cultures and traditions. The Christian who maintains that, say, the doctrines of the Vedanta or of Mahayana Buddhism are inferior to his own, must not forget that he bases his judgement upon standards which he has acquired from Christianity—so that his conclusion is foregone or, more plainly, prejudiced. It would seem that in the present state of our knowledge of other spiritual traditions than the Christian, there is no further excuse for religious provincialism. This knowledge is now so extensive that it is becoming hard to see how anyone can be considered theologically competent, in the academic sense, unless thoroughly well versed in traditions outside the Christian alone.

The third, and perhaps most important, defect, is that the official doctrines betray a strange anxiety to *prove* the literal factuality of the myth as a basis for *belief*. But this believing in the myth, this anxious clinging to it as fact and certainty, utterly destroys its value and power. A God conceptually defined, a Christ believed in as a factual rock, is at once changed from a creative image to a dead idol. The anxiety to believe is the very opposite of faith, of self-surrender to the truth—whatever it is or may turn out to be. In the *philosophia perennis* there never was any question of belief—of the fervent wish that truth be consoling—not because there is no wish to be consoled, but because of the clear understanding that the human being has emotions and desires of a nature so contra-dictory that they cannot be consoled by *any* truth! Further-more, the truth with which it is concerned is out of all relation to any beliefs or cherished ideas, since it is quite impossible to express it—save mythically or figuratively—in any positive statement. This truth is one which mythology divines but does not define, and any attempt to understand it by treating its statements as if they were of a precise, historical, or scientific character is—if ever there was one— a sin against the light.[1]

There are two—rather understandable—reasons why contemporary theologians, both Catholic and Protestant, close their minds to any interpretation of Christianity in the light of the *philosophia perennis*. One is the fear of a syncretism, of the growth of a "new religion" which will be a hodgepodge of the "best elements" of the existing traditions, a development which has indeed been advocated by people of theosophical inclinations. But because the essential features of the *philosophia perennis* are complete in every great tradition, an arbitrary syncretism of the "best elements" of all would undoubtedly leave out certain vital aspects of doctrine and symbol. By and large, a mythical tradition is not deliberately constructed; like every living thing, it *grows*—and an artificial syncretism would, in comparison, be a lifeless and rigid affair.

The other reason is a fear of the supposed "individualism" and "acosmism" of anything connected with mysticism. This is almost a case of the pot calling the kettle black, for what could be more individualistic than the claim of official Christianity to be the sole truth, or even the best version of the truth? The fact that such claims are made by a group makes them no less individualistic than when they are made by a single person. Such claims are, furthermore, as remote from the mind of any "seer of the Real" as anything could be, for it is transparently clear to him that his individuality is merely conventional, and that it is precisely to the degree that he is no more an individual that he enjoys knowledge of Reality. As

[1] To give the phrase its literal and proper meaning—to miss the point when it is luminously clear.

for "acosmism"—the notion that the whole conventional world is valueless and false—the *philosophia perennis* says no more than that "my kingdom is not of this world". The point is that conventions attain the value of art and beauty only when they are seen to *be* conventions, and are employed from a higher standpoint which is "not of this world". The conventions of time, space, multiplicity, and duality are false *until* they are seen to be conventional, whereafter they are "redeemed" and attain the full dignity of art.[1]

In the pages that follow, our main object will be to describe one of the most incomparably beautiful myths that has ever flowered from the mind of man, or from the unconscious processes which shape it and which are in some sense more than man. We shall not be concerned with how much of the myth is woven out of historical facts, and how much out of fiction—seeing that we have defined myth as any narrative, factual or fanciful, which is taken to signify the inner meaning of life. This is, furthermore, to be a description and not a history of Christian Mythology, which would require a work to itself, since our aim is to show what this flower is, and not how it might have been put together. After description, we shall attempt an interpretation of the myth along the general lines of the *philosophia perennis*, in order to bring out the truly catholic or universal character of the symbols, and to share the delight of discovering a fountain of wisdom in a realm where so many have long ceased to expect anything but a desert of platitudes.

Anyone who has studied Christianity by present-day methods employed in universities and theological schools must accustom himself to a rather unusual perspective in approaching Christianity as a coherent myth. Today,

---

[1] And one might note that the true artist does not rebel against the limitations of his media, but rejoices in the possibilities of how much can be expressed *with* such limitations. The conventions and limitations of art are not abolished, but only changed, when all their possibilities have been exhausted.

Christianity is almost invariably studied as an historical development out of Hebrew and Greek origins. If we were to follow this method, we would have to approach Christian Mythology through preliminary chapters on Babylonian, Egyptian, Hebrew, Assyrian, Persian, Graeco-Roman, Celtic, and Teutonic Mythology. But this kind of historical perspective was not the world-view of the Patristic and Scholastic ages, during which the Christian Myth came to full flower. I wish to describe the myth more or less as it would have appeared to a man living in the golden age of its power, say, the end of the thirteenth century.

For such a man, the centre of history was the appearance of Christ, and all history was read in terms of Christ. That is to say, the Old Testament was read backwards, and regarded as a prefiguring of the Incarnation and the Church. The story of the Creation and the Fall of Man was read and understood in terms, not of primitive Hebrew mythology, but of the highly developed dogma of the Holy Trinity and of the Angelology and Cosmology of St. Dionysius pseudo-Areopagite, St. Augustine, and St. Thomas.[1] Anyone who has visited the great mediaeval cathedrals of Europe or studied the pages of the illuminated manuscripts will have noticed an entire absence of historical realism in the mediaeval mind. The patriarchs and prophets as well as the figures of the New Testament wear the clothes and live in the dwellings characteristic of Western Europe between 900 and 1400. Incidents from the Old and New Testaments are juxtaposed according to the theory of "types", wherein the Tree of Knowledge stands opposite the Tree of the Cross, the Exodus opposite the Resurrection, the assumptions of Enoch and Elijah opposite the Ascension, and so forth. All this goes to show that the primary interest of the mediaeval mind was not so much the

[1] For example, *Genesis* does not say that the serpent who tempted Eve was the fallen angel Lucifer or Satan, nor that the angelic world was created before our world.

history as the symbolism of the Christian story. The Feasts of
the Church in which the faithful relived the events of this
story were not mere historical commemorations, but rather
ways of participating in the rhythm, the very actuality, of the
divine life. Of this life the historical events were the earthly
manifestations, the doing of the will of God on earth as it is—
per omnia saecula saeculorum—through all the ages of ages in
heaven.

A similar shift of perspective must apply to the ordering and
interpretation of the sources of the Christian Myth. A modern
Protestant would base everything on the Bible, but for a
Catholic the primary source of Christian revelation is "Christ-
in-the-Church", or rather the Holy Spirit himself informing
and inspiring the living Body of Christ. This gives rise to the
Catholic principle *lex orandi lex credendi*—the law of worship
is the law of belief. *Lex orandi*, the law of worship, is not mere
liturgical rule; it is the state of the Church *in* worship, which
is to say, in the very act of union with God here and now.
Thus the Church, in this authoritative position, promulgates,
first, the Liturgy. This includes primarily the Mass and the
Six other Sacraments, all of which are held to have been
instituted by Christ himself and thus to embody the earliest
and most basic law of the Christian life. Second in order come
the Holy Scriptures of the Old and New Testaments, and the
Apocrypha, considered to have been written or approved by
the Church in such a way that the authority of scripture derives
from the Church, and not *vice versa*. Third in order come the
Apostles' and the Nicene Creeds, being the Church's official
summary of the essential points taught·in both scripture and
tradition. Fourth in order comes another part of the Liturgy,
the Divine Office, contained in the Breviary and consisting of
the day-to-day worship of the Church outside the Mass
itself—composed of the Psalms with their seasonal antiphons,
the official hymns of the Church, and various lections from the
scriptures and the writings of the Fathers.

These sources, with the special perspective involved in their hierarchical arrangement, give the basic structure of the Christian Myth, and as the bare branches of a tree are filled in with innumerable leaves and flowers, this structure is enfoliated with the vast wealth of symbolism in art and ceremonial, of legend, hagiography, and tradition, to make—as a veritable Tree of Life—one of the most complete and beautiful myths of all time.

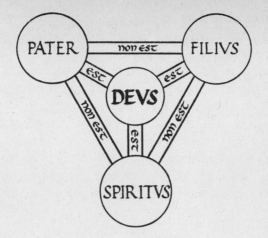

CHAPTER I

In the Beginning

In the beginning was the Word,
And the Word was with God,
And God was the Word.
He was in the beginning with God.[1]

[1] *John* I: I–2. "In the beginning", is *en archē* or *in principio*, the same as the "once upon a time" which begins all folk-tales. Mythology is the representation of the supernatural, the unthinkable and unknowable, in terms of sensible images having spatial and temporal dimensions, apart from which the mind cannot think at all. God is perforce represented as having existed from an everlasting past, from beginningless time. But it is a useful reminder of the relativity of all mythological images to make the following transposition of terms: Refer all references to the *beginning* of time to that which *underlies* time, so that God is not merely first in a series of events but the *ground* or *field* in which the series takes place—not in time but beyond time. Similarly, all references to God or heaven as *above* may be translated *within*—i.e. at the very centre of things, since "the kingdom of heaven is within you". For the myth is the outward and visible sign of the inward and spiritual fact—that is, of the unconscious origin of consciousness, of that which sees and knows, but does not become its own object of sight or knowledge. Myth portrays or divines that which we cannot

FROM all eternity there had always existed One whose secret and unutterable Name was YHVH—the Tetragrammaton of four Hebrew letters—meaning I AM.[1] There was never any time when I AM was not; he was not created by anyone, and before anything else had been created by him he existed alone through endless ages of ages, for which reason he was also known by the name Ancient of Days. In appearance he was pure light—not, however, the created light of the sun, moon, and stars—but Shekinah, the Light of Glory. Because man was subsequently created in the image of I AM, the appearance of his Glory was always considered as having the human form.

> His head and his hair were white like wool,
>   as white as snow;
> and his eyes were as a flame of fire;
> and his feet like unto fine brass, as if
>   they burned in a furnace;
> and his voice as the sound of many waters.
>
> And he had in his right hand seven stars;
> and out of his mouth went a sharp two-edged sword;
> and his countenance was as the sun when it
>   shines in its strength.[2]

comprehend because it is what we *are*. Hence God is I AM, or *Ens*—pure Being. Such a transposition of terms is, however, still mythological, for the notions of *underlying* and *within* are just as much borrowed from sensual, time-and-space imagery as *beginning* and *above*. Thus the philosopher should remember that all so-called metaphysical concepts (a contradiction in terms!) are strictly mythological.

[1] *Exodus* 3: 14. The Hebrew YHVH, perhaps pronounced Yahveh, was for centuries translated I AM, though modern scholars suggest that "I Will Be" is more accurate. But since we are dealing with Catholic and not early Hebrew mythology, we retain the sense in which the Christian mind has always understood it.

[2] *Revelation* 1: 14–16. All quotations from the Bible are based primarily upon the Authorized ("King James") Version because of the beauty of its language. However, at points where the translation is seriously inaccurate or where the language is so archaic as to mislead the modern reader, I have made minor alterations.

This One, then, Adonai, the Lord, El-Elyon, the Most High God, Sabaoth, the Lord of Hosts, had lived for always and always before the time when the worlds were first created. Before there were even any heavens or lights of the day and night, before all spirits and angels, the incalculable centuries and aeons of his life go back for ever and ever, shortened no whit by the fact that a thousand years in our time are but a day in his.[1]

One might imagine that a life stretching through so unthink-able an abyss of time would have been intolerably dull and lonely. Yet dull it was not—by any means—for the whole infinity of space was, as it still is for those who have eyes to see, filled with his radiance—in comparison with which the fire in diamonds and opals, the clarity of the sapphire sky, the splen-dour of sunset, and the light of all stars is just a dim and tawdry glitter. Nor was it lonely. For in some deeply mysterious manner, this One and Only I AM was three Persons, whom we shall discern if we look more intently into his image, and understand the symbolism of the two-edged sword which comes out of his mouth, and the seven stars which he holds in his hand.

The sword which comes out of his mouth is his Word, for "the Word of God is a sharp two-edged sword, piercing to the division of soul and spirit".[2] The seven stars in his hand are his sevenfold Spirit. In God, however, the Word and the Spirit are not mere effluences. They are Persons; and they are as much

---

[1] The very simile of a thousand years being a day in the sight of God is suggestive of the idea—not that time passes *faster* for God than for man—but that from the divine standpoint all the aeons of time are one "timeless Moment". It is a universal feature of the *philosophia perennis* that what we experience as the succession of time is an abstraction rather than a reality, and that the real state of the universe is eternal or timeless—a "moment" without past or future. Hebrew literature is very vague as to numbers, and uses the expression "a thousand" to mean any enormous number, or simply the principle of numerosity. Thus "a thousand days" may be taken as "all days", so that to God—i.e. in reality—all days are one day.

[2] *Hebrews* 4: 12.

persons and as much God himself as the white-haired Ancient of Days whom we must learn to recognize as but one of three Persons, namely, the Father. The other two are the Word, or the Son, and the Holy Spirit.

These three Persons were, then, the one God, and all three had existed together from all eternity, no one coming into being before or after the others. For always and always the Son was being generated or begotten by the Father, and for always and always the Holy Spirit was proceeding from the Father and the Son. Thus from time without beginning, I AM was "the Holy, Blessed (i.e. Happy), and Glorious Trinity, three Persons and one God". For this reason, God was not lonely since he combined within himself not one Person but three, and so constituted a community rather than an individual.

In these most remote beginnings it is difficult for us to make out the proper image of the Trinity, since we are speaking of a time when God the Son had not yet become Jesus the Christ, and when the Holy Spirit had not yet descended in the form of the fiery dove. It is most important to remember that the "only-begotten Son of God" was not *originally* Jesus the Son of Mary, and that before his Incarnation the Son was simply the Word (Logos) and the Wisdom (Sophia) of God—that is, the creative Power by which the world was to be made. To God the Son as the Divine Wisdom, the Church has applied the famous passage *Dominus possedit me* from the *Book of Proverbs*:

> The Lord possessed me in the beginning of his way,
> before his works of old.
> I was set up from everlasting,
> from the beginning, ere ever the earth was.
> When there were no depths, I was brought forth;
> When there were no fountains abounding with water.
> Before the mountains were settled,
> before the hills was I brought forth. . . .

When he prepared the heavens, I was there;
when he set a compass upon the face of the deep;
when he established the clouds above;
when he strengthened the fountains of the deep. . . .
Then I was by him, as one brought up with him;
and I was daily his delight,
playing always before him.[1]

Throughout all those endless ages before the world began, the Son was the object of the Father's love and delight, and the Holy Spirit was the Love that passed between them—so that the Divine Life was an eternal cycle or play of love. *Deus est caritas,* God is love—but love implies relationship, and this relationship is constituted by the Father as the Lover, the Son as the Beloved, and the Holy Spirit as the very Love.[2]

To form some image of the pre-mundane Trinity we must look through the eyes of those icon-painters of the Eastern Orthodox Church who have represented it in the form of three "angels" or winged Beings, and who show God the Son, not as Jesus, but as Sophia—a Being enthroned, crowned and winged, holding a sceptre, and seated in the midst of an aureole of three concentric circles blazing with stars.[3] Or perhaps we may think of it, with Dante, as the radiance of an

[1] *Proverbs* 8: 22–31.

[2] One of the *arcana*, or rather obscure mysteries, of Christian mythology is the fact that the Son as Wisdom, Sophia, is *feminine* and that the Church also applies the above passage from *Proverbs* to the Virgin Mary, since it is used as the Epistle on the Feast of the Immaculate Conception. The great cathedral of Constantinople, Hagia Sophia, is of course dedicated to God the Son under this aspect. We shall have more to say of this hidden feminine side of the Godhead when we come to consider the cult of the Virgin Mother.

[3] The Trinity represented by three "angels" is based on the story in *Genesis* 18 of the appearance of God to Abraham in the form of "three men". A famous icon of this type was painted by Rublev (*c.* 1410) and is now in the Tretyakov Gallery in Moscow. A splendid fifteenth-century icon of Holy Wisdom, as described above, is in the Carnegie Institute at Pittsburgh, the work of the Novgorod School. See *Russian Icons: The Collection of George R. Hahn* (Pittsburgh, 1944), Item 28, and plate.

eye wherein there somehow circulate three irises or rainbow rings, the whole "painted with the effigy of man"—*pinta della nostra effige.*[1]

Even before the creation of the spiritual and material universes, which revealed the extraordinary power and wisdom of the Triune God, his own inner life was so complete that absolutely nothing was lacking to him. He was neither lonely, nor bored. Because he had never at any time been created, he could never cease to be, for he was Being itself—I AM. Thus it was never necessary for him to labour in order to live. He neither suffered, ailed, nor died. He was under no constraint whatsoever to do anything or create anything, because there never had been nor could be any action more perfect nor any object more wonderful than his own existence—which was, furthermore, possessed of the most remarkable properties.

For God did not fill the immeasurable immensity of space by mere largeness. He was neither large nor small, but so filled space that all of him was in every place—except that it was only after the world had been made that anyone realized there were places. This did not mean that God multiplied himself in such a way that one of him was everywhere. There was still just one God, but somehow that entire one was—all of him—simultaneously at every point in space. Rather the same thing was true of the way in which he lived in time, for he had a way of knowing past and future happenings which required neither memory nor foresight. This was the ability to see the past and the future as if they were happening in the present, so that as well as being able to be in all places at once, God was able to know all times at once.

Because of this marvelous relation to space and time, he was all-knowing in the most comprehensive way imaginable. Even before he began to create the world, he was totally and clearly aware of every single, minute hair on the wings of every moth that would ever exist. He was as conscious of every leaf

[1] *Paradiso* xxxiii.

momentarily fluttering in the wind as if he were conscious of nothing else—his mind completely concentrated on every last detail of all things and all events, and on all of them at once—and this without the slightest effort. Thus he was able, with perfect ease, to have in mind not only the details of things but also the combinations of details, the constellations of events, their larger relationships and inner meanings, and so understood the unbelievable network of cause⁄and⁄effect which connects, for example, the cracking of a seed⁄pod with the explosion of a star a million years later.

An even stranger characteristic of his all⁄knowledge was that although he knew everything that would ever happen, this was not at all the same thing as determining everything that would happen. He knew beyond every shadow of doubt all the future deeds of angels and men, but this did not mean that he himself had fore⁄ordained those deeds. They were to be done quite freely and responsibly by the individuals concerned, and yet he knew exactly what they would do.[1]

Marvelous as were these properties of power and knowledge, the Triune God possessed three other attributes at which the Christian tradition has wondered still more—probably because they are still more difficult to explain. They are known

[1] From a strictly metaphysical standpoint, God does not fore⁄ordain anything, since for him there is no future. Thus one must be careful of how the myth is interpreted at this point. Catholic *theology*, as distinct from mythology, insists that free⁄will is the property of the created individual, and is exercised inde⁄ pendently of the will of God. It should be apparent, however, that the concept of individual free⁄will is meaningless, since unmotivated, uncaused, spontaneous action would be something possible only for the First Cause. If, then, the gift of free⁄will to creatures means anything, it means—as every metaphysical doctrine insists—that God gives *himself* to creatures, so that free⁄will is not the property of any creature in so far as he is an individual, but only in so far as the actual reality of his being, his true Self, *is* God and acts as God. To the extent, then, that creatures act freely they are performing what are essentially the actions of God. God himself is therefore the true actor, playing the many parts of the world⁄drama. But the drama is "play", not "reality", and "art" or "seeming" rather than "truth", as is indicated in the passage quoted above from *Proverbs* 8, where the Divine Wisdom is described as "playing".

respectively as holiness, love, and justice. The first is quite the hardest to understand because it is connected in the human mind with the fear of the unknown. For we are afraid when confronted with something which altogether surpasses our experience and comprehension, so that we have not the slightest idea how to deal with it. This fear is not necessarily negative—not just panic or terror; it is rather the feeling of awe, of strangeness, of "the creeps" which come over us in the presence of supernatural events and visitations. It is said, then, that the holiness of God inspires this kind of awesome fear in the saints and angels, giving them a shudder which is at the same time a thrill beyond the most ravishing of sensual pleasures. This is, perhaps, the only way of describing holiness, since it is of the essence of this quality that we do not know what it is, but only what it makes us feel.

Love, as we have seen, was always the predominant relationship between the three Persons of the Trinity, and, when the world had been created, it remained the basic attitude of God to each one of his creatures. Love is said to be the unreserved pouring out, or giving away, of oneself for the good of another. It is that of which *shekinah*, the divine radiance, is primarily the symbol—for as the sun gives its light without reservation, and without asking anything in return, so God "maketh his sun to shine upon the evil and upon the good, and sendeth his rain upon the just and upon the unjust". It was by love, then, that God created the worlds, for when he gave to other things the power of life and existence, he gave them himself. It is for this reason that Dante speaks of God as "the love which moves the sun and other stars". But this love is on no account to be confused with anything sentimental or doting, because it is inseparable from the awe-inspiring quality of holiness, so that "it is a terrible thing to fall into the hands of the living God"—in other words, just to be alive. Thus the love of God inspires a fear, which, if one does not flee from it, becomes a rapture enabling the mind to perceive it as light and splendour. But if this fear becomes panic, if one runs from it, the same radiance becomes the fire which is never quenched and the worm that dieth not, so that the damned who writhe in Hell are burned by the same fire which delights the angels in Heaven.

And then, from beginningless time, God was also justice. At root, justice is the quality of *order*, though of an order dictated by love. Despite the infinite ages of his existence and the inscrutable complexity of his works, God was never fickle or capricious, for "with him there is neither variableness nor shadow of turning". He would never contradict himself; he might always be relied upon to be completely consistent, so that a single, comprehensive, and perfectly logical law characterized all his works. It was by this law of justice that he was subsequently to govern all events whatsoever, so that, for always and always, every effect should have a sufficient cause, and facts—however complicated—should never be selfcontradictory. By no amount of power or ingenuity could the justice of God ever be set aside; one might intend, and even try, to break his law—just as one may try endlessly and fruitlessly to jump out of one's own skin or to draw a square circle.

Such, then, was the "image and likeness" of the Origin from which, in time, all created things were to spring. The tradition insists that there was, however, no necessity for God to create anything apart from himself because the inner life of the Trinity comprised all perfection, lacking nothing. But the superabundance of the divine love was so overflowing that the time came when, quite gratuitously and in total freedom from any constraint, the Holy Trinity created, out of nothing, a vast world of spirits. These were not, as it might seem, a multitude of sparks shaken loose from the central fire; they were not in any sense fragments of God. From beginningless time they were not. And then, by the sudden command of the Word, they appeared—circle upon circle, sphere upon sphere of lesser lights about the Light—points of substantialized nothingness, reflecting in a million ways the central radiance of the Trinity as if they had been great clouds of crystal fragments swirling about the sun.

From the moment of their appearance these spirits—the angels—were startled out of everlasting sleep into the lightning-shock of a direct, unshielded vision of the Glory. To be able to bear the exquisite pleasure-pain of this awakening, they at once protected their eyes with their golden and flaming wings—wings upon which they soared and danced and circled through and all about the Light which gave them birth. At the same instant, all the nine choirs or spheres into which they were divided, burst into the exultant hymn which they have never ceased singing to this day.

"Thou art surrounded by thousands of Archangels and tens of thousands of Angels, by the Cherubim and Seraphim that are six-winged, full of eyes, and soar aloft on their wings, singing, crying, shouting, and saying—

> "*Agios! Agios! Agios! Kyrie Sabaoth!*
> Holy! Holy! Holy! Lord of Hosts!
> Heaven and earth are full of Thy Glory!
> Hosanna in the Highest!"[1]

Now a real angel is not to be confused with the simpering creatures which a decadent Christian art now shows in Church windows and upon Christmas cards. Angels are not blonde girls with silver wings, floating around in white nighties—for "he maketh his angels spirits, and his ministers a flame of fire". The angels are, on the contrary, spirited and fiery, and belong to an order of creatures where there is neither male nor female.[2] They are not, as some have wrongly supposed, the kind of spirits which men become when they die; they are a special and separate order of creatures, immortal

---

[1] *Divine Liturgy of St. John Chrysostom.* Preface and Trisagion.

[2] According to Dom Albert Hammenstede, O.S.B., the noted Benedictine liturgist of Maria Laach, angels are not to be associated with harps and silver trumpets—the proper musical instrument for an angel being the trombone!

from the moment of their creation, and having the double function of enjoying and praising the glory of God, on the one hand, and of ministering between God and the material universe, on the other.

When the angels were created they were divided into nine orders, or choirs, the names of which—in descending rank—are as follows:

1. Cherubim
2. Seraphim
3. Thrones
4. Dominions
5. Authorities
6. Powers
7. Principalities
8. Archangels
9. Angels

The Cherubim and Seraphim are respectively the spirits of divine knowledge and love. The Cherubim are represented as heads only, having two wings—a symbolism appropriate to beings preoccupied with the knowledge of God. The Seraphim, the fiery spirits of love, are six-winged—two wings covering their faces, two covering their feet, and two for flight—and each carries a hexapteryx or fan in the right hand. The Thrones, who actually constitute the Throne upon which the All-Highest takes his seat, are shown as winged wheels.

> The appearance of the wheels and their work was like unto the colour of a beryl: and the four had one likeness: and their appearance and their work was as it were a wheel in the middle of a wheel. When they went, they went upon their four sides: and they turned not when they went. As for their rings, they were so high that they were dreadful; and their rings were full of eyes round about those four.[1]

[1] *Ezekiel* 1: 16–18.

All the members of this first group of three, the highest order of angels, are said to be "full of eyes, before and behind", and sometimes the heads of the Cherubim are described as having four forms—one like a bull, one like a lion, one like an eagle, and one like a man. These are, of course, the four "fixed signs" of the Zodiac—Taurus, Leo, Scorpio, and Aquarius—which later became the symbols of the Four Evangelists.[1]

Tradition has little to say about the next group of three, the Dominions, Authorities, and Powers—perhaps because their function, being mixed, is not so clear, for they stand mid-way between those angels concerned with the contemplation of God and those concerned with ministration to the material world. They are to be represented as clothed in green tunicles or dalmatics, the ecclesiastical vestments proper to Deacons when serving at the altar, beneath which they wear the white alb or chlamys flowing down to the feet, and gathered at the waist with a gold cincture. In their right hands they hold golden staves, and in the left seals inscribed with the X cross —the *Signaculum Dei* or "Seal of God".

The third and lowest group consists of the Principalities, Archangels, and Angels, represented chiefly as warriors equipped with such instruments as spears, axes, and swords, as well as instruments of skill and art such as measuring rods, harps, trumpets, and pipes. As we have said, these angels have the special duties of ministering between God and the material universe. They are the protectors and guardians of the laws of nature, of planets, nations, societies, institutions, and individual men—personifications of the omnipresent power of God, directing and ordering every detail of the world.

[1] Scorpio is interchangeable, in astrological symbolism, with the Eagle or Phoenix, because of the myth which associates both with death and resurrection through fire. The Cherubim are the spiritual prototypes of the Gospel writers, *Evangelists*, because it is through them that men receive the knowledge of Christ, as the Cherubim are concerned with the knowledge of God. In Greek, the word "angel" has the meaning of "messenger", and thus the Gospel is the good (εὐ) angel or message (ἄγγελος).

I. THE CREATOR MEASURING THE WORLD

(From a French "Bible moralisée". Probably Rheims, thirteenth century.)
God is represented in the form of the Christ, who, as the Second Person of the
Trinity, is the Logos "by whom all things were made". He is shown in the
act of "setting his compass upon the face of the deep", since it is by division
and measurement (*māyā*) that distinct "things" are recognized in the
continuum of life.

2. THE CREATION OF THE WORLD

This remarkable Christian *mandala* is a thirteenth-century mosaic upon the vault of the atrium in St. Mark's, Venice. Reading anti-clockwise, the subjects are as follows: *Inmost ring*, (1) The Spirit upon the face of the Waters, (2) the Separation of Day and Night, (3) the Creation of the Firmament, (4) the Division of the Waters, (5) the Trees of Life and Knowledge. *Middle ring*, (1) Creation of the luminaries, (2) of fish and birds, (3) of plants and herbs, (4) of Adam from the dust, (5) the Sabbath, (6) the Spirit breathed into Adam, (7) Adam brought into Eden where the Four Rivers, represented as men, flow from the Two Trees. *Outer ring*, (1) Adam's Dominion over Nature, (2) the Creation of Eve, (3) the Naming of Woman, (4) Adam and Eve in the Garden, (5) the Temptation and Eating of the Fruit, (6) they hide their nakedness with leaves, (7) they hide from God, (8) who discovers them, (9) rebukes them, (10) gives them clothes, and (11) expells them from Eden.

The Principalities are rather remote, in the sense that they govern such vast spheres as natural laws and great areas of the universe. The Christian tradition names only four of the Archangels—Michael, Gabriel, Raphael, and Uriel—and the general function of the Archangels may be surmised from the respective duties of these four. Michael is the messenger of divine judgement, and Gabriel of divine mercy. In the Last Days at the end of the world, Michael is destined to vanquish the Devil and to drive him down to the bottomless pit of fire. And at the final judgement of the living and the dead, it is Michael who holds the terrible scales in which the souls are to be weighed. Gabriel is the messenger of good news, and was thus the Archangel of the Annunciation, who came to the Virgin Mary with the news that she was to be the mother of Christ. Raphael is the angel of healing, the dispenser of divine mercy to the sick, while Uriel, the Fire of God, is the minister of prophecy and of the interpretation of God's will to the minds of men.[1]

The Angels—the generic name for the whole company of spirits being used in particular for the lowest choir—are specially charged with the protection of individual men, each human being having, at birth, a guardian angel assigned to him as minister of divine guidance and guard against the powers of darkness. As the guardian angel is the bearer of divine love and wisdom to each man, so in turn he is the bearer of the individual's prayers to God.

The angels of every order are winged to designate their spiritual nature, as well as the instantaneous manner in which they discharge all their activities. For an angel is where it thinks, and thus any number of angels can stand on the point of a pin because any number of angels can think of the point

[1] Jewish tradition preserves the names of three other Archangels, making seven altogether. These are Chamuel, the Seer of God, Jophiel, the Beauty of God, and Zadkiel, the Justice of God. The names of all seven are Hebrew in form, the final *-el* being the general Hebrew word for a god, a divine being, or of something belonging to God.

of that pin. As thought can move faster than light, jumping instantaneously from earth to the utmost nebulae, so likewise the angels can move from heaven to earth, and from end to end of the universe in almost no time at all. Furthermore, angelic thought is said to be many times faster than human thought because it does not require the cumbersome instrumentality of material images, which take time and effort to form within the mind.[1]

In the beginning, in that first moment of created time in which the angelic choirs were made, the whole of God's creation was perfect in every respect. Because the realm of spirits was, however, finite and creat*ed* it was naturally not as perfect as God himself, yet it was nonetheless as perfect, as godlike, as finite things could possibly be. And in so far as it was godlike, every created spirit was endowed with that most divine of all properties—autonomy, the power of self-direction without compulsion, otherwise known as the freedom of will. Lacking this power, created spirits would have been incapable of the one thing which their Creator wanted them to have, the one thing which so intimately constituted his own essence—the capacity of love. For love exists only when it is given freely, without any duress.

In allowing creatures to possess the divine property of freedom, God was well aware that he had undertaken an immense risk. For if one is free to love, one is also free to hate.

[1] The traditional sources of information about the angels are principally as follows: The Vision of Ezekiel in *Ezekiel* 1, various parts of *Revelation*, the *Book of Tobit* (Raphael), *Esdras* 2 (Uriel), an eleventh-century work entitled the *Hermeneia* by the Greek monk Panselinos, and, most important of all, the *Celestial Hierarchies* of the sixth-century Syrian monk known as St. Dionysius the Areopagite, in Migne's *Patrologia Graeca*, vol. iii. Angels, as their name indicates, are the "messengers" between God and men, though, at the same time, their function is also the contemplation of the Beatific Vision of God himself. In other words, the angels are the "insights" that come into conscious-ness suddenly, giving intimations of hitherto unsuspected levels of reality. "An angel told me" means that I did not think it out by myself, but rather that it came to me all of a sudden.

As soon as freedom is granted, there remains no guarantee of the way in which it may be used. Anything can happen—save the one thing which is impossible by definition, the overthrow of God himself, without whom even freedom cannot be exercised. The God who lent this dangerous gift to his angels knew, by his vision of the future, exactly how they would use it. He knew that the gift would be abused to the limit. He understood vividly, to the last hideous detail, the enormities of wickedness which the bestowal of this gift was to involve. But he knew also that, in spite of the worst that was to happen, the final end which he had in mind would be so splendid as to make the risk entirely justified.

Now among the angels which God had created, there was one so surpassingly beautiful that he was named Lucifer, the Bearer of Light. He is generally thought to have been an Archangel, but some suppose that he must have been much higher in rank—perhaps one of the Cherubim or Seraphim who reflect the immediate and most intense glory of the divine radiance. Since an angel is, like God, aware of himself, one of the first things that Lucifer noticed was the unbelievable grandeur of the being which God had given him. He realized that it would really be impossible for the Almighty to create anything more excellent—that he, Lucifer, was really the crowning triumph of God's handiwork.

He looked again into the heart of the Holy Trinity, and as his gaze went deeper and deeper into that abyss of light he began to share the divine vision of the future. And there, to his complete amazement, he saw that God was preparing a far higher place in heaven, an honour more glorious than the rank of Cherub and Seraph, for creatures who—by comparison with angels—were coarse and crude in the extreme. He saw that he was to be outclassed in the hierarchy of heaven by beings with fleshly and hairy bodies—almost animals. He saw that, of all things, a *woman* was to be his Queen. Far worse than this, he saw that Logos-Sophia, God the Son himself was to become man, and to set one of those "vile bodies" upon the very Throne of Heaven.

At all this Lucifer was at once inflamed with a mystery called Malice. Out of his own heart, by his own choice, by the free and unconstrained exercise of his own will, he preferred his own angelic glory to that of the Divine Purpose—which was to "corrupt itself" with humanity. With all the wisdom and foreknowledge possible to an angel, Lucifer could see at once what his malice would involve. He could see, beyond any power of mortal imagination, the everlasting damnation which must inevitably follow from rebellion against God. He realized quite clearly that such rebellion was, as it were, to throw himself with all his might, for ever and ever, against a wall of adamant. Nevertheless, he considered it more noble to rebel and rebel for ever than to surrender the pride of his angelic dignity, and to pay homage to a Body less luminous and spiritual than his own. He was convinced that God's wisdom had gone astray, that the Creator had forgotten himself, and he determined to have no part in such *lèse majesté*, such an undignified aberration in the otherwise beautiful scheme of creation. Certainly he would have to submit to the utmost wrath, to complete rejection from That which was, after all, the Being of his being. But one thing he need not surrender, the one thing which God had given him as his very own, for all eternity—his own will.

Along with Lucifer, there were many other angels who felt the same way—according to one authority 7,405,998 of them— and all together, with Lucifer at their head, they turned their backs upon the Beatific Vision, flying and falling from the Godhead towards that ever-receding twilight where Being borders upon Nothing, to the Outer Darkness. It was thus that they put themselves in the service of Nothing rather than the service of Being, and so became the nihilists who were to do their utmost to frustrate the creative handiwork of God, and most especially to corrupt the fleshly humanity which he intended to honour. In this manner a whole host of the angels became devils, and their prince became Satan, the Adversary, and Beelzebub, the Lord of Flies.

Yet because God was infinite, because the *shekinah* reached out for ever and ever, the devils found no escape from his light. Turning from it they found it facing them. Above and below, and around on every side, they rushed towards darkness and found—always—the inescapable Light, the hated Love which began to burn them like a raging fire, so that the only escape lay inwards, to the solitary, isolated sanctuary of their own wills. Therefore this place of isolation and solitary confinement, where the light of God torments and gives no gladness, became the place of Satan's dominion, the Kingdom of Hell. Here he ruled over his own angelic hierarchy with its Powers, Principalities, Archangels, and Angels of Night—Mephistopheles, Ashtaroth, Abaddon, Mammon, Asmodeus, and Belphegor.[1]

Something must be said here as to the true nature of angelic evil, since most people are not aware of any greater evils than lust, cruelty, murder, drunkenness, greed, and sloth. From the angelic point of view these "sins of the flesh" are as far from real evil as conventional goodness is removed from true sanctity or holiness. Very few human beings have the courage, the persistence, the very *asceticism* necessary for the perfect service of Satan—which requires that one perform miracles of darkness, as the saints perform miracles of light. From this standpoint, characters such as Jenghiz Khan, the Marquis de Sade, Heinrich Himmler, and Jack the Ripper are mere blunderers. The true Satanist must always have the outward aspect of an angel of light, and will never, under any circumstances, resort to the cruder, violent types of evil. He must be so clever that only an expert in holiness can discern him, for in

[1] Anyone wishing to acquaint himself further with the hierarchy of Hell might consult de Givry's *Witchcraft, Magic and Alchemy* (London, 1931), esp. Chapters 1, 2, and 10.

this way he may far more effectively mislead the sons of men and please his infernal Master, whose supreme craft lies in Deception, and subtle confusion of the truth.

In some ways the Devil is the most significant character in this whole story, for nowhere but in Catholic Christianity do we find a real Power of Darkness. The Satan of Judaism and Islam is rather an angel ministering the wrath of God; the Asuras of Hinduism and Buddhism are simply dark aspects of the divine, which is in itself beyond good and evil. One of the special distinctions of Christianity is that it takes evil more seriously than any other religion. While not allowing the Principle of Evil the rank of equal and opposite to the Principle of Good, as in pure dualism, it insists that evil is in no sense whatsoever of divine origin. It takes its rise exclusively from the finite, created world, but at the same time constitutes an appalling danger of eternal consequence—which God permits but does not condone. The true Christian is, therefore, unceasingly on his guard against this dread reality, and, for all his faith in God, walks through life with the sense that living is a real adventure because it contains a real danger of infinite subtlety and horror. "Brethren, be sober, be vigilant, for your Adversary the Devil, as a roaring lion, walketh about seeking whom he may devour; whom resist, steadfast in the faith." These are the opening words of Compline, the regular prayer of the Church which, day after day, brings the work of worship to its close for the night.

A Christianity without the Devil is, then, lacking in something which is of the essence of the Christian consciousness. It is true that in the Middle Ages the Devil of popular mystery plays became a sort of buffoon, and that as time went on his horns and cloven feet, borrowed from Pan, provoked more mirth than terror. But in a more serious mood the Christian mind conceives Lucifer not as an ugly old goat-man but as an angel of dark beauty and deceptive glory—a supernatural, psychic entity which plots against our welfare with a cleverness far beyond the range of the most intricate human intellect. Against this Power no amount of purely human effort or good will is of the slightest avail, for the most heroic man made holiness is so easily netted in its own pride, and confused by its self interested motivation. Against the wiles of an archangel the only protection is the Grace of God.

This conception, so marvelously peculiar and sinister, brings into sharp contrast the Christian sense of the goodness of God. For what the Christian consciousness sees in all the trappings of glory, of *shekinah*, of the blinding radiance of the Trinity, is not so much beauty, or even truth, as goodness. Beauty has seemed a deceptive attribute, shared alike by God and Satan, who also knows the truth—and trembles. What belongs essentially and exclusively to God is inflexible righteousness, and historical Christianity simply has not tolerated any notion of God as an Absolute "beyond good and evil". Thus the Being of being, the Ultimate Reality, has—for the Christian mentality—a definite character, a specific and particular will, such that goodness does not exist merely in relation to evil but is, from everlasting, the very essence of God. As we shall see, this conception is as monstrous and sinister, in its own way, as that of the Devil. It represents the crucial point at which historical Christianity is "aberrant" among the great traditional doctrines of the world, though the aberration is not so much from any defect of the myth as from the minds of those who have been its official interpreters.[1]

[1] To the extent that myth is a figurative expression not only of the very foundations of human life, but also of unconscious contents of a more superficial character, the orthodox conception of the Devil has its own particular significance, which will be discussed in the following chapter. See further, A. K. Coomaraswamy's article "Who is Satan and Where is Hell?" in *Review of Religion*, xii, 1 (New York, 1947), pp. 76–87, in the course of which he observes, "For anyone who holds that 'God made the world', the question, Why did he permit the existence in it of any evil, or that of the Evil One in whom all evil is personified, is altogether meaningless; one might as well enquire why he did not make a world without dimensions or one without temporal succession."

We must now imagine the purely spiritual light of the Trinity, surrounded by its nine choirs of bright angels, floating over an abyss of dark and formless water—the symbol of the *prima materia*, the elemental substance out of which everything was to be formed.

> In the beginning God created the heaven and the earth.
> And the earth was without form, and void; and darkness was upon the face of the deep.
> And the Spirit of God moved upon the face of the waters.[1]

For the "heaven and earth" which God first created was a formless mass. Before he made anything else he made matter— *materia, matrix, mater*—as the maternal womb of the universe, for it is a general principle in mythology that material is the feminine component and spirit the masculine, their respective symbols being water or earth and air or fire. In the Christian myth every new creation is from water and the Spirit, for out of this conjunction the world is made, the Christ is born, and man is recreated through Baptism. The sacred texts make this symbolism peculiarly vivid:

> The Spirit of God moved upon the face of the waters.[1]

> Who for us men and for our salvation came down from heaven, and was incarnate by the Holy Spirit of the Virgin Mary.[2]

> Except a man be born of water and the Spirit, he cannot enter into the kingdom of God.[3]

> O God, whose Spirit in the very beginning of the world moved over the waters, that even then the

[1] *Genesis* 1: 1-2.   [2] *The Nicene Creed.*   [3] *John* 3: 5.

nature of water might receive the virtue of sanctification. . . . By a secret mixture of thy divine virtue
render this water fruitful for the regeneration of
men, to the end that those who have been sanctified
in the *immaculate womb* of this divine font, being born
again a new creature may come forth a heavenly
offspring.[1]

In the beginning the Spirit conceived, the waters gave birth,
and the world which was born from their conjunction was the
first material image of the Word, of God the Son, the Logos
who was the ideal pattern after which the creation was
modeled. After the world had been corrupted by Satan, the
Spirit conceived again, and that which was born from the
immaculate womb of the Virgin Mother Mary, Star of the Sea,
was the Word himself in human flesh. Yet again the Spirit
conceives, and that which is born again from "the immaculate
womb of this divine font" is a man christened, a member of the
Body of Christ, an *alter Christus*—for "to them gave he power
to become the sons of God".[2]

The story goes on to tell us that when God had created
Prima Materia, Chaos, the Earth Mother, he formed the
universe from her in six days—days, it may be, by divine
reckoning, which are periods of "a thousand years" in the
Hebrew tradition, and 4,320,000 years in the Hindu.

On the first day, he created light, material light which must
be distinguished from the spiritual and uncreated light of the

---

[1] Prayer for the Blessing of the Font, from the Liturgy of Holy Saturday
in the *Roman Missal*.

[2] In the same way the texts of Mahayana Buddhism describe the world of
things as the waves raised on an ocean by the wind. Cf. *Brihadaranyaka
Upanishad*, iii. 6, it is asked, "Since all this world is woven, warp and woof, on
water, upon what is water woven, warp and woof?" And the answer, "On
wind". So also *Chandogya Upanishad*, vii. 10. 1, "It is just water made solid that
is this earth, this atmosphere, this sky, that is gods and men, animals and birds."
The significance of this symbolism will be discussed in ch. III, when we come
to consider the role of the Virgin Mary.

Trinity, as well as from the supernatural light of the angels. At the same time he divided light from darkness and day from night.[1]

On the second day, he created the firmament of Heaven, the colossal dome (or sphere) of brass within the midst of the waters of chaos, so that it divided the upper waters from the nether waters—the waters above the firmament from those below.[2]

On the third day, he created the earth in the very centre of the firmament, and divided it from the waters so that the former became the dry land, and the latter the oceans. And on the under-side of the earth at the Antipodes he created the seven-storey mountain of Purgatory. Within the earth, like a vast funnel reaching down to its very centre, he created the pit of Hell, surrounded with its nine rings of "pockets" or valleys, corresponding to the nine orders of the heavenly choirs above. Into the very depth of this pit he cast Lucifer and his angels, and some say that the mountain of Purgatory was made when the earth itself shrank from the falling Devil.[3] On the same day, he created all trees, plants, flowers, and grasses to bear fruit for men and beasts, and herbs for the healing of diseases.

[1] The important symbol of *division*, of God setting his compass (dividers) upon the face of the deep, is discussed below, ch. III.

[2] Water has a dual role in mythology, for sometimes it is the fountain of life and at other times "the depths" into which one should dread to fall. Thus to fall into the "nether waters" is to regress to a pre-human state, to be swamped by unconscious contents and to lose all rational control. For there are two ways of becoming ego-less or un-self-ish: to descend into the lower waters so that one is not *even* an ego, and to ascend into the upper waters by the increase of consciousness, thus outgrowing the illusion of individual isolation.

[3] The Mediaeval picture of the universe is not quite that of *Genesis*. In the former the firmament was spherical, since it was known that the earth is a globe, but in the latter it is a dome, and the dry land of the earth is divided from the nether waters. The brazen firmament is the Hebrew-Christian equivalent of the World Egg, originally laid by the Divine Bird upon the primaeval waters, as in the Egyptian, Orphic, and Hindu mythologies. It is of interest that the Devil lies at the very centre of the created universe—indicative, perhaps, of the feeling that the individual ego is the true centre of man, since, as we shall see, "I-ness" is what the Devil primarily represents.

FIG. I THE CREATION OF THE ANIMALS
Woodcut from
the *Meditations* of Turrecremata, Rome 1473

On the fourth day, he created the sun, moon, and stars, and set them within seven crystal spheres, within the firmament and around the earth. In the first sphere he set the Moon, as a light for the night, in the second Mercury, in the third Venus, in the fourth the Sun, as a light for the day, in the fifth Mars, in the sixth Jupiter, and in the seventh Saturn. And round and about the outside of the seventh sphere he set the stars of the Zodiac, so that on this day the Sun lay under the Sign of the Ram, where it lies also at Easter, when the world was redeemed by the Sacrifice of the Lamb of God.

On the fifth day, he created all fish and birds.

On the sixth day, he created the beasts of the earth, and, finally, Adam—the man. He formed Adam from the dust and clay of the earth; he made him in his own image, and breathed the breath of his own divine life into his nostrils so that the man became a living soul.[1] He made Adam the ruler of the earth, the head of nature, commanding all beasts, birds, fish, and plants to be subservient to him. One by one, God brought all those creatures into Adam's presence, and to each one Adam gave a name.

On the seventh day, Saturday, the Sabbath, God rested, and rejoiced in the knowledge that everything which he had made was good. According to Clement of Alexandria, the six days of creation and the seventh of rest are to be understood as a kind of simultaneous radiation from a centre.

> There proceed from God, the heart of the world, indefinite extensions—upwards and downwards, to right and left, backward and forward. Looking in these six directions, as at a constant number, he completes the creation of the world, of which he is the beginning and end. In him the six phases of time have their end, and it is from him that they receive their indefinite extension. And that is the secret of the number seven.[2]

For the number seven signifies God himself, the heart or centre of the six rays, sometimes called the Seventh Ray. In other words, in the six days God manifests himself outwardly, but on the seventh he returns back into himself. And this is a day of rest because the heart and centre of God is "unmoved", just as in a wheel the spokes turn but the hub remains fixed.[3]

[1] God's breath (*ruach Adonai*) is the spirit, and is thus God himself residing within the vessel of clay, the two together constituting a living soul (*psyche*, *nefesh*). The symbolism indicates that Adam is the first incarnation and Christ the second, for as Christ is conceived of the Spirit and born of the Virgin Mother, Adam is the creation of the Spirit breathed into virgin matter.

[2] *Stromata*, vi. 16.

[3] What Clement actually describes is the three-dimensional cross, which, when represented on a plane surface appears as the six-pointed star✱, and this, curiously enough, is the earliest form of the Christian monogram for Christ, made by the superimposition of the initials of the Greek name IHCOYC XPICTOC. It is for this reason that symbols of the sun—the astronomical

The tradition maintains that Adam, the primordial man, was the perfect man as God originally designed him. He was physical and yet immortal, and all creatures of the earth obeyed him. The animals served him and the plants fed him, and there was no need for him to labour for his livelihood. He was thus in perfect harmony with his natural surroundings, and constantly aware of the presence of God. For this material image of himself God planted a garden—Eden—in the centre of the world, which was to be the earthly counterpart of Heaven, since all things which were below were to mirror those which were above. In Heaven there is "a pure river of the water of life, clear as crystal, proceeding out of the throne of God. . . . In the midst of the stream of it, and (branching out) on either side of the river, was the tree of life, which bare twelve fruitings, and yielded her fruit every month. And the leaves of the tree were for the healing of the nations."[1] So also in Eden, "The tree of life (was) in the midst of the garden, and the tree of the knowledge of good and evil. And a river went out of Eden to water the garden."[2]

However, Eden was not quite like its heavenly prototype. There was the extra tree, the Tree of Knowledge. Yet this must be taken to represent the same risk which was taken in the creation of the angels with free will. For Adam, too, was endowed with this freedom, and the Tree of Knowledge may perhaps be regarded as a kind of materialization of the negative potentiality within that freedom—the very real possibility that Adam might choose his own will rather than God's. "And the Lord God commanded the man, saying, Of every tree in the garden thou mayest freely eat, but of the Tree of the Knowledge

imago Dei—may be either four- or six-rayed stars, according as to whether the sun is shown in two or three dimensions. Thus the creation of the world in six directions and three dimensions is the primordial crucifixion of the Logos, the slaying of the Lamb at the foundation of the world (*Revelation* 13: 8). Creation is a sacrificial act in the sense that it is God's assumption of finite limitations, whereby the One is—in play but not in reality—dismembered into the Many.

[1] *Revelation* 22: 1–2. [2] *Genesis* 2: 9–10.

of Good and Evil, thou shalt not eat of it, for in the day that thou eatest thereof thou shalt surely die."[1]

After this, the Lord God took another risk. He decided that it was not good for Adam to be alone, for of all the beasts of the field, none was sufficient to be a companion for him. So he put Adam into a deep sleep, and, taking out one of his ribs, fashioned from it the Woman, Eve. In this manner, then, was completed the creation of the First Parents of our race— immortal, free from all conflict and sorrow, innocent, naked, and unashamed.[2]

It was then that Lucifer entered the garden. He assumed the form of a serpent, and entwined himself about the Tree of Knowledge. In due time, Eve came to the part of the garden where the Tree was standing, and there beheld the golden fruit and the splendid snake with shining scales, twisted around the trunk of the Tree. And the Serpent Lucifer murmured to Eve, saying, "Yes? Hath God said, Ye shall not eat of every tree in the garden?" And Eve replied, "We may eat of the fruit of the trees of the garden. But of the fruit of the Tree which is in the midst of the garden, God hath said, Ye shall not eat of it, neither shall ye touch it, lest ye die."

"Ye shall not surely die," answered the Serpent. "For God

---

[1] *Genesis* 2: 16–17.

[2] After "going to sleep" Adam became divided, no longer androgyne, but two-sexed. It was this that made it possible for him to fall. For when God first entered (breathed his spirit into) Adam, the indwelling spirit was "awake" and aware of its proper divinity, of its substantial unity with God. But this putting of Adam into a deep sleep is the Spirit's voluntary self-forgetting—a further extension of the sacrificial character of the creation, as when an actor, playing a part, forgets his proper identity and identifies himself with the *persona* he has assumed. In the actual myth the generation of Eve and the Fall succeed one another, but myth extends in narrative what is simultaneous in reailty. (Note that in Plato's *Symposium* the order is reversed—division into two sexes is the penalty for the fall.) It need not be supposed that this division of man refers to the biological origin of two sexes. In mythology male and female, *yang* and *yin*, signify duality rather than sexuality, and the Fall is the subordination of the human mind to the dualistic predicament in thinking and feeling—to the insoluble conflict between good and evil pleasure and pain, life and death.

knows that in the day ye eat thereof, then your eyes shall be opened, and ye shall be as gods, knowing good and evil." So when Eve saw that the tree was good for food, that it was pleasant to the eyes, and a Tree to be desired in that it would make one wise, she took and ate the fruit, and then went and gave some to Adam, so that he ate as well. At once the eyes of both of them were opened, and they knew that they were naked. In the shame of this discovery they plucked fig-leaves, and, sewing them together, made aprons.

It was, at this time, the cool of the day, and apparently it was God's custom to descend from Heaven at this hour and walk in the garden. Hearing him coming, the pair went and hid themselves amongst the trees, fearing that he would see them in their nakedness. But God called them out of their hiding-place, and, seeing the aprons of fig-leaves, demanded, "Who told thee that thou wast naked? Hast thou eaten of the Tree, whereof I commanded thee that thou shouldst not eat?" And Adam, searching rather desperately for an excuse, replied, "The woman thou gavest to be with me—*she* gave me of the Tree, and I did eat." Whereupon God turned to Eve—"What is this that thou hast done?" "The serpent", she answered, "beguiled me, and I did eat."

Hearing all this, the divine wrath of the Lord God was aroused, and he pronounced a solemn and terrible curse upon the Serpent, and upon Adam and Eve—a curse which affected the whole realm of nature because Adam was its head and lord. He condemned the Serpent to go always upon its belly in the dust, and to be in perpetual enmity with the human race. He condemned Eve, and all her female offspring, to bring forth children in pain and sorrow, and to be subject to her husband. As for Adam, for Adam's sake the Lord God cursed the very earth so that it would no longer bring forth fruit for him without sweat and toil, so that it would bring forth not only fruit but also thorns and thistles. And finally, he pronounced the curse of death and of expulsion from the garden—"For dust thou art, and unto dust thou shalt return. . . . Behold, the man is become as one of us, to know good and evil. And now, lest he put forth his hand and take also of the Tree of Life, and eat, and live for ever. . . ." Without a further word the Lord God expelled the pair from the garden, to till the ground from which they were taken. And at the eastern entrance to the garden, to guard the way to the Tree of Life, he set a Cherub with a sword of fire which turned every way.

From this moment death, suffering, and evil entered the material world—the outward and visible signs of something still worse, of the Fall of the world from Grace, of separation from the divine life of God, incurring the sentence passed upon Lucifer—the sentence of everlasting damnation.

Tradition, not scripture, adds a further word to this story. In the course of time one of the sons of Adam, named Seth, procured a branch of the fatal Tree. Versions of this story differ very much, for some accounts say that Adam himself brought it from Eden when he was expelled, and used it throughout his life for a staff. Others say that what Seth acquired was not a branch of the Tree of Knowledge, but seeds from the Tree of Life, given to him by the angel sentinel.[1] But despite the differing details, the theme is clear—a portion of one of the Trees came out of the garden, and subsequently had a most miraculous history.

It became the famous rod of Moses, which turned into a serpent to confound the Egyptian magicians, with which he divided the waters of the Red Sea so that the children of Israel could flee the hosts of Pharaoh in safety, upon which he hung *nehushtan*, the brazen serpent, so that all who beheld it were delivered from a plague of snakes, and with which he struck the rock in the wilderness so that it gave forth water. It became a beam in the great temple built by Solomon the Wise. It

[1] For the various versions see A. S. Rappoport, *Mediaeval Legends of Christ* (New York, 1935), ch. 11.

3. THE TREE OF JESSE

(British Museum, Nero MS., *c.* twelfth century.) From the phallus of the
recumbent Jesse springs the Tree of Life, with its stem consisting of David,
St. Mary, and the Christ. The many-petaled flower at the top contains the
Dove of the Spirit, and the figures on either side are two prophets, perhaps
Elijah and Isaiah.

4. THE ELEVATION OF THE HOST AT HIGH MASS

Taken in a monastic church, this photograph shows the solemn moment when the Host (the sacred Bread) has been consecrated as the Body of Christ and is raised for adoration. The three monks at the altar are the Priest (standing, and wearing the chasuble), the Deacon (kneeling by the Priest, wearing the dalmatic), and the Subdeacon (kneeling behind the Priest, wearing the humeral veil over the tunicle).

The four monks kneeling to the right of the altar are (left to right) the Thurifer in the act of censing the Host, the Master of Ceremonies, and two acolytes, one of whom is ringing the Sanctus Bell. The two in the foreground are acolytes with candles.

passed, in time, to the carpenter's shop of Joseph, the foster-father of Jesus, and from him it was acquired by Judas the Betrayer, who, in the end, turned it over to the Roman soldiers who used it for the Cross upon which they crucified the Christ—for the Cross which became the Tree of Salvation.

Herein we discover one of those marvelous networks of correspondences which do so much to illumine the sense of the myth. For Eden is not only the mirror of Paradise above: it is also a reflection of Christ, wherein all the events of man's Redemption are seen in reverse. Over against the Tree of Knowledge, from which came death, is the Tree of the Cross, from which came eternal life. The parallel is brought out in the Proper Preface for the Mass at Passiontide:

> Who didst set the salvation of mankind upon the Tree of the Cross, so that whence came death, thence also life might rise again, and that he who by the Tree was vanquisher might also by the Tree be vanquished, through Christ our Lord.

The Theme of the Cross as the true Tree of Life is taken up again in the Mass of the Presanctified on Good Friday—

> *Crux fidelis, inter omnes*
> *Arbor una nobilis:*
> *Nulla silva talem profert*
> *Fronde, flore, germine.*
> *Dulce lignum, dulces clavos,*
> *Dulce pondus sustinet.*

> Faithful Cross, the one Tree noble above all: no forest affords the like of this in leaf, or flower, or seed. Sweet the wood, sweet the nails, sweet the weight it bears.

Over against Adam stands Christ, the Second Adam, for "the first man Adam was made a living soul; the last Adam a quickening spirit."[1] "For as in Adam all die, even so in Christ shall all be made alive."[2] Over against Eve stands Mary, who bore the fruit of Life as against the fruit of death, and the Breviary hymn *Ave, maris stella* plays on the very reversal of Eve's name:

> *Sumens illud Ave*
> *Gabrielis ore,*
> *Funda nos in pace,*
> *Mutans Evae nomen.*

> Receiving that Ave from the mouth of Gabriel,
> establish us in peace, changing the name of Eva.[3]

Opposite the Serpent Lucifer, entwining the Tree, there stands, again, Christ—a type of whom is seen by Christian symbolism in the *nehushtan*—the Serpent of Bronze which Moses hung upon his staff for the healing of the plague, and which was kept for many years in the Ark of the Covenant in the Holy of Holies of Solomon's Temple.

With the Fall of Adam and his expulsion from Eden, the Christian story has stated its problem. It has represented the whole plight of man and of the created universe—the sense that things are not as they should be, that death and pain are imperfections, the sense of separation from the divine, of conflict with nature, of guilt, anxiety, and impotence of will, since "the good that I would, I do not; but the evil which I would not, that I do". From now on the story turns to the extrication of man from the tangle in which Lucifer has involved him, to his Salvation from Death and Hell.

---

[1] 1 *Corinthians* 15: 45.　　　[2] 1 *Corinthians* 15: 22.
[3] Vesper hymn in the Common of Feasts of the B.V.M.

CHAPTER II

God and Satan

BECAUSE the foregoing story is the Christian account both of
the very beginnings of the universe and of the origination of the
great life-problem, evil, we cannot go further without trying to
understand something of the meaning behind the story. For
there really is no more important story in the whole history
of Western civilization. It is not only the genesis of the
Christian myth as such: it is also a clue to the entire mentality
of Western culture, which, for more than fifteen hundred
years, regarded it as the serious and sober account of the
world's origin.

From the start, Christian mythology involves some problems
of interpretation which are hardly found elsewhere. These are
due to the fact that the myth proper contains a large admixture
of theology, which, in the Western world, is a strange confusion of two types of knowledge—metaphysic and science.
Any attempt to describe and interpret the world-view of

Christianity is doomed to hopeless confusion if we do not begin with some distinctions between different types of knowledge—distinctions which have almost entirely escaped the Western mind.

Myth itself is simply a "numinous" story. Theology is an intrusion into the story of certain interpretations and comments, and of morals drawn from the story—as that the story itself is fact in the historical sense, or that the Lord God is the Ultimate Reality in the philosophical or metaphysical sense. The Hebrew Bible does not contain assertions of this nature, but Catholic doctrine most certainly does. To understand what theology has done to the myth, we must first try to see the distinction between the oddly assorted components of theology—science and metaphysic.

It is now generally agreed that science—a legacy of the Greeks—is the knowledge of events, things, or facts, and is thus essentially a history, a record of what has been as a basis for the prediction of what will be. Furthermore, "events" or "things" are parts of experience, of sense-data, which have been isolated, named, and classified by the process of reflective thought which, because it involves memory, perceives certain regularities and orders in the manner wherein experience is presented to us. Thus the language of science consists of positive statements of fact: it is an analysis of past experience.

Metaphysic,[1] on the other hand, is the apprehension of a reality prior to any facts. We have suggested that, of the many valid interpretations of myth, the metaphysical is the most basic. In the words of Joseph Campbell:

[1] The singular form is used to distinguish it from the "metaphysics" of Aristotle, Descartes, Spinoza, Kant, and Hegel, which constitute a viciously circular attempt to make factual statements about that which transcends facts—in other words, to make that which is metaphysical an object of scientific knowledge. In modern Western thought, something of an approach to a true metaphysic may best be found in the "meta-linguistics" of B. L. Whorf and others. See his "Language, Mind, and Reality" in *ETC* (Chicago, Spring 1952).

All mythology, whether of the folk or of the literati, preserves the iconography of a spiritual adventure that men have been accomplishing repeatedly for millennia, and which, whenever it occurs, reveals such constant features that the innumerable mythologies of the world resemble each other as dialects of a single language.[1]

Thus far, however, we have described the nature of metaphysic in somewhat traditional terminology which is peculiarly foreign to the modern mind. But the vast importance of the subject to a proper grasp of mythology requires an attempt to define it in a manner more suited to present ways of thinking. As a "pre-factual" knowledge it is concerned with what we know directly and immediately, as distinct from what we know by reflection, inference, and abstraction. This is not to say that its concern is with uninterpreted sense-data. It is far more fundamental. For the very notion that the foundations of experience are sense-data is already an opinion, an interpretation of experience based upon memory and reflective thought. The word "metaphysic" itself is the clue to its meaning: it is the knowledge of that which is "beyond" (*meta*) "nature" (*physis*)— that is to say, of the way in which we experience before we ascertain the *nature* of our experiences by reflection—by remembering, naming, and classifying. Strictly speaking, then, metaphysic has no language, and its content is incommunicable or ineffable.

In one sense, however, there is no need to communicate metaphysical knowledge because it is already the ground of what every man knows—what he knows before he knows anything else. It is the origin, the *sine qua non*, the basis of all other knowledge. But it is at the same time a neglected knowledge, because the mind is distracted by things that come after—somewhat as considerations about the past and future

[1] In his Foreword to Maya Deren's *Divine Horsemen* (London and New York, 1953), p. 1.

distract us from the immediate present. Therefore metaphysical knowledge is communicated, not by direct description, but by a removal of distractions and obstacles. When these are out of the way, it is possible for the mind to attend one-pointedly to the only reality which it knows, veritably, immediately, now.

Nearly every great culture of the world has held this type of knowledge in the highest esteem, even when it was enjoyed only by an *élite* minority. For knowledge of this kind is the essential corrective, the "balast of sanity", for a species whose chief instrument of adaptation to the world is memory and reflective thought, the power of abstraction. It preserves the human mind from slavery to, as distinct from mastery of, the conventions of thought, and from the anguish and confusion which follow from treating certain abstractions, such as the ego, as realities. It keeps our consciousness in touch with life itself, and preserves it from the emotional frustrations which attend the pursuit of such purely abstract mirages as "pleasure", the "future", or the "good".

A formal metaphysical doctrine—such as the Vedanta and various types of Buddhism—employs, therefore, a negative language in order to convey the realization that reality, life itself, is *not* any fact or thing, since the division of experience into things is a convention of language and thought. One cannot, for example, point to the *difference* between two fingers. One can point to that which is called "fingers" but not to the difference, since the latter is an abstraction. Thus a metaphysical doctrine asserts that the world of reality is *un*differentiated, without, however, meaning that it is numerically one, or uniform. In the same vein, it asserts that reality is eternal, which is to say non-temporal rather than everlasting, since time is a concept, a theory, abstracted from memory. It asserts, too, that this reality is infinite, which means not "boundlessly large" but indefinable. It goes on to say that from this reality all things (i.e. differentiations) are produced out of that which is "no-thing" by the Logos, which is word-and-thought.[1]

These assertions begin to sound like theology; but, from the Christian standpoint, theology does not mean anything of this kind. It seems quite incongruous to use the name "God" to signify *that* which we experience immediately, before thought has sundered it into a world of things. This may be what Hindus mean by "Brahman" and Buddhists by "Tathata" (that-ness), but it is certainly not what the majority of thoughtful Christians have understood as God the Father. The problem arises, however, because the theologians really want to say that God is a fact, a thing—albeit the first fact and the first thing, the Being before all beings. Had it been clear that theology was not speaking of facts, the conflict between theology and natural science could never have arisen. But when, during the era of the Renaissance, this conflict first arose neither the theologians nor the scientists realized that there might have been any profound difference between the languages they were speaking. Theologians and scientists alike understood themselves to be talking about "objective realities", which is to say—things and events. Yet—to add to the confusion—the language of St. Thomas, St. Albert the Great, and St. Bonaventure was *also* metaphysical. They *said* that God was not in the class of things, that he was not an event in time, that he was not a body, that he had no parts or divisions, that he was eternal, infinite, and all the rest. But it is very clear that with some few possible exceptions, such as Eckhart and Erigena, the scholastics were still trying to talk about a thing—a very great thing, beyond and including all other things.[2]

[1] Thus B. L. Whorf has pointed out that for a people, such as the Nootka Indians, whose language contains only verbs and no nouns, the world contains no things: it consists entirely of processes. See *Four Articles on Metalinguistics* (Department of State, Washington, D.C., 1951).

[2] This is clear in the Thomistic identification of God with Being. For the purely metaphysical doctrines of India, as well as for St. Dionysius pseudo-Areopagite (from whom St. Thomas derived more of the words than the

The confusion has its historical roots in the fact that Christian dogma is a blend of Hebrew mythology and history with Greek metaphysic and science, complicated by the fact that Greek metaphysic was never so clearly formulated as Indian, and was always in danger of being identified with highly abstract thought. Indeed, the Western metaphysicians from Aristotle to Hegel have been—above all things—the great abstractionists, the *thinkers*. In this respect they are at the opposite pole from any traditional metaphysic, which is radically empirical and non‑conceptual. It is possible, then, that the Greeks derived a number of metaphysical doctrines from India, but, for the most part, mistook their nature and treated them as concepts— as abstractions which have an objective existence on a "higher plane" than material things! It seems to have escaped the Greek mind that a metaphysical term such as "eternity" is not a concept at all. It is the negation of the concept of time. It involves no positive statement. It merely points out that the notion of reality as extended through past, present, and future is a theory and not a real, first‑hand experience.

As a result, then, Christian dogma combines a mythological story which is for the most part Hebrew, and a group of metaphysical "concepts" which are Greek, and then proceeds to treat both as statements of fact—as information about objec‑ tive realities inhabiting (*a*) the world of history, and (*b*) the "supernatural" world existing parallel to the historical, but on a higher plane. In other words, it talks about mythology and metaphysic in the language of science. The resulting confusion has been so vast, and has so muddled Western thought, that all our current terms, our very language, so partake of the confusion that they can hardly straighten it out. It may, there‑ fore, help the reader if we make a brief summary of the types of knowledge involved.

meaning), the highest Reality is "neither being nor non‑being"—for the simple reason that both "being" and "non‑being" are conceptual abstractions—like thing, spirit, matter, substance, and form.

1. SCIENCE. The record or history of facts, which are the parts of experience designated by nouns and verbs. However, "parts" is already a noun, so that the reality or realities which science discusses remain ultimately undefined.[1]

2. METAPHYSIC. The indefinable basis of knowledge. Metaphysical knowledge or "realization" is an intense clarity of attention to that indefinable and immediate "point" of knowledge which is always "now", and from which all other knowledge is elaborated by reflective thought. A consciousness of "life" in which the mind is not trying to grasp or define what it knows.

3. METAPHYSICS (Greek and Western). Highly abstract thought, dealing with such concepts as being, nature, substance, essence, matter, and form, and treating them as if they were facts on a higher level of objective existence than sensually perceptible things.

4. MYTH. A complex of images or a story, whether factual or fanciful, taken to represent the deepest truths of life, or simply regarded as specially significant for no clearly realized reason.

5. THEOLOGY. An interpretation of combined myth and metaphysics (3), in which both are treated as objective facts of the historical and scientific order.

The Christian account of the primal beginnings, taken simply as myth, is without doubt a marvelous tale, full of magic, poetry, and splendour. The wonderful King of kings who was alive for ever before time began, the creation—out of nothing—of the nine choirs of angels, the dark mystery of the villainous Lucifer, the six days of the making of the world, the First Man in the paradise-garden, Eve, the Serpent, and the Terrible Tree,—all this is as good a tale as ever was told,

[1] Since Hilbert, for example, mathematicians no longer attempt to define a point. Contemporary science more and more accepts the principle that it must work with a number of basic unknowns, signified by undefined terms.

and ranks with the marvels of the *Arabian Nights*, of the *Puranas*, of the *Iliad* and *Odyssey*, of Hans Andersen and Grimm. But—one must hasten to say—this is in no sense leading up to the conclusion that the story should be treated as *mere* poetry or *mere* fairy-tale, having no other function than entertainment.

There is no more telling symptom of the confusion of "modern thought" than the very suggestion that poetry or mythology can be "mere". This arises from the notion that poetry and myth belong to the realm of fancy as distinct from fact, and that since facts equal Truth, myth and poetry have no *serious* content. Yet this is a mistake for which no one is more responsible than the theologians, who, as we have seen, resolutely confounded scientific fact with truth and reality. Having degraded God to a mere "thing", they should not be surprised when scientists doubt the veracity of this "thing"—for the significant reason that it seems an unnecessary and meaning-less hypothesis. (An excellent illustration of the point that "things" are really hypotheses.) Certainly, the poets and myth-makers have little to tell us about facts, for they make no hypotheses. Yet for this very reason they alone have something really important to say; they alone have news of the living world, of reality. By contrast, the historians, the chroniclers, and the analysts of fact record only the news of death. They tell us what, precisely, did happen. And because "life" as we live it goes repetitively round and round—"history repeats itself"—what, precisely, did happen is the best basis for pre-dicting what, precisely, will happen. Such information is, then, the supremely valuable information for those who have no other interest in life than to continue—to keep on keeping on.

Myth does not supply us with facts in the sense, therefore, that it gives us no useful hypotheses for predicting the future—the use of prediction being to continue, to keep on "living". Because, for so many centuries, the theologians have confused eternal life with everlasting life, and salvation with temporal immortality, our culture is utterly hypnotized into the notion that mere continuity, survival, is a good—if not the supreme good. Hence we value practical facts above all other knowledge because, above all else, we need to earn our livings, to adapt ourselves to events, to master the operations of nature, to provide for the future, to benefit posterity . . . to what? Obviously, to keep on going on, to keep on consuming and accumulating, longer and longer, more and more. Convinced that, in this fashion, we are practical, that we are getting somewhere, we do not notice that we are covering the same ground again and again—not because we love the ground so much that we want to return to it, but, on the contrary, because we want to move away from it, to that grass on the other side of the fence which is always greener.

Yet pleasure and pain are relative, and the grass on the other side soon feels like the grass on this side. To retain the sensation of getting somewhere we must soon find yet another pasture and another fence over which to cast our envious glances. It is thus that we feel alive only in terms of the sensation of moving from the less to the more—that is to say, by running *around* faster and faster. The principal reason for this practical madness is that we are not alive at all. We are dead with an immortal, continuing death, which is perhaps what the myth means by everlasting, eternally recurring damnation.[1] And we are dead because each man recognizes himself simply and solely as his past. His "I", his continuity and identity, is nothing but an abstraction from his memory, since what I know of myself is always what I *was*. But this is only tracks and echoes, from which the life has vanished. If the only self which I know is a thing dead and done, a *was*, a "has-been",

[1] By this interpretation the Christian myth of everlasting torture and frustration presents a marvelous parallel to the Greek myth of the punishments of Ixion, Sisyphus, and Tantalus—Ixion bound to the ever-turning wheel, Sisyphus pushing the rock to the hill-top from which it ever rolls down, and Tantalus pursuing the feast which always eludes him.

and I am ever reluctant to admit that I am dead, my only recourse is to work and struggle to give this "has-been" a semblance of life—to make it continue, move, get somewhere. But because it is dead, and has all the fixity and permanence of an unchangeable fact, this "I" can only go on being what it was. Like a machine, it can only repeat itself *ad nauseam*, however fast it may be run.

Thus when the dead man talks, he gives us the facts; he tells all and says nothing. But when the living man talks, he gives us poetry and myth. That is to say, he gives us a word from the unconscious—not from the psychoanalytical garbage-can, but from the living world which is not to be remembered, of which no trace can be found in history, in the record of facts, because it is not yet dead. The world of myth is past, is "once upon a time", in a symbolic sense only—in the sense that it is *behind* us, not as time past is behind us, but as the brain which cannot be seen is behind the eyes which see, as behind memory is that which remembers and cannot *be* remembered. Thus poetry and myth are accounts of the real world which *is*, as distinct from the dead world which *was*, and therefore *will be*. The form of myth is magical and wonderful because the real world is magical and wonderful—in the sense that we cannot pin it down, that we do not understand it because it under-stands us.

For these reasons the significance of myth is totally lost when we try to approach it through factual analysis—whether as "scientific" anthropologists or psychologists or as theologians. Above all things, then, one must refrain from approaching the Christian myth *historically*. It is simply not to be explained by reference to its Babylonian, Egyptian, Hebrew, and Greek antecedents, because they do not explain anything. The explanation of ten o'clock is not to be found in nine, eight, seven, six, five, four, three, two, and one; it is to be found in the moving hand upon the dial. The other and older myths are cited, not as if they themselves in any way explained the Christian myth, but because they illumine it by showing the work of the same hand—the hand which is not behind *in* time, but the hand which is, now, behind time.

The theological analysis destroys the myth in just the same way as the "scientific" analysis, because theology is a pseudo-science—or science a pseudo-theology, I am not sure which. In spite of the vital power of its myth, Christianity began to die in the moment when theologians began to treat the divine story as history—when they mistook the story of God, of the Creation, and the Fall for a record of facts in the historical past. For the past goes ever back and back into nothing; it never leads to its Creator, to its explanation—at least, not in the backward direction. For the past is the creation, the empty echo, of the Now. Time does not flow forward from a Creator who *made* the world; it flows backwards, like the tail of a comet, from a Creator who *makes* the world, and whom no one can remember.

And here we discover the reason why God has to be conceived in the human image—or rather, in the image of the human mind. It is not simply that we know of nothing higher than the human mind in the scale of evolution, so that every other image of God would be inferior to our own. The deeper reason is that the mind, in its unknown depths, is our point of contact with that real "world" which escapes all definition. Elsewhere we behold that world superficially, from the outside, through our senses. But in the mind we *are*, and feel from the inside, the reality which elsewhere seems only a foreign "object". Through our senses reality appears as a known, but in the mind it is a knowing. Upon the outside, reality can be plastered with labels, giving us the illusion that we know what it is. But the mind, the source and origin of consciousness, always escapes the label. It is too close to be accessible, and thus can never be made into an object or thing.

It is at this point, then, that we find what the myth calls "God", or what the metaphysical doctrines call the eternal and infinite. This is the realm from which myth and poetry speak to us. It is immensely important to distinguish this from any kind of "subjective idealism" or psychologism. In saying that God is the knowing but ever-unknowable "ground" or source of the mind, we are not saying that reality is "mental" or "subjective". On the contrary, that reality which we apprehend subjectively as mind is also what we know objectively as "things". It is both subjective and objective, or better, neither subjective nor objective. In the mind—as minds—we are that which, otherwise, we only see. It is simply the point of most intimate contact with reality, and all the pride of knowledge is put to confusion by the fact that at the point where we feel reality most intimately we understand it least.

For I never know my "own" act of knowing. I do not understand how it is done. I did not create the mechanism by which it functions. It goes on as independently of any volition or control on my part as the clouds moving above my head, or the atoms vibrating in the stones at my feet. I have to admit, then, that it is meaningless to say that *I* do it, or that *I* know. "It" does it; "it" knows. And this "it", whether as the ground of the mind or as the indefinable basis of what our senses perceive as structures and "things", is that which articulates the myths, just as it articulates the shapes of trees, the structure of the nervous system, and every other process beyond our so-called conscious control.[1]

The myth is revelation, consisting of "the mighty acts of God", because myth wells up spontaneously within the mind

---

[1] Though I use the word "it", I do not wish to imply the singular number, or any notion of a sort of uniform "stuff" out of which all things are made. For that which is truly indefinable escapes every concept whatsoever. In the words of St. Dionysius, the father of all Christian metaphysic, "We say that he (God) is neither a soul, nor a mind, nor an object of knowledge . . . neither is he reason, nor thought, nor is he utterable or knowable; neither is he number, order, greatness, littleness, equality, inequality, likeness, nor unlikeness; neither does he stand or move, nor is he quiescent; neither has he power, nor is power, nor light; neither does he live, nor is life; neither is he being, nor everlastingness, nor time, . . . nor wisdom, nor one, nor oneness, nor divinity, nor goodness, . . . nor any other thing known to us." *Theologia Mystica*, V.

according to the same involuntary processes which shape the brain itself, the foetus within the womb, and the molecular pattern of the elements. For myth is the complex of images eventually assumed by all involuntary imagination, since, left to itself, imagination takes on a structure in the same manner as the body and the brain. Thus with their fascinating unanimity the myths tell us that the world proceeds out of the invisible and the unknown by articulation, by the power of the Word or Logos, which is "God of God, Light of Light, true God of true God, begotten not made, being of one substance with the Father; by whom (i.e. the Word) all things were made."[1]

So, too, Hindu mythology maintains that everything was called into being by *Vak*, which is speech, or *shabda*, sound. Indeed, the Hindus insist that the roots of their sacred language, Sanskrit, are not merely the roots of verbs and nouns, but the roots of things themselves, which come into being by the utterance of the primordial words. In the Chinese tradition the formative principle of the world is called *Tao*, which originally meant "speech", the creative power of the Great Ultimate (*t'ai chi*) which is represented by an empty circle. Obviously, it is impossible for the mind to recognize any things or structures in its experience without the ability to number and to name—prior to which the "objective" world is simply that Chaos or *prima materia*, which God created in the beginning of time. One must suppose that, for instance, to a cat there is not any thing to be known as a field, containing another distinct thing to be known as a tree. The field is just a state where life becomes green, and the tree where it goes up in such a fashion that a dog cannot follow. Before logic, before the recognition of orders in experience through name and number, there is no thought and thus no things, and it is not by chance that there is an etymological relation between *thing* and *think*, as between the equivalent Latin words *res* and *reor*, German *Ding* and *denken*, the Greek *rhema* and *rheo*.

[1] *The Nicene Creed.*

Thus "primitive" thought is not so primitive as one might suppose in perceiving a mysterious identity between things and their names—a perception which underlies the Hebrew restrictions against the utterance of YHVH, the Name of God. The convention is equally preserved in modern society, where a man who is not classified, who has no name or belongs to no nation, does not legally exist. In the same way, modern logical philosophy often takes the position that a term without logical meaning cannot correspond to any physical reality. Thus the term "God" is illogical in so far as it is predicated of "all" things, as in the sentence "All things were made by God", for in strict logic that which is predicated of everything is predicated of nothing. It follows, then, that if "God" has no logical meaning, no God exists—a conclusion highly disturbing to theologians so long as they insist upon God as a fact, which exists, as distinct from the mythical symbol of a metaphysical reality, a no-thing, having neither existence nor non-existence.

The moment, then, that the theologians started to explain God, they began to lose all contact with him. They treated the language of myth as the language of fact. They rationalized God, and degraded him to the level of a dead, fixed thing— dead because all things are past, inhabiting only the world of memory. Almost from its earliest beginnings Christian orthodoxy began to insist on the scientific rather than the metaphysical or mythical interpretation of the divine revelation. This was largely due to the fact that during the era in which Christianity arose, both the Hebrew and Graeco-Roman cultures were much preoccupied with a craving for salvation in terms of individual immortality. Both cultures had developed in such a way as to increase that vivid sense of the ego, of individual isolation, which—ever since—has been so peculiarly characteristic of the Western mentality.[1]

---

[1] It is often noted that the earlier forms of both Greek and Hebrew religion almost ignored the problems of an individual survival of death. The places of the departed, the Greek Hades and the Hebrew Sheol, were realms where the

To the extent that the human mind identifies itself with the individual ego, it is confusing its life with its past since the ego is an abstraction from memory. Hence history and facts become more valuable than reality. Because the ego and its values have no real life, the real present becomes empty, and existence a perpetual disappointment, so that man lives on hope and prizes nothing more than continuity. In this general misplacement of value God, too, becomes a fact, a historical entity, since past and fixed facts seem now more real, more certain and sure than anything else.

It is at this point, too, that God is identified with Absolute Goodness, with morality. For goodness, in this sense, is the kind of action which we know by memory and experience, as a matter of fact, to lead to survival. The good can always be recognized because it is simply the abstract name for positive content of memory, and "good action" is the law, the method of returning more and more to the safe ground we have known. Morality is the wisdom of experience, of memory, which cannot tell us how to live, but only how to go on being dead. This is why even St. Paul insists again and again that the Law of Moses cannot give life, that a goodness which is the mere obedience of a precept always presupposes and fosters its own opposite—evil and sin. "For when we were in the flesh (i.e. the world of fact), the motions of sins, which were by the law, did work in our members to bring forth fruit unto death. But now we are delivered from the law, that being dead

dead continued only as shadows and memories. Thus Hades and Sheol were "the past", so that beyond death there was no expectation of any real life for the individual. Early Hebraism distinguished between *nefesh*, the individual soul, and *ruach*, the spirit, which God had originally breathed into Adam. At death the body returned to the dust, the *nefesh* to Sheol, but the *ruach*, being essentially divine, was reabsorbed in God. See *Ecclesiastes* 12: 7. It was not until some two centuries before Christ that the Hebrew mind became concerned with individual immortality, conceived not merely as the survival of the *nefesh*, but as resurrection, in which the body was restored as well as the soul. Even while Christ was alive, however, the powerful sect of the Sadducees was opposed to the resurrection doctrine.

wherein we were held, in order that we should serve in newness of spirit, and not in the oldness of the letter."[1]

For in the world of fact and past experience good and evil are as relative to one another as pleasure and pain. The good which we remember is recognized in contrast with the evil which we remember. Without evil good cannot be recognized. Therefore, as the mind ever returns to the good which it has known, it necessarily re-creates the evil—not only because the two are mutually related, but even more because the remembered good is a dead good, breeding evil as its particular corruption. The good which is *not* in relation to evil is always a grace unsought, a gift unsolicited, for—as with happiness—the act of reaching for it pushes it away. Naturally, however, the mind which is ever seeking more and more of the remembered good does not *intend* to re-create the evil. For such a mind is self-deceived, confusing itself with its past, its life with its death, and thus does not realize that it condemns itself to action in a mechanical repetitive circle. When, therefore, such a mind conceives its rationalized, moralistic God, this God must of necessity be accompanied by a Devil whom he *does not intend* to create. Furthermore, the whole art of this Devil will lie in deception, and the whole problem of evil will be lost in unfathomable mystery. For the origination of evil is a problem and a mystery because man identifies himself with his past, and does not realize it.

Yet a myth is an extraordinarily difficult thing to kill, for it continues to be devastatingly revealing even when one has tampered with it, and changed its form by rationalistic or moralistic interpretation. We have suggested that the Devil is in many ways the most significant figure in the whole Catholic myth, bearing in mind that the Christian Devil is the product of Catholic moral philosophy, working upon the earlier Hebrew myth of the Dark Angel who simply personifies the wrathful aspect of God. For the theological Devil is a

[1] *Romans* 7: 5–6.

symbol which, without any conscious intention, reveals the whole confusion of the mentality which produced it.

The story of the Fall of Adam foreshadows what the later myth of the Fall of Lucifer makes vividly clear—that the mentality which produces them is one increasingly confused by self-consciousness. No sooner do Adam and Eve eat the fruit of the Tree than they become painfully aware of their nakedness; the shame and the awkwardness of the self-conscious mentality is here revealed in its beginnings. With the Fall of Lucifer this predicament has become far more appalling. The theological myth states that Lucifer fell because he loved himself more than God, because he became infatuated with his own created beauty. Consequently the essence of all malice is equated with love of self, as distinct from love of God.

But the confusion of the self-conscious mentality is its failure to see that it is not really self-conscious at all. It is a mentality baffled by what is, in itself, the marvelous and indispensable gift of memory. Upon memory rest all the achievements of human culture. Yet it is not really so surprising that the human memory should be a source of confusion—for the very reason that it is so clear, so sensitive, and so retentive that it can create the most persuasive illusions of reality. To the extent that they are recognized *as* illusions, memory serves us well—just as the mirror serves us well when we do not confuse the reflection with the thing reflected. But when what is remembered is mistaken for what *is*, for reality, we are as confused as if we were trying to drive a car looking *only* into the rear-vision mirror.

For theology there is, then, a very deep mystery in Lucifer's origination of evil. The Christian consciousness cannot understand Lucifer's mistake because it is making the same mistake itself. It *thinks* that it is self-conscious, and that it can commit the evil of self-love. But in actuality the "self" which we know and love is not the self at all. It is the trace, the echo, of the self in memory, from which all life, all selfhood, departs in the moment that we become aware of it. Self-consciousness is thus a feat as impossible as kissing one's own lips.

So long as this mistake remains undetected, the mind is condemned to wander in a veritable maze of illusions and shams. Even in its most heroic efforts to be genuine and honest it is self-deceived, and this comes out nowhere more clearly than in the urgency with which the Christian consciousness struggles to repent and to be truly contrite—to transform its own will. For the self which we perceive in memory and take for our own is always a liar, and nowhere more so than when it says that it is a liar. The reason is simply that self-conscious-ness is itself a lie, a deception, in that it is not true. When, therefore, the penitent says, "I am a sinner", his statement is as problematic as the famous paradox of Eubulides, "I am lying"—a statement which is false if it is true. The problem in the "I am lying" paradox is that one is trying to make a state-ment about the statement one is making—which is impossible. Similarly one cannot think about the thought one is thinking, or know the self which is knowing. The mind falls for this kind of nonsense only because memory provides the convincing illusion of achieving the impossible. Thus the Christian peni-tent is always tormented by his inability to repent honestly—to achieve a contrition which is genuine, and which does not have the same motivation as the sin. Perpetually he finds that his will mocks him with masks, that the honest act of the will has a dishonest intent, for ever and for ever in an exasperating infinite regression.

Thus it is not at all surprising that the Christianity mentality is profoundly haunted by the Devil, for it finds the Liar everywhere—even in admitting the lie. No one is more acutely aware of his sinfulness than the Christian saint, because he realizes that he is proud of his humility—and worse, proud because subtle enough to realize that he is proud. Obviously, then, the Devil is credited with an almost infinite intelligence for subtle falsification, whereas in truth this is not subtlety at all, but merely the endless maze of confusion resulting from an unperceived mistake.

In the end we must face the inevitable conclusion that the most deceptive of all the masks of the Liar is the very figure of the absolutely righteous God. Not infrequently, Christians have had the uncomfortable intuition that the theological God is a monster and a bore. Men are commanded to forgive the offences of their brethren even when they are repeated until "seventy times seven", but God does not forgive one offence save on the condition that you repent and grovel. Men are taught that it is an evil to do good works in order to be praised, but the moralists' God demands to be praised for ever and ever. Men are taught that the very essence of evil lies in egotism and selfishness, but the Lord is entitled to bluster, "I am the Lord, and there is none else! Me only shalt thou serve!" and is, furthermore, said to have been occupied from all eternity with nothing but the love and contemplation of his own excellence. Granting even that the excellence of God is such that it is a "which than which there is no whicher", so that there is nothing more admirable to contemplate, even for God himself, the whole concept is profoundly monstrous unless there can be one redeeming condition.

This condition is that God may remain eternally surprised at himself, eternally a mystery to himself, so that he is genuinely amazed at his own glory, so that he does not know how he manages to be God. "Let not your left hand know what your right hand doeth." Only this will free God from the vicious circle of the great lie. God is only lovable if he is not pretending to be self-conscious—to be impossible. Fortunately, the purely mythological God fulfils this condition. He creates the world, and then—surprise!—sees that it is good. But in devising the theological God, the theologians let their logic run away with their sanity. God had to be omnipotent and omniscient, and so it seemed illogical that he should not have the most absolute knowledge and control of himself. Yet, after all, it was at this point that their logic crashed along with their sanity. If God has to control himself, he is not God. If he has to know, to illumine, himself, he is not light. And a God who does not perform the contradiction of knowing himself as an object is still omniscient, knowing all *things*, since he himself is not in the class of things.[1]

As we have seen, the myth of necessity reveals God in the human image—since no higher image is available. But the image of God is always modified by the kind of man, the type of mentality, in whose terms it is cast. Thus the image of the Christian God is in terms of the Western and Christian mentality—a type of human consciousness which is to an extraordinary degree "split" into "I" and "me". Three of the greatest moulders of Christianity—St. Paul, St. Augustine, and Martin Luther—were aware of the problems and contradictions of self-consciousness almost to the point of torment, and yet never perceived the underlying fallacy upon which the illusion is based.

As a result Christianity has not been able to deliver the Western world from the split-mindedness, the schizophrenia, which renders it such a danger to human culture as a whole, the more so since it is equipped with immense technological power. On the contrary, Christianity has been expounded by an orthodox hierarchy which has consistently degraded the myth to a science and a history, and resisted the metaphysical interpretation which other great orthodox traditions have always allowed. Thus "theologized", the myth is unable to

---

[1] It does seem strange that, to the best of my knowledge, theologians have overlooked this point, in view of their handling of analogous problems relating to the divine omnipotence. When asked, "Could God make himself cease to exist?" they have always replied that the question is nonsense, in that it asks whether Being could be the same as Nothing. The same reply—that the question is nonsense—should have been given to the question, "Does God, or can God, know himself?" The failure to give the same answer is, of course, due to the fact that the theologians thought that they knew themselves.

liberate Western man from history, from the fatal circle of a past which repeats itself faster and faster, from a life which loses all touch with reality in its increasing absorption in the arid fantasies of abstraction. For the living God has become the abstract God, and cannot deliver his creatures from the disease with which he is himself afflicted.

Though the human being is an organism which exists only in terms of a marvelously intricate and intimate relationship with its social and natural environment, the Western conscious-ness feels itself to exist primarily as the ego—a dissociated island of awareness, detached from the very body which it inhabits, let alone the environment. It follows, then, that the Western God is likewise a discarnate ego—a detached *soul*[1]— existing in total separation from the physical universe just as Western man feels himself to be separate from his own body.

Furthermore the division of the human mind into "I" and "me" presents the problem of self-control in such a way as to lead to endless confusion—since the human being tries to dominate and regulate his emotions and actions, which are concrete, with the force of an ego and will, which is purely abstract. As a result, man is thrown into a state of conflict with himself which can never be resolved in the terms in which it is proposed. Good-intentioned "I" wrestles with wayward "me" like a rider on an unbroken horse. "I keep under my body, and bring it into subjection; lest that by any means, when I have preached to others, I myself should be a cast-

[1] Primitive Christianity (St. Paul) had a trichotomous conception of man's nature, such that he was held to consist not only of body (*soma*) and soul (*psyche, nefesh*), but also of spirit (*pneuma, ruach*). It is very clear that spirit was something of a supra-individual nature—a divine element transcending the ego. With the development of Christian theology the distinction between soul and spirit was virtually obliterated, so that as spirit became identified with soul the whole supernatural order became identified with the merely psychic—i.e. the world of things existing on a higher level or in a more subtle state than material bodies. The conception of God underwent the same degradation. God became naturalized, and fell from the rank of a metaphysical reality to that of a psychic being, a cosmic ego.

away."[1] But this conflict between "I" and "me" is not so much a self-consciousness as an unconsciousness—a failure to see that the righteousness of "I" has the same motivation as the sinfulness of "me", both alike being attempts to save, to continue, myself—the illusory abstraction from memory.

This conflict is reflected in the irreconcilable war between God and Satan, where the absolutely righteous God is, after all, the final mask of the Devil—just as the "good" motives of "I" are a disguising of the "selfish" motives of "me". The myth itself contains a number of strong hints as to the ultimate identity of God and Satan, but this is the one thing to which the theological interpretation is most resolutely opposed—because it coincides with the special blind-spot of the Western mind. For the Christian consciousness has always taken a peculiar delight in judging and condemning, in having a "scape-goat" upon which to vent the full fury of its indignation. Yet this familiar psychological mechanism is easily recognized as the "protest complex", whereby the insincerity of one's motives is conveniently hidden by violent condemnation of the same insincerity in others. Nothing advertizes the inner identity of God and Satan so much as the uncompromising enthusiasm wherewith the partisans of God do battle with their Satanic enemies.

But the myth itself belies the theology. Reconsider the Preface of the Cross from the *Roman Missal*:

> Who didst set the salvation of mankind upon the Tree of the Cross, *so that whence came death, thence also life might rise again*, so that he who by the Tree was vanquisher might also by the Tree be vanquished, through Christ our Lord.

The poison of evil and death comes into the world, into the heart of the First Adam, through the Serpent on the Tree. Healing comes through the Second Adam, Christ crucified

[1] *I Corinthians* 9: 27.

FIG. 2 ENGRAVED GEM FROM AN EARLY CHRISTIAN RING
(After Didron)

on the Tree of the Cross—of which Christian imagery discovers a "type" in *nehushtan;* the brazen serpent which Moses erected in the wilderness so that all who looked upon it were delivered from a plague of serpents. The process is homoeo-pathic—*similia similibus curantur*, likes are healed by likes.[1]

Let us remember, also, the myth which identifies the Wood of the Cross with the staff or beam taken from the Tree of Eden, so that the Cross which is *medicina mundi* is of the same Tree which bore the fruit of knowledge, the poison of death.

Now the serpent-and-tree is a common mythological theme, for one calls to mind not only the World Ash, Yggdrasil, of Norse mythology, with the worm Nidhug at its roots, but more particularly the Kundalini symbolism of Hindu Yoga. One thinks, too, of the Aesculapian symbol of the Caduceus, of the two serpents entwined about the rod—one of poison and the other of healing—a symbol which passed into Christianity

---

[1] The identification of Christ with the *nehushtan*-serpent is based on *John* 3: 14, "As Moses lifted up the serpent in the wilderness, even so must the Son of Man be lifted up." Thus Christian art often employs the motif of the serpent on the cross as an emblem of Christ. See the engraved stone from Gori's *Thes. Diptych.*, vol. iii, p. 160, reproduced also in Lowrie's *Art in the Early Church*, pl. 33a (New York, 1947). Cf. Tertullian, *De Idolatria*, iii; also St. Ambrose, *De Spiritu Sancto*, iii. 9, "Imago enim crucis aereus serpens est: qui proprius erat typus corporis Christi: ut quicunque in eum aspiceret, non periret."

when it was adopted for the bishop's pastoral staff in the Eastern Churches.[1]

In the symbolism of Kundalini-Yoga the "tree" is the human spine considered as a flowering plant. At the top, within the head, is the thousand-petalled lotus *sahasrāra*, emblem of the sun beneath the dome of the firmament, arche-type of the skull, since here as in almost all mythologies man is seen as the universe in miniature. At the root of the spinal-tree, at the sexual organs, there sleeps the serpent Kundalini entwined about the phallus. So long as the serpent remains at the root of the tree, asleep, man is "fallen"; that is to say, his divine consciousness is asleep, involved in the darkness of *māyā*, since at this stage the divine has identified itself with the finite world. But when the divine consciousness awakens, Kundalini ascends the tree and passes up to the thousand-petalled lotus in the head.

Thus the serpent has two roles, which, in Hindu mythology, correspond to the two "movements" in the eternal play (*lila*) of God: the one where God (*Vishnu*) sleeps, and dreams that he is the multiplicity of individual beings, and the other where God awakens and realizes his proper divinity. Downward in the roots, the serpent is the divine One asleep, enchanted by his own spell; upward in the sun-lotus, the serpent is the same divine One disenchanted, free from the illusion that he is divided into many "things". Therefore the dual role of the serpent in Christian mythology might suggest the same idea— that Lucifer and Christ are two distinct operations of the Divine, respectively the "wrath" and the love of God, the

---

[1] See British Museum, *Guide to the Early Christian and Byzantine Antiquities* (London, 1903), p. 87. Possibly the crook-shaped pastoral-staff of the Western Church has a similar origin, for it closely resembles the serpentine *lituus*, or divining-rod, shown in an Etruscan sculpture reproduced in Murray's *Dictionary of Christian Antiquities*, vol. ii, p. 1566—an object which, again, resembles the official "sceptre" or *nyoi* carried by Buddhist abbots in the Far East. One must recollect the story that, as a sign of the power of God, Moses' staff was changed into a serpent to confound the Egyptian magicians.

shadow and light of the world drama. Interpreted in this fashion, the Fall would stand for man's forgetting of his divine nature, for involvement in the illusion of individuality. Salvation would be the recollection (*anamnesis*) of his divinity, the awakening or birth of Godhead in man.

But, as one can only expect, theology will admit nothing of this kind, since it is the product of a mentality still very much under the spell of illusion. Yet, as a result, whole areas of Christian dogma do not make sense, or, at least, sense only of a very tortuous kind. If it is maintained, for example, that the Fall of Adam involves the whole human race, this is only because Adam—Man—is inclusive of each particular man. Contrariwise, there can only be Redemption for the human race if Christ, the Second Adam, is likewise inclusive of each particular man—if the Incarnation of God in the man Jesus is representative of God in every man, as Adam represents Lucifer in every man. Yet, with rare exceptions, the theologians insist that the Godhead is incarnate in one man only—the historical Jesus. This confinement of the Incarnation to a unique event in the historical *past* thus renders the myth "dead" and ineffective for the *present*. For when myth is confused with history, it ceases to apply to man's inner life. Myth is only "revelation" so long as it is a message from heaven—that is, from the timeless and non-historical world—expressing not what *was* true once, but what *is* true always. Thus the Incarnation is without effect or significance for human beings living today if it is mere history; it is a "salvific truth" only if it is perennial, a revelation of a timeless event going on within man always.[1]

[1] This problem will be discussed more fully when we come to the proper part of the story. The orthodox theological explanation of how the race is saved by the Incarnation of God in Christ is peculiarly confused, because the myth was rationalized according to the inadequate categories of Greek philosophy. Thus when God became man, he was held to have united himself with human *nature*, but not with any human *person*, since Christ was human in nature, but divine as to his person. Consequently, God has united himself with the nature of each man, but not with the person of each man. This would make sense if theology would go on to state that the person (*nefesh, psyche*, soul) is not the real

Still more repugnant to the theologians is the perception of the divine in Lucifer, the realization that the two serpents are one—Lucifer in descent and Christ in ascent. The nearest which the Church approaches to anything of this kind is the embarrassing passage which is sung on Holy Saturday at the blessing of the Paschal Candle:

O truly necessary (*certe necessarium*) sin of Adam, which the death of Christ has blotted out. O happy fault (*O felix culpa*), which merited such and so great a Redeemer.

With this one might compare the words of *Isaiah* 45: 7, "I am the Lord and there is none else. I form the light and create the darkness; I make peace and create evil. I, the Lord, do all these things."

The tragedy of Christian history is that it is a consistent failure to draw the life from the Christian myth and unlock its wisdom. This whole failure is epitomized in the problem of Lucifer, who should have remained the symbol, not of "deliberate malice", but of the necessary "dark side" of life, of shadow revealing light by contrast, of darkness as the Light (*luci-*) Bearer (*fer*). He would correspond to what the Chinese call *yin* as distinct from *yang*, the dark, negative, and feminine aspect of life, in complementary opposition to the light, positive, and masculine—the two represented together as the interlocked commas or fish, one black and one white, one ascending and one descending. In the West, this same symbol

man, but only the abstract and illusory man. But it takes the very opposite standpoint, and insists that it is the *psyche* precisely which has to be saved, and since this is that part of man's being which Christ did *not* assume, the salvation of the soul remains an impossibility. Yet the Gospels do not actually propose the salvation of the *psyche*. Cf. *John* 8: 21, "Whither I go, *ye* cannot come", and thus to ascend to heaven man must "deny him-self" (*Mark* 8: 34) because "no man hath ascended up to heaven, but he that came down from heaven, even the Son of Man which is in heaven". (*John* 3: 13.) Similarly, in *Matthew* 16: 25, "Whosoever would save his *psyche* shall lose it"; and in *Luke* 14: 26, "If any man come to me, and hate not . . . his own *psyche* also, he cannot be my disciple."

FIG. 3 DESIGN FROM AN ENGRAVED GEM IN THE BRITISH MUSEUM

(Early Christian) The two birds suggest *Mundaka Upanishad*, 3. 1. 1., "Two birds, fast bound companions, clasp close the self-same tree. Of these two, the one eats sweet fruit; the other looks on without eating." (Trs. Hume.) These birds, in the Hindu figure, are respectively the *jiva* (ego) and the *atman* (true Self), the spirit enchanted and disenchanted.

is found as the zodiacal sign of Pisces, and the two opposed fishes are a common motif of early Christian gems—Christ himself being the ascending fish.[1]

A truly problematic evil arises in human life when the necessary dark side of existence is not accepted and "loved" along with the light—that is, when the human mind sets itself such goals as the total retention of pleasure and the total elimination of pain. Paradoxically, devilish behaviour is the necessary consequence of not coming to terms with Lucifer, of refusing to admit that life is willy-nilly a coincidence of opposites. Thus, in the complex picture of Christian mythology, Lucifer has a double role. He is the necessary negative or

[1] Serpent and fish are often mythological equivalents, being alike legless. The Greek ιχθυς, by a play on the letters, suggested Christ, since each letter would be the initial letters of the phrase ιησους (Jesus) χριστος (Christ) υιος (Son) θεου (of God) σωτηρ (Saviour). But, as Austin Farrer remarks in his *Rebirth of Images*, "The name ιχθυς for Christ was also a play on letters, but it would not have been made unless the result had appeared to mean something." p. 64 n.

dark aspect of life, personifying the "wrath" of God—the dark angel Samma‑el. He is *also* the Liar, the illusion of self‑consciousness and self‑love, personifying the mistake, the missing‑of‑the‑mark,[1] which the human mind has made in confusing its identity with a "self" abstracted from memory. In both roles he is a "disguise" of God. In manifesting a universe of relativity, the metaphysical "absolute", the unde‑fined, appears as the defined, and positive is defined in relation to negative, life in relation to death, light in relation to darkness —God appearing as two‑faced like Janus. In becoming "enchanted" or identified with the abstract and illusory self, that which suffers the enchantment is the ever‑unknown "ground" of the human mind—the *ruach* or *pneuma*—which is always divine in principle, and which never "really" becomes the individual save in seeming, in dream. Thus Lucifer is God seeming to be self‑conscious, to be an ego, an individualized *thing*.

Both these senses of the myth have been missed by Christian theology, so that what is now personified or symbolized by the theological Satan is not one of the aspects of God but the very illusion of "self", in which orthodox Christianity most fervently believes. After all, it is not so surprising that that which it professes to hate most enthusiastically turns out to be identical with the ideal which it tries to love, the monstrously righteous God. Such predicaments are the inevitable penalty for the pursuit of a mirage, or for running after a shadow. For the zeal with which you follow measures the speed with which it eludes your grasp.

In sum, then, the tragedy of Christianity is the confusion of its myth with history and fact. For this is the realm of the abstract and the dead—of the seeming self. Degraded to this realm, Christ and Lucifer alike became images of the ego, of the past and dead man who does not liberate but only binds. For this predicament the myth goes on to offer its own un‑heeded solution.

---

[1] To miss the mark is the original meaning of ἁμαρτάνω, to sin.

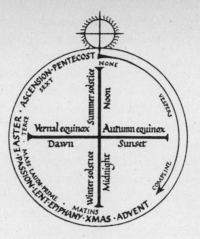

CHAPTER III

Advent

FROM the very beginning, of course, the Lord God had fore-
seen what Lucifer and Adam would do, and that by their
disobedience the whole universe would become subject to
death and corruption. Therefore in the secret counsels of his
wisdom he had already prepared the remedy, which was to
consist in the extraordinary act of descending into his own
creation, becoming himself a creature—man—and, by making
the life and death of created being his own, deliver it from the
curse. For in taking the risk of creating beings with freedom
of action, the Lord God was prepared to suffer the risk himself,
and to experience the whole burden of anguish which it
would involve. This is the real reason for the Christian's
veneration of Christ. It is not simply that he is a great teacher,
wonder-worker, and exemplar, but much rather that Christ is
God himself sharing the fate of his erring creatures.

For the modern Protestant, who begins to learn his religion

from Bible stories, there is a very long interval between the Fall of Adam and the Birth of Christ, because a large part of his religious education consists in learning the story of the *Old Testament*—so much so that there are many respects in which Protestantism is often more of a Hebraism than a Christianity. But in traditional Christianity the religion is learned less from the Bible than from the cycle of the Christian Year, which is a ritual re-living of the life of Christ. Within this cycle the events of the *Old Testament* are interwoven in such a way that they form, not a continuous story, but a system of oracles or prophecies.

From this point of view, history begins with Adam and begins again with Christ, so much so that what happens in between occurs within an epoch of darkness wherein God is known only through "types and shadows". That is to say, the *Old Testament*—the Law of Moses, the Prophets, and the history of Israel—is significant to the Catholic mind only because it is a symbolical foreshadowing of Christ. Thus the *Old Testament* stories enter into the Christian story in so far as they seem appropriate "types" of the various "mysteries" of the life of Christ which are celebrated through the course of the Christian Year. As an excellent example of the way in which the *Old Testament* is used as a source-book of typology, the reader should turn to the Liturgy of Holy Saturday in the *Roman Missal* and go through the section entitled "The Prophecies", noting how both events and actual quotations from the Prophets are used as a prefiguring of the Christian mysteries.[1]

[1] The reader will find it much to his advantage to have a copy of the *Roman Missal* available for reference as he goes through this book. Very inexpensive editions are available, but he should be careful to acquire the *Daily Missal* and not the *Sunday Missal*, since the latter is very much abridged. The *Missal* is divided into the following sections: (1) the Ordinary of the Mass, consisting of the unchanging parts of the Mass which are recited daily; (2) the Proper of the Time, consisting of the parts of the liturgy appropriate to the seasons of the Christian Year; (3) the Proper of the Saints, consisting of the variable parts of the Mass recited on the feasts of the saints; (4) the Common of Saints, consisting

It must be understood that with the Fall of the Angels and of Man the whole created universe of time and space, material and immaterial, became corrupt—so much so that at one period the deeds of men became so evil that the Lord God sent a flood upon the earth which destroyed all except Noah and his family, who floated upon the waters in an Ark built at the commandment of God. For Christianity, the Ark of Noah is naturally a type of the Church—the Nave or Ship of Salvation, wherein men are saved from the Flood of everlasting damnation. However, when God the Son came into the world as Jesus of Nazareth, the universe was redeemed from this curse, and time itself became holy so that the very years are reckoned from his birth—*Anno Domini*, in the Year of the Lord. Furthermore, the seasons of the year are themselves transformed from the pagan Spring, Summer, Autumn, and Winter to the Christian Advent, Christmas, Epiphany, Lent, Passiontide, Easter, and Pentecost.

However, because the sun itself in both its daily and annual course is seen as a type of Christ, the Sun of Justice, the Christian Year is rather significantly integrated with the cycle of the sun. The Christian Year begins about four weeks before Christmas, which coincides approximately with the Winter Solstice—the time when, in the Northern Hemisphere, the sun is at its lowest meridian and is about to begin once more its upward journey to the midheaven. Anciently this time was sometimes known as the Birth of the Sun, being, as it were, the midnight of the year, from which point the sun begins to rise. According to tradition, then, Christ was born at midnight at the Winter Solstice.

of Masses for certain general types of saints rather than particular individuals; (5) Votive Masses for special needs and occasions; (6) Masses for the Dead. The Liturgy of Holy Saturday will be found under (2), the Proper of the Time. It might also be useful to the reader to have available a translation of the *Breviary*. For this purpose I would suggest either *The Short Breviary* (St. John's Abbey, Collegeville, Minn.) or *The Monastic Diurnal* (Oxford University Press, London, 1940).

The Vernal Equinox, corresponding in the daily cycle to sunrise, is the approximate season of Easter, the feast of Christ's Resurrection, the actual day of Easter being the Sunday following the first full moon after the Vernal Equinox. As the sun climbs to the midheaven after the equinox, the Church celebrates—forty days later—the Ascension of Christ into heaven, and in another ten days Pentecost or Whitsunday, the feast of the descent of the Fire of the Holy Spirit upon the Church. The solar symbolism is obvious, except that the Church keeps no seasonal feast at the Summer Solstice, and observes only the course of the sun in its rising. The other half of the year is mostly occupied by the somewhat formless season of "Sundays after Pentecost", which end only at the beginning of Advent, and during which the Church rehearses the ministry and the miracles of Christ upon earth.

Christianity in practice is therefore the annual re-living of the Christ-life, symbol of the union of the Christian with Christ in his birth, his labor, his passion, his resurrection, and his ascension in glory. Other concepts of Christianity-in-practice are post-mythical, being of a rationalized, historical, and moralistic character, and are thus beyond the concern of a study of Christian Mythology. In its Protestant form Christianity is increasingly rationalized, and, with the exception of Christmas and Easter, the Christian Year is almost wholly forgotten.[1] In this conception, Christianity is no longer a symbolical re-living of the Christ-life, but rather an imitation of his character based on a reading of the Gospels as history and biography—to the exclusion of all miraculous and mythological elements.

Thus the Christian Year introduces its presentation of the Christian life with the season of Advent, which, to some extent, corresponds with the "historically" vast period between

---

[1] The story is told of a Scotch Presbyterian minister receiving a letter from a Catholic priest, dated January 17th, St. Anthony's Day, and replying with a letter dated, January 20th, Washing Day.

the Fall of Man and the Birth of Christ. Strictly speaking, Advent has a double theme. It corresponds to the epoch between the Fall and the Incarnation in so far as it is a preparation for Christmas, a season of longing for the appearance of the Redeemer who will save the world from the Fall and its curse. But, by analogy, it looks forward also to the Second Coming of Christ at the end of time, "to judge the living and the dead and the world by fire". For our purposes, however, we must relegate this event to the end of the story, and consider Advent as the season of preparation for Christmas, when the Church casts its mind back to the time before the first Christmas, and shares the longing of the fallen universe for release from its darkness.

> O Dayspring, Brightness of the Light eternal,
> and Sun of Justice, come and enlighten those who
> sit in darkness and the shadow of death.[1]

At such a time, then, it is appropriate to remember the Age of Wandering, as the time between Adam and Christ was called, during which the Lord God raised up a Chosen People to be a type of the Church and to prepare the world by prophecy for the coming of the Saviour. Thus, during the

---

[1] The Great Antiphon, *O Oriens*, sung during Advent at Vespers on December 21st. From the *Breviary*. In addition to the annual "hallowing of time" by means of the Christian Year, there is also a diurnal timehallowing by means of the Hours of Prayer to be found in the *Breviary* as distinct from the *Missal*. This is why the shorter form of the *Breviary*, excluding the nighttime service of Mattins, is often called the *Diurnal* or *Book of Hours*. The Offices or Canonical Hours, as these services of prayer are called, are as follows:

> *Prime*, between 3 and 6 a.m.
> *Lauds*, immediately follows.
> *Terce*, between 6 and 9 a.m.
> *Sext*, between 9 a.m. and Noon.
> *None*, between Noon and 3 p.m.
> *Vespers*, between 3 and 6 p.m.
> *Compline*, about 9 p.m.

second week of Advent, the Mass opens with the words of the prophet:

> People of Sion (Jerusalem), behold the Lord shall come to save the nations; and the Lord shall make the glory of his voice to be heard in the joy of your heart. (*Introit*, from Isaiah 30.)

As the liturgy goes on, the same theme recurs—

> Out of Sion, the loveliness of his beauty, God shall come manifestly. (*Gradual*.)
>
> Arise, O Jerusalem, and stand on high, and behold the joy that cometh to thee from thy God. (*Communio*.)

At the same time the Epistle for the Day, from *Romans*, begins with St. Paul's words on the *Old Testament*: "Whatsoever things were written aforetime were written for our learning, that, through patience and strengthening of the Scriptures, we might have hope." Seeing, then, the entire *Old Testament* as the hope of Christ, the mind of the Church goes back again to the beginning of the world, and calls upon Sophia, the Divine Wisdom, the Word, to reform the universe of which he was at first the ideal form:

> O Wisdom, who came forth out of the mouth of the Most High, and reachest from one end to another, mightily and sweetly ordering all things; come and teach us the way of prudence.[1]

In this light the entire story of the generations of Adam and of the Chosen People, from the Fall through Abraham and Moses to the Return from Babylon, is seen as a rehearsal in shadow-play for the manifestation of Christ. We saw that the very events of the Fall—the Serpent, the Tree, and its Fruit— were the reverse reflection of Christ's Passion. Thus, even

[1] Great Antiphon at Vespers, December 17th.

though they laboured under the darkness of evil, the actions of men and angels could not help but resemble, in however distorted a fashion, the pattern of the Christ-life upon which the universe was originally designed.

The discreditable incident of the two sons of Adam, Cain and Abel, was a prefiguring of the Old Israel and the New. For both sons offered sacrifice to the Lord God, and when Abel's was accepted and Cain's refused, Cain slew his brother as, in a later time, the Jews crucified Christ—so that Cain's unacceptable sacrifice was a type of those ancient offerings of bulls and goats which did not cleanse the Chosen People from sin, while Abel's sacrifice foreshadowed the perfect and acceptable sacrifice of Christ. The mysterious assumption of the patriarch Enoch into heaven prefigured the Ascension of Christ, while Jesus as the High Priest of Heaven was fore-shadowed in the remote figure of Melchizedek, King of Salem, who "brought forth bread and wine" and made offerings to "the most high God".

The patriarch Abraham, as father of the Hebrew people, is a type of God the Father, and his barren wife Sarah who miraculously gave birth to Isaac are respectively types of Mary and Jesus—a symbolism further suggested by Abraham's willingness to offer Isaac as a sacrifice when commanded by God to do so.[1] The twelve sons of Jacob or Israel—grandsons of Abraham—from whom were descended the twelve tribes of Israel, stand for the Twelve Apostles of Christ, from whom the Church is descended.[2]

Much of this typology centers around the whole history of the descent and enslavement of the children of Israel in Egypt, their deliverance by Moses, and their journeying through the wilderness to the Promised Land. The descent into Egypt prefigures both the flight of Joseph and Mary into Egypt to escape from Herod with the child Jesus, and the descent of Christ into Hades after his crucifixion.[3] The Exodus, the

---

[1] *Genesis* 18: 1–16; 22: 1–13.   [2] *Genesis* 35: 16–26.   [3] *Genesis* 46.

deliverance from Egypt, finds Moses in the role of Christ, and represents both the salvation of the human race from the Kingdom of Satan and the Resurrection of Christ from death. In particular this typology centers around the Passover Feast.[1] The Latin term for Easter is *Pascha*, from the Hebrew *Pesach*, the Passover, and the first Passover was the immediate occasion of the deliverance of Israel from Egypt. The sacrifice of Christ is seen in the sacrifice of the paschal lamb, whose blood was spread upon the door-posts of the Israelites to deliver them from the Destroying Angel, who was to slay the sons of the Egyptians. This terrible visitation persuaded the Egyptian king to release the enslaved people, and their miraculous escape across the Red Sea is the figure of Christ's Resurrection.

> *Ad regias Agni dapes,*
> *Stolis amicti candidis,*
> *Post transitum Maris Rubri,*
> *Christo cantamus Principi.*

> At the royal feast of the Lamb,
> clothed in white robes,
> after the crossing of the Red Sea,
> we sing to Christ our Prince.[2]

In general, the wanderings of the children of Israel in the wilderness on their way to the Promised Land, "flowing with milk and honey", are taken as a type of the Church Militant— that is to say, in its long period of struggle between the Resurrection of Christ and his Second Coming, and the final entry into the Promised Land foreshadows the Church Triumphant in its final attainment of Heaven. During their wanderings the Chosen People are guided, in the day, by a pillar of cloud and, at night, by a pillar of fire—symbols of the

---

[1] *Genesis* 11–14. See also my *Easter—Its Story and Meaning* (New York, 1950), ch. 6.
[2] Vesper hymn for Eastertide, from the *Breviary*.

guidance of the Church by God the Holy Spirit. They are refreshed by water from the Rock, which Moses struck with his rod, typifying the sacrament of Baptism. They are fed upon the mysterious Manna, the bread from Heaven, which is the fores:.adowing of the Host, the consecrated Bread of the Mass. They are taught by the Law revealed by God to Moses upon Mount Sinai, and in its turn the Church is taught by the doctrine of Christ delivered in the Sermon on the Mount.[1]

The next great group of typological symbols is connected with David, conqueror of Jerusalem, who unified and stabilized the tribes of Israel as a single kingdom after many years of struggle and strife in their new homeland. As David was the founder of the earthly kingdom of Israel, so Christ is the founder of the heavenly kingdom, the fulfilment of the Hebrew hope for the Messiah who would restore the glories of the days of David. Hence the Christ, as duly prophesied, was born of the line of David in Bethlehem ("House of Bread") where David himself was born.[2] The Father of David was the shepherd Jesse, of whom the prophet said, in a later day,

> There shall come forth a rod out of the stem of Jesse,
> and a branch shall grow out of his roots:
> and the Spirit of the Lord shall rest upon him.[3]

And with an illuminating pun the Church takes up the theme in the *Missal*—

> *Virga Jesse floruit:*
> *Virgo Deum et hominem genuit:*
> *pacem Deus reddidit, in se*
> *reconcilians ima summis.*

---

[1] For the wanderings, see *Exodus* 16–40, *Deuteronomy* 1, 2, 3 and 34. Entry into the Promised Land, *Joshua* 1–5. Incidentally, Joshua, who in the end leads the people into the Promised Land, is the Hebrew form of the Greek name Jesus.

[2] 1 *Samuel* 16: 1–13.   [3] *Isaiah* 11: 1–2.

The verge of Jesse hath blossomed:
A virgin hath brought forth God and man:
God hath restored peace, reconciling
in himself the highest with the lowest.[1]

Naturally, David's victory over the Philistine giant, Goliath, is likened to Christ's triumph over Satan,[2] the fact that he was originally a shepherd-boy makes him a type of the Good Shepherd, his power of healing with music pre- figures Christ the Healer,[3] and his eventual setting up of the Throne of Israel in Jerusalem makes him the type of Christ the King, who reigns enthroned in the New Jerusalem on high.[4]

Other figures and events from the *Old Testament* playing an important part in this scheme of typology may be listed briefly as follows:

TYPE	MYSTERY
The Assumption of Elijah the Prophet;[5]	The Ascension of Christ
The miracles of the Prophet Elisha:	[fishes
The multiplication of the widow's oil[6]	The miracle of loaves and
Raising the Shunamite's son[7]	The raising of Lazarus
Jonah and the Whale[8]	The Death and Resurrection
The deliverance of Shadrach, Meshach, and Abed-nego in the furnace[9]	Salvation from Hell
Susanna and the Elders[10]	Persecution of the Church by the Jews and Pagans
Tobias and the Fish[11]	The Healing Christ

The juxtaposition of the *Old Testament* type and the *New Testament* mystery was always a favourite convention of

---

[1] Annunciation B.V.M. The Alleluia when the Feast is in Paschaltide.
[2] *1 Samuel* 17.
[3] *1 Samuel* 16: 14-23.
[4] *2 Samuel* 5: 6-12. Cf. *Revelation* 3: 12.
[5] *2 Kings* 2: 8-13.
[6] *2 Kings* 4: 1-7.   [7] *2 Kings* 4: 8-37.
[8] *Jonah* 1 and 2.
[9] *Daniel* 3.   [10] *Story of Susanna* (Apoc.)
[11] *Tobit* (Apoc.) 6: 1-8.

Christian art, as when the opposite walls of a nave would be painted with the related scenes from the two *Testaments*. Often they were represented side-by-side in double panels of stained glass, or worked together into the design of initial ornaments in illuminated manuscripts.

A more general typology than this symbolism of particular events was connected with the two great *Old Testament* institutions of Sacrifice and the Law—institutions embodying the promise but not the fact of salvation. In the *Old Testament* the self-offering of man to God represented in the burning of bulls and goats upon the altar was, from the Christian standpoint, an ineffectual shadow of the only offering which can restore human nature to its proper union with God. For the perverted human will cannot make a genuine surrender of itself to the divine will, so that there can be no true sacrifice unless God himself enters into man, and, as man, makes the "full, perfect, and sufficient" sacrifice which was consummated in the death of the God-man upon the Cross. Similarly, the Law given to Moses is one which the human will is incapable of obeying. It serves only to "convict man of sin" by setting a standard to which he fails to attain. Thus in the new covenant of the Christian dispensation the ancient sacrifices are replaced by the Crucifixion, of which the Sacrifice of the Mass is a continuing re-collection,[1] and the Law gives way to the mystery of Grace, the power of God which enables the human will to perform works beyond its own capacity.

Because this long, long epoch of types and shadows embodies the promise, and man's expectation, of a Redeemer, the liturgy of the Advent season refers again and again to "captive Israel", to "the people that walked in darkness", and their

---

[1] *Anamnesis*, usually translated as "memory", "memorial", or "recollection", is no mere reminder of a chronologically past event. Strictly speaking, *anamnesis* is much more than the simple sign of a fact distant (in time) from itself; it is rather the actual "re-collection" of a truth which eternally *is*, so that to recollect the sacrifice of Christ is to make it really and effectively present.

hope of deliverance. This is the theme of the great Advent hymn *Veni Emmanuel*—

> O come, O come, Emmanuel
> And ransom captive Israel,
> Which mourns in lowly exile here,
> Until the Son of God appear.
> Rejoice! Rejoice! Emmanuel
> Shall come to thee, O Israel!

Its words are based on the seventh of the Great Antiphons of Advent, in which the ancient types are repeatedly presented.

> O Adonai, and Leader of the House of Israel, who appeared in the bush to Moses in a flame of fire, and gave him the Law upon Sinai: Come and redeem us with an outstretched arm.[1]

> O Root of Jesse, standing as an ensign for the people, at whom kings shall shut their mouths, unto whom the Nations shall seek: Come and deliver us, and tarry not.[2]

> O Key of David, and Sceptre of the house of Israel; that opens and no man shuts, and shuts and no man opens: Come, and bring the captives out of prison, those that sit in darkness and in the shadow of death.[3]

> O King of Nations, and their Desire; the Cornerstone, who makest both one: Come and save mankind, whom thou hast formed of clay.[4]

[1] Vesper antiphon for December 18th.

[2] December 19th. The root, stem, rod, or verge of Jesse, the father of David, whose flowering is the birth of Christ, is another form of the Tree of Life, and is associated with the Virgin Mary whose family tree is traced back to Jesse.

[3] December 20th. The Key of David is the type of the "keys of the kingdom" later entrusted to St. Peter, who, as supreme representative of the priestly office, is charged with the binding and loosing of souls, with giving and withholding absolution from sin.

[4] December 22nd. The "Cornerstone, who makest both one" is a particularly

Because the final reference of the "once upon a time" of the myth is to that "time behind time" encountered in the depths of our consciousness, there is a particular significance to the Advent theme of "captive Israel". Its understanding is the necessary introduction to the miraculous Coming of Christ, whether we are considering the First Advent from the Virgin's womb or the Second Advent "in the clouds of heaven". A proverb says that "man's extremity is God's opportunity", suggesting that the necessary condition for a miracle is a state of *impasse* which only a miracle can solve. The Coming of Christ is associated with a number of striking symbols of the impossible: the rod blossoms, the virgin bears a son, and he "whom the heaven of heavens cannot contain" is found within the womb.

> Wonder beyond time's wonders—
> Eternity shut in a span,
> Summer in winter,
> Day in night,
> Heaven on earth,
> And God in man.

In short, the Coming of Christ is out of all continuity with anything that happened before. It is a complete reversal of the order of cause and effect, of the determination of the present by the past, since he comes to birth out of all relation with the continuity of human generation—having no father.

For the redemption of captive Israel, liberation from Hades, the forgiveness of sins, release from the self-love of Lucifer, from the "Old Adam", and from the bondage of "Egypt" and

interesting symbol of the divine as the "reconciling principle" in which the "pairs of opposites" are transcended. The symbol is widespread, and is found in China as the *tai ch'i*, the Great Ultimate—literally, the Great Ridgepole—underlying and uniting *yang* and *yin*, the positive and negative principles. See A. K. Coomaraswamy's article "Eckstein", in *Speculum*, vol. xiv (1939), pp. 66–72.

"Babylon" is in every respect a deliverance from the *past*. Salvation is always the ending of the mind's fascinated identification with the dead and unchanging image of what it was. It is a complete reversal of the "natural" order of things, a *metanoia*—the Greek word for "repentance" meaning precisely a "turningaroundofthemind", so that it no longer faces into the past, the land of the shadow of death, but into the Eternal Present.

So long as the mind is captivated by memory, and really feels itself to be that past image—which is "I"—it can do nothing to save itself; its sacrifices are of no avail, and its Law gives no life. For it is under the spell of death, identified with an impotent abstraction so that, in the language of symbolism, it is "formed of clay", or wandering in the wilderness, in "a dry and barren land where no water is". And under this spell it remains, hopelessly and helplessly captive, just so long as this dead image continues to give any illusion of life, so long as one thinks or feels that "I" is able to do anything in the way of a creative act. Therefore the necessary condition for the miracle is the realization that this "I" can do nothing—the discovery of its total and inescapable captivity. The "I" must confess that it is mere dust, that "there is no health in it", for liberation from the "I" is impossible so long as one retains any hope in its powers. While this hope persists one is still under the spell of death, turned into a pillar of salt like Lot's wife who looked *behind* on the way from Sodom.

> Even thus shall it be in the day when the Son of Man is revealed. In that day . . . he that is in the field, let him likewise not return back. Remember Lot's wife. Whosoever shall seek to save his soul shall lose it.[1]

---

[1] *Luke* 17: 30–33. "The day when the Son of Man is revealed" is, of course, the Last Day, the day when time comes to an end—as indeed it does *eternally* in this Now, wherein alone we are truly alive.

Follow me, and let the dead bury their dead.[1]

No man, having put his hand to the plough, and looking back, is fit for the kingdom of God.[2]

On the other hand, the miracle can come to pass if all hope in the "I" is abandoned, if that wherein man thought his life consisted is seen beyond any doubt to be unreality and death. The one thing, then, which is the indispensable preparation for the miracle of man's becoming "no longer I, but Christ", for the birth of Godhead in man, is the confession of "sin"— not, however, in the current sentimental sense of the word, but in the true metaphysical sense of *hamartanein*, "to miss the mark", to be off the point. The mark or point here—equivalent to the "strait and narrow gate" or the "needle's eye" which is the entrance to heaven—is the timeless, eternal moment wherein our real life consists.[3] To be "off the mark" is to be identified with the past, and thus "the soul that sinneth shall die". Repentance in "dust and ashes" is simply the clear admission that everything which I know (remember) as myself is dead, and can do nothing. The "I" which *is* the past can give no salvation from the past.

---

[1] *Matthew* 8: 22, and *Luke* 11: 60.

[2] *Luke* 11: 62. These, and many other passages, suggest quite clearly that eternal life consists in deliverance from the past, and thus from time in general, the whole notion of time being built upon our memory of the past. Cf. *Matthew* 6: 34, "Be not anxious for the morrow", and in *Luke* 24: 5–6, the words of the angels to those who sought the body of Christ in the sepulchre—"Why seek ye the living among the dead? He is not here, but is risen."

[3] The "point" is the *bindu* of the Hindu tradition, or the *ekaksana*, the "one moment", of the Buddhist, which is the same as Dante's *punto a cui tutti li tempi son presenti*, "point at which the whole of time is present", in *Paradiso*, xvii. 17–18. Cf. Plutarch, *De Iside et Osiride*, 77: "The principle of knowledge, that is conceptual, pure and simple, flashes through the soul like lightning, and offers itself in a single moment's experience to apprehension and vision." So, also, St. Paul in 1 *Corinthians* 15: 51–52, "We shall not all sleep, but we shall all be changed, in a moment, in the twinkling of an eye."

For this reason, then, Advent gives a special emphasis to the mission of St. John the Baptist, the Forerunner of Christ—

> The voice of one crying in the wilderness: Prepare
> ye the way of the Lord, make straight in the desert
> a highway for our God.[1]

For immediately before the public appearance of Christ there came the desert-prophet John, the son of a barren woman, Elizabeth, "preaching the baptism of repentance for the remission of sin". The imagery of Advent achieves a marvelous combination of spiritual and seasonal themes, the arid ground of the desert waiting for the winter rains corresponding to St. John's baptism in the wilderness, to the coming of the "Day-spring from on high" to "those that sit in darkness", and to the miracle of discontinuity—the blossoming rod— which is to liberate man from the arid past and revive him with the water of eternal life.

> Drop down dew, ye heavens, from above, and let the
> clouds rain justice; let the earth be opened and
> bud forth a Saviour.[2]
> The wilderness and the solitary place shall be
>   glad for them;
> and the desert shall rejoice, and blossom as the rose.
> It shall blossom abundantly, and rejoice even with
>   joy and singing. . . .
> For in the wilderness shall waters break out, and
>   streams in the desert.
> And the parched ground shall become a pool, and
>   the thirsty land springs of water.[3]

[1] *Isaiah* 40: 3, quoted in *John* 1: 19 et seq., which is the liturgical Gospel for the Third Sunday in Advent.
[2] Introit for the Fourth Sunday in Advent, based on *Isaiah* 45: 8.
[3] Lesson for Ember Saturday in Advent, from *Isaiah* 35: 1–7.

FIG. 4 GLORIFIED MADONNA

A Spanish woodcut of the late 15th century, from the Biblioteca Universitaria, Valencia. The Virgin is surrounded with roses; the Christ-child holds a rose; and the kneeling figures of the two *imperia*, spiritual and temporal, hold rosaries, as do the two monks above. The symbolism is of the Virgin as *Rosa Mundi*, Rose of the World—that is, of the created order, *māyā*, which flowers from its divine Centre.

Yet the rain must have a way to enter into the dry ground. The earth must be opened. To "make straight in the desert a high-way for our God" in conformity with St. John's cry for repentance, the ground must no longer remain closed. The whole mystery of the "opening of the earth", which, from the metaphysical standpoint, is the "passive" admission that "I can do nothing", is contained in the all-important figure of the Virgin Mary, upon whom the mind of the Church fastens more and more as Advent draws to its close.

O Virgin of Virgins, how shall this be? For neither before thee was any seen like thee, nor shall there be after. Daughters of Jerusalem, why marvel ye at me? The thing which ye behold is a divine mystery.[1]

In Christian mythology the figure of the Mother of God is second only in importance to that of Christ himself, and at times popular devotion has seemed to want to raise her to an even higher eminence. From every standpoint—theological, historical, or metaphysical—her role in the Christian scheme is crucial, because she is that without which there would be no Christ. Her consent—"Be it unto me according to thy word"—was the necessary condition of the Incarnation, and thus she is the vital bridge between death and life, sin and holiness—the "mediatrix of all graces", by whose openness to the Spirit the miracle of redemption could be achieved. Rather obviously, she takes the place of Isis, Astarte, Ceres, Aphrodite, Cybele, Inanna, Maya Shakti, and all the great Mother Goddesses of the Earth known to ancient history, for Catholic piety has endowed her with their titles—Mother of God and Queen of Heaven.

Ave, Regina caelorum,
Ave, Domina Angelorum:
Salve radix, salve porta,
Ex qua mundo lux est orta.

Hail, Queen of Heaven!
Hail, Lady of the Angels!
Salutation to thee, root and portal,
whence the light of the world has arisen.[2]

Tradition traces her ancestry back to Jesse, the father of

[1] Great Antiphon for December 23rd in the ancient English Use of the *Sarum Breviary.*
[2] At Compline, Final Antiphon B.V.M.

David, and even to Abraham himself, so that she represents a culmination of the entire history of the Chosen People—the Tree sprung from the Root of Jesse and the Seed of Abraham, whose own wife, Sarah, brought forth her son miraculously in her old age.[1] But behind this earthly descent the Church discerns her heavenly origin, according her a mysterious kinship with Sophia, the Divine Wisdom, in the time before time was. It is presumably with reference to this premundane origin that, at the Feast of the Assumption of the Virgin, the Lesson at Mass is taken from *Ecclesiasticus 24, In omnibus requiem*:

> In all things, I sought rest; and I shall abide
>   in the inheritance of the Lord.
> Then the Creator of all things commanded, and
>   spake to me;
> and he that made me rested in my tabernacle.
> And he said to me: Let thy dwellings be in Jacob,
>   and thy inheritance in Israel,
> and take thy root in my elect.
> From the beginning, and before the world,
>   was I created,
> and unto the world to come I shall not cease to be;
> and in the holy dwelling-place I have ministered
>   before him.
> And so was I established in Sion, and in the holy
> city likewise I rested,
> and my power was in Jerusalem;
> and I took root in an honourable people, and in
>   the portion of my God his inheritance,
> and my abode is in the full assembly of saints.

[1] The genealogies of Christ given by *Matthew* and *Luke* trace the descent of Christ through Joseph to David and Abraham. But mediaeval writers such as de Voragine argue that since Joseph was *not* the natural father of Jesus, and that since Jesus *was* of the line of David, it must follow that Mary also was of the same line—an opinion in which St. John of Damascus likewise concurs, tracing Mary's descent through David's son Nathan.

> I was exalted like a cedar in Libanus, and as
>   a cypress-tree on mount Sion;
> I was exalted like a palm-tree in Cades, and
>   as a rose-plant in Jericho;
> as a fair olive-tree in the plains, and as a plane-tree by
>   the water in the streets was I exalted.
> I gave a sweet perfume like cinnamon and aromatic
>   balm;
> I yielded a sweet odour like the best myrrh.[1]

It would seem that the association of the Virgin with Sophia, the Second Person of the Trinity, is that she is his feminine, though material, counterpart, consort, and image—being that Prima Materia which was the original Womb of Creation. For the Virgin is both Bride and Mother of God the Son— Bride in so far as she represents the universe and the Church, destined for an eternal union with Christ, and Mother in so far as the Son takes from her his human nature when he enters into the Womb and is born in the world. The nuptial symbolism of the relationship between God and the world is both ancient and very widespread in mythology and mysticism alike. No doubt it has historical origins in ancient cults of fertility, where the fertilization of the Earth Mother by sun and rain from Heaven was seen in analogy with human procreation. No doubt it is sometimes—in mysticism—a "compensatory fantasy" for the celibate life. But a sexually self-conscious culture such as our own must beware of its natural tendency to see religion as a symbolizing of sex, for to sexually uncomplicated people it has always been obvious that sex is a symbol of religion. That is to say, the ecstatic self-abandonment of nuptial love is the average man's nearest approach to the self-less state of mystical or metaphysical experience. For this reason the act of love is the easiest and most readily intelligible

---

[1] *Ecclesiasticus* 24: 7–15. The lesson *Dominus possedit me* from *Proverbs*, quoted in the first chapter, where the words are also those of Sophia, is used at the Mass of the Immaculate Conception.

illustration of what it is like to be in "union with God", to live the eternal life, free from self and time.[1]

The importance of the nuptial symbolism of the *unio mystica* explains the presence in Holy Scripture of that great Hebrew love-poem *The Song of Songs* or *Canticles*, consistently interpreted in Christianity as the dialogue between Christ the Bridegroom and his Bride, the Church or the human soul, of which the Virgin is the supreme type. *Canticles* is therefore one of the most important sources of both symbols of the Virgin and liturgical devotions in her honour.

> Who is she that riseth up as the morning, fair
> as the moon, clear as the sun, and terrible as
> an army with banners?[2]

> I am black, but comely, O ye daughters of Jeru-
> salem; therefore the King delighteth in me, and
> hath brought me into his chambers.[3]

> Lo, the winter is past, the rain is over and
> gone: rise up, my love, and come away.[4]

From this poem the Church derived such symbols of the Virgin as the Rose of Sharon, the Lily, the Enclosed Garden, the Sealed Fountain, and the Ivory Tower, and its glowing language runs through the whole liturgy like a thread of gold in a woven tapestry.

> Whither is thy beloved gone, O thou fairest
> among women? Whither is thy beloved turned
> aside?

[1] Thus, much of the Freudian interpretation of mythology is valid only for those Western sub-cultures where the repression of sex has led to its obsessive over-valuation. The notion that the sexual experience is so much the *summum bonum* of human life that it is the final, inner meaning of all mythological symbols, is a point of view which seems quite fantastic to those for whom sexual realization is as natural and usual as eating and sleeping.

[2] Feast of the Assumption, antiphon at Lauds, from *Canticles* 6: 10.

[3] Common of the B.V.M., antiphon from *Canticles* 1: 5 and 4.

[4] Common of the B.V.M., antiphon from *Canticles* 2: 11 and 10.

> A bundle of myrrh is my well-beloved unto me;
> he shall lie all night betwixt my breasts.

> Stay me with flagons, and comfort me with
> apples; for I am sick with love.[1]

The forty-fifth *Psalm* is another source of the poetry of the Virgin, and the Church's conception of her glory has no doubt been enhanced by the language of the scriptural passages which seemed applicable to her:

> Thou art fairer than the children of men:
>   grace is poured into thy lips;
>   therefore God hath blessed thee forever. . . .
> All thy garments smell of myrrh, and aloes, and
>   cassia, out of the ivory palaces, whereby
>   they have made thee glad.
> King's daughters were among thy honourable women:
>   upon thy right hand did stand the queen
>   in gold of Ophir.
> Hearken, O daughter, and consider, and incline
>   thine ear;
>   forget also thine own people, and thy
>   father's house;
> So shall the king greatly desire thy beauty:
>   for he is thy Lord;
>   and worship thou him. . . .
> The King's daughter is all glorious within:
>   her clothing is wrought of gold.
> She shall be brought unto the King in raiment
>   of needlework:
>   the virgins her companions that follow her
>   shall be brought unto thee.
> With gladness and rejoicing shall they be brought:
>   they shall enter into the King's palace.

[1] Compassion of the B.V.M. (Friday after Passion Sunday), antiphons from *Canticles* 6: 1, 1: 13, and 2: 5.

The ultimate picture of the Virgin in the fullness of her heavenly glory comes from the vision of St. John at Patmos:

> And there appeared a great wonder in heaven: a Woman clothed with the sun, and the moon under her feet, and upon her head a crown of twelve stars.[1]

Upon this passage Catholic art bases its iconography of the Virgin reigning as Queen of Heaven after her assumption—with the crescent moon beneath her feet, and the twelve stars forming an aureole about her head.

Despite its richness and complexity, the symbolism of the Virgin gives a definite picture of her role in the scheme of Christian mythology. The Virgin Mother is, first of all, *Mater Virgo*—virgin matter or the unploughed soil—that is to say, the Prima Materia prior to its division, or ploughing, into the multiplicity of created things. As Star of the Sea, *Stella Maris* (*mare*=Mary), the Sealed Fountain, "the immaculate womb of this divine font", she is likewise the Water over which the Spirit moved in the beginning of time. As the "Woman clothed with the sun, and the moon under her feet", she is also everything signified in other mythologies by the goddesses of the moon, which shines by the sun's light, and appears in the night surrounded (crowned) with stars. As the Womb in which the Logos comes to birth she is also Space, signified in the common artistic convention of clothing her in a blue mantle, spangled with stars. As the Jesse Tree, the Cedar of Libanus, the Cypress of Mount Sion, the Palm of Cades, and the Olive of the Plains, she is also to be identified with the Axle-Tree of the World, with the serpent at its roots—"it shall bruise thy head, and thou shalt bruise its heel"[2]—and bearing alike the fruits of death and life.[3] As the Rose and the Lily

---

[1] *Revelation* 12: 1.　　　　　　　　　　[2] *Genesis* 3: 15.

[3] The Virgin has also been associated in another way with the Tree of the Cross, upon which Christ performs the feminine-redemptive function of

she is the open cup of the flower, symbol of the receptive, passive, feminine aspect of man's spiritual transformation—represented also in the Chalice or Graal which receives the life-blood of Christ.

The Virgin Mary in Christianity thus typifies everything signified by Māyā in Hinduism and Buddhism—that is, the female *shakti*, or consort, of God, the world which "God so loved", or the finite manifestation of the infinite. The word *māyā* is derived from the root *matr-*, to measure, from which in turn come μήτηρ (mother), metre, matrix, *mater*, and matter, for *māyā* is that "no-thing", which, when measured or divided, becomes things. The Divider ("I came not to bring peace, but a sword") is the Logos, who "set a compass on the face of the deep",[1] who "divided the light from the darkness",[2] and created the firmament to "divide the waters from the waters".[3] Thus it is prophesied of Mary, "A sword shall pierce through thy own soul also",[4] since in all the great traditions creation is always through a sacrifice: the multiplicity of things is the One dis-membered and divided. By yet another sacrifice the One is re-membered—"Do this in re-membrance (*anamnesis*) of Me"—for the original Unity is restored when the sacrifice is repeated, because the repetition is a recollection of what was done "in the beginning".

The story of the creation of the world by the dismemberment or division of the feminine Chaos, Prima Materia and Virgin Matter, has one of its earliest forms in the Babylonian tablets—

When in the height heaven was not named
And the earth beneath did not yet bear a name,
And the primeval Apsu, who begat them,
And Chaos, Tiamat, the Mother of them both,—

"giving himself up" to death—to Non-being and Night. Death is always a return to the Womb in the sense of going back to the No-thing out of which one came, and it is of interest that the bone behind the uterus is the *os crucis*, popularly known as the Holy Bone, *kreuzbein*, etc.

[1] *Proverbs* 8: 27.   [2] *Genesis* 1: 4.   [3] *Genesis* 1: 6.   [4] *Luke* 2: 35.

Their waters were mingled together,
And no field was formed, no marsh was to be seen;
When of the gods none had been called into being,
And none bore a name, and no destinies were ordained. . . .

The Lord stood upon Tiamat's hinder parts,
And with his merciless club he smashed her skull. . . .

Then the Lord rested, gazing upon her dead body,
While he divided the flesh . . . and devised a cunning plan.
He split her up like a flat fish into two halves;
One half of her he stablished as a covering for heaven.[1]

Chaos-Tiamat is represented as a dragon or serpent because, before the division, she is "footless" or unmeasured. She is the "no-thing" which by the measurement, the *māyā*, the "art" of the Word is made to appear as things.

In Christianity, however, theology has consistently repressed a truth which in other traditions is abundantly clear. For when the primal Mother is dis-membered into "things", it is only then that she becomes *created*. Prior to her apparent division into parts by the art or *māyā* of the Word, she is uncreated and divine, being simply the female aspect of Godhead.[2] But for theology this is blasphemy and heresy, since theology, as distinct from myth, is the creation of individuals who cannot see this truth for the very reason that they are still spell-bound, enchanted by the Word which makes the Many *seem* to be different from each other and from the One, and the creation separate from the Creator. Yet whereas the individual theologian

[1] L. W. King, *The Seven Tablets of Creation* (London, 1902). Note, again, the repeated association of the creation of things with "naming", for it is always the "Word of God which is a sharp two-edged sword" which is the instrument of division.

[2] Christian official theology having ever been one-sided, and unable to grasp the riddle of the "compass" which God set upon the "face of the deep". For the compass, the dividers, is "two" at the points and "one" at the pivot, so that he who holds it at the pivot is above and beyond the "pairs of opposites" which include being and non-being, Father and Mother.

remains spell-bound, it is otherwise with the folk, the common man.[1] For more than six hundred years theology has fought a steadily losing battle with the Catholic folk-mind, which, step by step, is persuading the official Church to recognize the true divinity of the Virgin.

This is the obvious tendency behind the promulgation of the Immaculate Conception and the Assumption of the Virgin as dogma, belief in which is "essential to salvation", and one can hardly doubt that these will in due course be followed, first, by the dogma that she is Mediatrix of All Graces, and, ultimately, by some dogma to the effect that she must receive *latria*—the worship proper to God himself—by virtue of her assimilation to the Godhead.[2] This will be the victory of what was apparent long ago at Chartres and today in Mexico, where the Virgin of Guadaloupe is—in practice— honoured far above the Father and the Son, and whose icon stands before the worshippers in its own right, representing the Virgin alone without even the Christ Child in her arms.[3] Furthermore, the shrine of Our Lady of Guadaloupe is a basilica, and ranks third among all the shrines of Catholic Christendom.

The dogma of the Immaculate Conception of the Virgin—

[1] In the proper meaning of a now debased usage, for the "common man" is the Man common to us all, which Jung would call the "collective un- conscious". He is the man who is a "nameless nobody", not being this or that particular individual. Hence the monastic and, in general, initiatory practice of giving up one's proper name when entering into religion, and receiving instead a "Christian" name—i.e. one of the names of the Common Man, Christ, who—as even theology insists—is not a particular human person, not *a* man but man. It is only in the Nestorian heresy that Christ is held to be *a* man.

[2] Worship is of two kinds—*latria*, the adoration of the Godhead, and *dulia*, the veneration of the saints, though the reverence paid to the Virgin is already called *hyperdulia*. One might venture the guess that some further step in the divinization of the Virgin is contained in the parts of the Fatima visions remaining unpublished.

[3] See the marvelous treatment of this problem in the section dealing with Mexican culture in F. S. C. Northrop's *Meeting of East and West* (New York, 1946).

not to be confused with that of the Virgin Birth of Christ—is
to the effect that Mary was conceived without inheriting the
taint of Original Sin which has descended to all other human
beings from Adam and Eve. It is no wonder that the proper
Mass for the feast of this mystery has, as its Epistle, the *Dominus
possedit me* passage from *Proverbs* 8, in which Sophia, the
handmaid of Logos, declares that she was "set up from eternity",
and that "he who shall find me shall find life".[1] For the
miracle whereby the Virgin is free from Original Sin, that she
never "missed the mark" or was "off the point", is clearly that
she is of heavenly or divine origin. Like the Son, she was
"begotten before all the worlds", for "I was set up from of old,
before ever the earth was".

The dogma of the Assumption maintains that, after her
death, the Virgin Mary was assumed bodily into heaven, where
she was subsequently crowned—"more glorious than the
Cherubim and Seraphim"—to reign with Christ for ever
and ever.

> The most ineffable Trinity itself applauds her with
> unceasing dance, and since its grace flows wholly into her,
> makes all to wait upon her. The most splendid order of
> the apostles extols her with unspeakable lauds, . . . un-
> willing Hell itself howls to her, and the wanton demons
> shriek her praise.[2]

The mysterious and altogether peculiar nature of the Assumption is still clearer in the following passage from St. John
of Damascus:

> O Blessed Virgin, thou hast not gone to heaven as
> Elias did, or as Paul, who went up to the third heaven;

[1] The *Tract* of this Mass also identifies her with the City of God, in view
of which it is interesting to read the vision of *Ezekiel* 40, in which the Holy City
is *measured* by "a man whose appearance was like the appearance of brass"—i.e.
the Son of Man.

[2] From the *Homilies* of Gerardus, quoted in de Voragine's *Golden Legend*,
trs. Ryan and Ripperger (London and New York, 1941), vol. ii, p. 458.

thou hast mounted even to the kingly throne of thy Son!
The death of the other saints is blessed because it brings
them to blessedness, but this is not true of thee: for not
thy death . . . has bestowed upon thee the security of thy
blessedness, since thou art the beginning and the middle
and the end of all the blessings that surpass the mind of
man! Hence death has not beatified thee, but thou hast
glorified death, dispelling its sadness and turning it to joy![1]

We are here within sight of the recognition that the Assumption is the revelation of what the Virgin was from the
beginning—the one who reigns eternally with Christ, Sophia
as the consort of Logos, divine Matrix of the universe. All the
honours and symbols of this estate are present, and the only
thing lacking is the precise theological definition.

We are now in a position to see what light the figure of
the Virgin throws upon the metaphysical problem of man's
redemption from time, death, and the past. A widespread
symbolism likens the creative movement of life to the passage
of a bird through the sky: the point is that it leaves no trace,
because the sky is always "pure and immaculate". Similarly,
the real world and the real life of man is an eternal present
having neither a past nor a future; it "moves" through the Void
like a bird or dancing spark which leaves nothing behind.
For this reason, the memories which give the impression that
there is an "I", a conditioning past whose dead hand rules the
world, are shadows without any substance. It is for this reason
that Ruysbroeck says, "We must found all our lives upon a
fathomless abyss"; for this is, in truth, how they *are* founded—
upon an abyss in which nothing "sticks" or leaves any trace,
since all things past are as unreal as "the footprints of a star".
This abyss in which nothing leaves any stain is the Virgin,
the Immaculate Womb wherein Creation comes to birth,
and which, after birth, remains "ever Virgin" and spotless.

[1] *Ibid.*, pp. 463–4

Thou art all fair, O Mary; there is no spot in
thee. . . . Thy raiment is white as snow, and thy
countenance like the sun.[1]

As the Prima Materia, the No⁄thing out of which all things
were made, the Virgin has always represented our own true
nature—the human nature which she gave to the Christ in
bearing him. Thus the redemption of man from time depends
on the realization that his own true or real nature is, from the
beginning, immaculate: he *has* no past, and the stain which he
seems to leave behind him, and which is everything that makes
up his individuality, is a seeming only. In reality it is not there;
in reality there is only the spark of eternity in the trackless abyss.
"The Moving Finger writes, and, having writ, moves on"—yes,
but in truth it writes on the sky. Of all this there is perhaps no
more eloquent symbol than the fact that our earth and the
whole host of heaven are suspended in emptiness. Time and
space are the same void. "Look!" said Meister Eckhart. "The
person who lives in the light of God is conscious neither of
time past nor of time to come but only of the one eternity. . . .
Therefore he gets nothing new out of future events, nor from
chance, for he lives in the Now⁄moment that is, unfailingly,
'in verdure newly clad'."[2]
Unfamiliar as such an interpretation of the Virgin may be,
it comes naturally enough, without "stretching" the symbols,
and is precisely the interpretation which brings the Christian
myth into its proper relation with the other great mythological
traditions—as a form of the *philosophia perennis* rather than a
strange abnormality. As the deep upon which God set his
compass, the waters upon which the Spirit moved, the Womb
in which the Logos was made flesh, the Immaculate and
Ever⁄Virgin Mother is clearly that "nothing" in which "things"
are made to "seem" by *māyā*, by measurement and division,

---

[1] Immaculate Conception B.V.M., antiphons at the Hours.
[2] R. Blakney, *Meister Eckhart* (New York, 1941), pp. 209–10.

just as what we call time and space are abstractions created by measurements upon the fathomless void. From another point of view, she is that which passively, willingly, without resistance submits to the Dividers and the Sword, offering no obstacle to the free play of the divine *māyā*; "Be it unto me according to thy word". She is thus the Open One—the Rose, the Lily, the Womb, the Sky. And out of this "being nothing" there comes, paradoxically and miraculously, fruitfulness—the Tree and its Fruit, the Rod of Jesse which blossoms and bears the Christ.

This miracle is what "I" can never understand; for "I" always thinks it must *do something* to be fruitful and creative. It does not understand the famous "law of reversed effort", whereby creative action at one level of one's being depends upon inaction at another. Only when the "I" is seen to be nothing, a shadow unable to move even a grain of dust, the Man in us comes to life "in a moment, in the twinkling of an eye".

CHAPTER IV

Christmas and Epiphany

SHE who was, from the beginning, the Virgin of virgins and the Immaculate Mother of the universe, appeared in due time as Mary, the daughter of Joachim and Anna. According to St. Jerome, Joachim was from the town of Nazareth in Galilee, and Anna from the City of David—Bethlehem; and the two were just and godly folk who divided their wealth into three parts—one for the Temple, one for the poor, and one for their own needs. Anna, however, was barren and lived for twenty years with her husband without bearing him a child. But, moved to compassion by their holy lives, the Lord God at last sent his angel with the news that there would be born to them a daughter. They were to give her the name Mary, and to dedicate her from infancy to the service of God, for, said the angel, "as she will be born to a barren mother, so will she herself, in a wondrous manner, bring forth the Son of the Most High, whose name shall be called Jesus, and through whom will come salvation to all the nations".

When the child was three years old, her parents took her to the Temple at Jerusalem, and left her in the company of the Temple virgins, with whom she grew up until she was fourteen—constantly visited by the angels and enjoying always the mystical vision of God. Now that she had become a woman, it was the proper custom that she should be returned to her home and given in marriage. But Mary told the High Priest that it could not be so with her, since she had promised her virginity to God. Perplexed, and seeking guidance from the Most High, the High Priest entered into the sanctuary of the Temple, and, as he prayed, a Voice came forth from the inmost shrine of the Holy of Holies, commanding that all the marriageable men of the House of David should come to the Temple and each one lay a branch upon the altar. One of these branches, said the Voice, would burst into flower, and he to whom it belonged was to take the Virgin Mary as his wife. And so it came about that the branch which blossomed was that which belonged to Joseph, a carpenter from Bethlehem. This branch was no doubt that ancient cutting from the Tree of Eden, which, according to another legend, had been handed down among the patriarchs of Israel until it had at last found its way to Joseph; and now, as it blossomed upon the altar, the Holy Spirit appeared from heaven in the form of a dove, and rested upon it.

Joseph was therefore espoused to Mary—whereafter he returned to Bethlehem to prepare for the wedding, and she to her home in Nazareth.[1] One day when Mary was at prayer

---

[1] It is of interest that "Nazareth" means "branch", though St. Bernard understood it to mean "flower", and said that the Virgin was the Flower who willed to be born of a flower, in flower, in the season of flowers. As Christ is the Fruit of the Flower—the Mystic Rose, so in the traditions of India the *avatars* or incarnations of God are commonly represented as born from or enthroned upon the lotus. I have in my possession an old Chinese Buddhist print of an *arhat* (awakened sage) holding in his hand a small bottle from which arises a lotus

FIG. 5 THE ANNUNCIATION

Spanish woodcut, about 15th century. Note the inner border, where the Tree of Life grows out from the Skull (lower left). Cf. Figs. 8 and 9.

she found herself, suddenly, in the presence of a shining being, robed in white and carrying a lily in his hand—none other than the Messenger of God, Gabriel the Archangel, who greeted her crying, "Hail, full of grace, the Lord is with thee! Blessed art thou among women!" And as Mary was troubled, wonder-ing at the meaning of this vision, the Archangel spoke again: "Fear not, Mary, for thou hast found favour with God. Behold, thou shalt conceive in thy womb, and bring forth a Son, and shall call his name Jesus.¹ He shall be great, and shall

bearing the figure of the Buddha as a baby—the bottle being a recognized symbol of *Tathagata-garbha*, the womb of the Buddha-nature, which is *sunyata*, the primal "no-thing" or Void.

¹ This is the Greek form of the Hebrew Jehoshuah, Joshua, or Jeshua, meaning "YHVH is Salvation". The original Greek is written IHCOYC, abbrevi-ated in Christian symbolism as IC, IHC, or IHS.

be called the Son of the Highest; and the Lord God shall give him the throne of his father David, and he shall reign over the House of Jacob for ever; and of his kingdom there shall be no end."

And Mary answered, "How shall this be, seeing that I know not a man?"

Again the Archangel spoke: "The Holy Spirit shall come upon thee, and the power of the Highest shall overshadow thee. Therefore also that holy thing which shall be born of thee shall be called the Son of God."

To this Mary responded with the words which have ever been regarded as the "opening" of Matter to Spirit, Earth to Heaven, so that the Incarnation of God could be possible: "Behold the handmaid of the Lord; be it unto me according to thy word."[1]

At this instant the Second Person of the Trinity, God the Son, the Eternal Word by whom all things were made, was conceived in the Womb of the Virgin.

> Great is the mystery of the inheritance. The womb of her that knew not man is become the temple of the Godhead; by taking flesh of her, he was in no way defiled.

> A great and wondrous mystery is made known to us this day: a new thing is done in both natures: God is made man. That which was, remained. That which was not, he assumed; suffering neither con-fusion nor division.[2]

---

[1] The foregoing account of the Annunciation is, of course, based on *Luke* 1: 26–38. To avoid the unnecessary re-telling in detail of a story told incomparably well in the original, it would be best if the reader would, before proceeding with this chapter, read the whole Nativity Story as it is found in *Luke* 1: 5 to 2: 52, and *Matthew* 1: 18 to 2: 23.

[2] Office of St. Mary on Saturday, antiphons at Vespers and Lauds. "Both natures" are the divine and the human, being and non-being, "that which was" and "that which was not", the All (Logos) and the Void (Sophia).

Whereupon Mary went to visit her cousin Elizabeth, who had meanwhile conceived in her old age the son who was to be St. John the Baptist, and while the two women rejoiced together, Mary, out of the fulness of her heart, spoke the words which for so many centuries have been the great Vesper canticle, *Magnificat*:

> My soul doth magnify the Lord: and my spirit hath rejoiced in God my Saviour.
>
> For he hath regarded the lowliness of his hand/maiden; for behold from henceforth all generations shall call me blessed.
>
> For he that is mighty hath magnified me: and holy is his Name.[1]

Joseph and Mary were duly married, and Joseph was at once astonished to find that she was already with child. But, while he slept, an angel appeared to him in a dream, foretelling the nature of the child which his young wife was to bear, so that his mind might be at rest. Close to the time of her delivery, it was necessary for them to make a journey from Nazareth—where they had lived since the wedding—to the city of Bethlehem. The Roman Emperor Augustus had ordered a census for purposes of taxation, for which every man had to repair to his own home/town. Because of the crowds present in the city for the census—though some attribute it to their extreme poverty—there was no room for Joseph and Mary at the inn. They were thus compelled to lodge for the night in a cattle/manger which, according to most traditions, was in a cave close to the inn.

Precisely at midnight there occurred the event which, for Christendom, marks the very centre of time, and from which the years are numbered backward to the Creation and forward

---

[1] *Luke* 1: 46–55. At Solemn Vespers incense is brought in and blessed before the *Magnificat* is sung, and, during its singing, the officiant and his deacons or acolytes cense the altar.

to the Last Day—the entrance of eternal life being ever in that Moment which separates past and future. The Virgin gave birth to the Child who is true God and true man, in whom time and eternity are one.

> While all things were in quiet silence, and night
> was in the midst of her course, thine almighty Word,
> O Lord, came down from thy royal throne:
> alleluia![1]

In the middle of the centuries, at the depth of the year—the Winter Solstice, in the midst of the night, and in the cave—the depth of the earth, the King of kings and Light of lights was born in circumstances of the most extreme humility, amidst the animals in a crib of hay.

> The Virgin today brings forth the Superessential,
> and the earth offers a cave to the Unapproachable.
> . . . I behold a Mystery strange and wondrous
> (*paradoxon*): the cave is Heaven, and the Virgin is
> the throne of the Cherubim; in the confines of the
> manger is laid the Infinite.[2]

The tradition holds that at the moment of the Lord's birth all Nature was still as if time itself had missed a beat and paused

[1] Sunday within the Octave of the Nativity, antiphon at Vespers. The preparatory condition for the *unio mystica* is invariably *silence* and the very *depth* of night—silence or "the prayer of quiet" being the state which comes about when it is clearly seen that "I" can do nothing, which is also midnight in the sense of a kind of despair. But this is "despair" in the special sense of being "de-spirited" or "de-spirated", that is to say "blown out", which is the literal meaning of the term *nirvana*. It is the "sigh of relief" which comes after "I" has reached the limit and discovered its impotence, so that it "gives up the ghost". Then, "I live; yet no longer I, but Christ". Cf. the opening words of the *Divina Commedia*, "Nel mezzo del cammin di nostra vita mi ritrovai per una selva oscura, che la diritta via era smarrita". This extremity of man must always be reached before the divine life can begin.

[2] Collect and Dismissal Hymn from the *Menaion*, proper of the Greek Liturgy for December 25th. "Superessential" is *hyperousion*, St. Dionysius' peculiar word for the divine nature which is above every conception (essence) which the mind can form, including those of "being" and "non-being".

FIG. 6 THE NATIVITY

Spanish woodcut, *c.* 15th century

in its course, and that the shock of a stillness so strange and sudden was known to all creatures so that, for a moment, there was a universal revelation of the Incarnation of God. According to the *Golden Legend*, "it was revealed to every class of creatures, from the stones, which are at the bottom of the scale of creation, to the angels, who are at its summit". It was made known to stone by the sudden crumbling of the "Eternal Temple of Peace" in Rome, concerning which the oracle of Apollo had prophesied that it would stand until the day when a virgin gave birth to a child. It was made known to water, for in the same night a spring that flowed in Rome was changed into a fountain of oil. It was made known to plants, for the vines of Cades suddenly flowered, bore grapes, and produced their wine. It was made known to animals, to the ox and ass present at the manger. It was made known to the birds, for at midnight the cock crew as at dawn. It was made known to the angels, for the whole Host of Heaven had come down to earth and shone around the cave with a brilliance that turned night into day. Hardly had that intense throb of silence passed when all the nine choirs of heaven cried out, singing——

> *Gloria in excelsis Deo*—Glory be to God on high,
> and on earth peace to men of good will!

And, by the angels, it was made known also to men through the shepherds of Bethlehem, to whom the Messenger of God came as they watched their sheep, saying: "Fear not; for, behold, I bring you tidings of great joy, which shall be to all people. For unto you is born this day in the city of David a Saviour, who is Christ the Lord."

It is impossible to tell the whole story of the Nativity and its surrounding events in a chronologically consistent order. Not only are there differences in the accounts of *Matthew* and *Luke* which are hard to reconcile, but the Church Calendar also has a confused order, due in part to the fact that it was not until the fourth century that the feast of Christmas (December 25th) was widely separated from the feast of the Epiphany (January 6th), commemorating the visit of the Magi. The memorial of the Massacre of the Holy Innocents, which would be expected to follow the visit of the Magi, falls on December 28th, so that popular imagination has to associate the Magi with Christmas as well as Epiphany. The Nativity was ultimately fixed upon December 25th because of the irresistibly appropriate symbolism of associating the Birth of the Sun of Justice with the pagan prototype of the Brumalia, the feast of the Birth of the Unconquered Sun—*Natalis Invicti Solis.*

> *Nam post solstitium, quo Christus corpore natus*
> *Sole novo gelidae mutavit tempora brumae,*
> *Atque salutiferum praestans mortalibus ortum,*
> *Procedente die, secum decrescere noctes*
> *Jussit.*

FIG. 7 THE ANGEL AND THE SHEPHERDS OF BETHLEHEM

Woodcut from de Alliaco's *Tractatus Exponibilium*, Paris 1494

For it is after the solstice, when Christ born in the flesh with the new sun transformed the season of cold winter, and, vouchsafing to mortal men a healing dawn, commanded the nights to decrease at his coming with advancing day.[1]

Thus in the complete symbol of the Nativity there are gathered round the Virgin with her Child not only the adoring host of angels with Joseph, the shepherds, the ox and the ass, but also the three Magician-Kings representing the nations of the earth—Caspar, Melchior, and Balthasar—and above all the blazing Star of the Epiphany, of the Manifestation of

[1] Paulinus of Nola, *Poema* xiv. 15–19.

Christ to the world.[1] Tradition gives a number of varying stories of the Magi, representing them as Chaldean or Persian astrologers, as Zoroastrian sages, and as kingly types of the great races of the world—white, negro, and mongolian. The point is always, however, that they represent both the Gentiles as well as the height of human wisdom and dignity, whereas the shepherds represent the Jews and the humble peasantry— constituting together a symbol of the homage of mankind to the Incarnate God. Their gifts of gold, frankincense, and myrrh are usually understood to be offerings appropriate to Christ: as King, the gold of tribute, as God, the incense of worship, and as Sacrificial Victim, the myrrh for embalming the body.

According to the version of *Matthew*, the visit of the Magi was followed immediately by the flight of the Holy Family into Egypt. For as the Magi had followed the mysterious Star of the Epiphany from a distant land, they went to Jerusalem before proceeding to Bethlehem, since the former was the notable holy city in which they might have expected the Christ to be born. Here they had taken counsel with Herod, the King of Judaea, and the priests and scribes of the Temple, and were directed to Bethlehem in accordance with the prophecy of Micah that the Christ would be born in the city of the "House of Bread". Herod, fearing that so great a King of kings would usurp his own throne, requested the Magi to return to him after they had found the Child, that he also might go and worship him, though his real intent was to put him immediately to death. Thus, when the Magi were warned by God in a dream not to return to Herod, the latter, as soon as he had discovered their deception, gave orders for the slaughter of all male children in Bethlehem under two years old. But, again in a dream, the angel of God had in the meantime warned Joseph to flee with the Virgin and Child into Egypt, and remain there until it was safe to return.

---

[1] According to the *Golden Legend* the Greek form of their names was Appellioss, Damaskos, and Amerios, and the Hebrew Galagat, Sarachin, and Malagat.

It is of great interest that the *Matthew* story works out a typological correspondence between the life of Christ and the history of Israel. For the flight into Egypt corresponds to the Egyptian captivity of the tribes of Israel, while Joseph, like Joseph the son of Jacob, is a dreamer of prophetic dreams. Furthermore, the whole Gospel is divided into five books corresponding to the five books of the Pentateuch, since the Gospel is to be the New Law superseding the Old Law of Moses. Likewise the great Sermon of Christ is given, not, as in *Luke*, on a plain, but on a mountain as upon Mount Sinai Moses received the Old Law from God.[1]

Luke does not record the flight into Egypt. The Nativity is followed by the events which would normally attend the birth of a Jewish child—Circumcision, eight days after birth, and, later, the ceremony of the Purification of the mother, together with the Presentation of the child in the Temple. The Church keeps these two feasts on January 1st (Circum cision) and February 2nd (Purification of the Blessed Virgin Mary). The former feast typifies the submission of the Incar nate God to the "ordinances of the flesh", that is, to the law of nature, as well as the formal bestowal of the Name of Salva tion, Jesus.

> Thou, O compassionate Lord, being by nature God, didst without change take upon thyself the form of man, and, to fulfil the Law, wast willing to submit to circumcision in the flesh, in order that darkness should cease, and that thou mightest roll away the thick veil of our sufferings.[2]

[1] The "five books" of *Matthew* will be found as follows: (1) chapter 3: 1 to 7: 29; (2) 8: 1 to 11: 1; (3) 11: 2 to 19: 2; (4) 19: 3 to 26: 2; (5) 26: 3 to the end. The closing sentence of each book begins with the phrase, "And it came to pass that when Jesus had made an end of . . ." The Pentateuch comprises the first five books of the *Old Testament—Genesis, Exodus, Leviticus, Numbers,* and *Deuteronomy,* the so called "five books of Moses".

[2] The *Menaion,* dismissal hymn for January 1st.

In the cycle of the Christian Year the rites of the Incarnation are governed by the solar calendar, since they are connected with the Birth of the Sun, and so fall upon fixed dates. On the other hand, the rites of the Atonement, of Christ's Death, Resurrection, and Ascension, are governed by the lunar calendar, for there is a figure of Death and Resurrection in the waning and waxing of the moon. The rites of the Incarnation begin with the solemn celebration of the Midnight Mass of Christmas—a feast which is unique in that it requires three masses. The first, at midnight, is centred upon the mystery of the appearance of Light in the depth of darkness, of God "who hast made this most sacred night to shine forth with the brilliance of the true light", and of him who is begotten "from the womb before the day-star". The second is at dawn, the Aurora Mass, which with the rising sun celebrates the illumination and transfiguration of the world, opening with the Introit *Lux fulgebit*—"A light shall shine upon us this day, for our Lord is born to us". The third, during the day, celebrates the eternal generation of the Divine Word from the Father, since the Child born this day is he who in the beginning created all worlds.

Twelve days later, the Feast of the Epiphany, of the Manifestation of Christ's glory, commemorates three events—the Adoration of the Magi, the Baptism of Christ by St. John, and the first miracle—the transformation of water into wine at the wedding-feast in Cana. These three events all have to do with the beginnings of "the power and the glory", for the transformation of the water is the beginning of the works of power, the Baptism with the descent of the fiery Dove is the beginning of Christ's ministry, and the tribute of the Magi is the beginning of the "kingdom which shall have no end".

The Gentiles shall walk in thy light, and kings in the brightness of thy rising. . . . The multitude of camels shall close around thee, the dromedaries of

Midian and Ephah: all they from Saba shall come, bringing gold and frankincense, and showing forth praise to the Lord.[1]

Finally, the rites of the Incarnation reach their climax with the Feast of the Purification on February 2nd, otherwise known as Candlemas. For at this time the Church blesses all the lights to be used in its ceremonies throughout the year, since it was at Christ's Presentation in the Temple that Simeon called him "the Light to lighten the Gentiles, and to be the glory of thy people Israel", in the canticle *Nunc dimittis* which is now sung nightly at Compline:

> Lord, now lettest thou thy servant depart in peace; according to thy word.
> For mine eyes have seen thy salvation; which thou hast prepared before the face of all peoples.
> To be a light to lighten the Gentiles; and to be the glory of thy people Israel.

As the choir chants this hymn, all the clergy and people assembled for Candlemas receive the blessed candles before the altar, and then go in procession with them around the church, singing:

> O daughter of Sion adorn thy bride-chamber, and welcome Christ the King: greet Mary with an embrace, who is the gate of heaven; for it is she who bringeth the King of Glory, of the new light. She remains a virgin, bearing in her hands the Son begotten before the day-star; whom Simeon received in his arms, declaring him to the people as Lord of life and death, and Saviour of the world.

During the Mass which follows, all hold their lighted candles during the chanting of the Gospel as well as from the Elevation

[1] *Isaiah* 60, used for the Lesson and Gradual of the Mass.

to the Communion, while the bread and wine—mystically changed into the Body and Blood of Christ—remain upon the altar. The Sun which first shone in the cave has now given forth an ocean of stars.

The entire theme of the Incarnation is the transformation of manhood into God—the birth or awakening of the divine and eternal nature in man as his true Self.

> O wondrous interchange! The Creator of man-
> kind, taking upon him a living body, vouchsafed
> to be born of a Virgin: and proceeding forth without
> seed as Man, hath bestowed upon us his own Deity
> (*largitus est nobis suam Deitatem*).[1]

This, however reluctantly and grudgingly admitted by theology, is the actual dogma of the Incarnation, and the dogma is always that which constitutes the authentic form of the myth—the rest being individual opinion. The dogma of the Incarnation, as fully formulated by the General Council of Chalcedon in A.D. 451, declares the Christ to be one Person in two Natures. The Person[2] is God the Son, who is, from all eternity, of the divine nature—"God of God, Light of Light, very God of very God". By reason of his Birth from the Virgin Mary he is also endowed with human nature and

---

[1] Office of St. Mary on Saturday, antiphon at the Hours. "Without seed" is the exact equivalent of *asamprajñāta*, the word which Patanjali employs for the state of consciousness, the *samādhi*, in which the divinity of the true Self (*ātman*) is fully realized. It is described as a state of consciousness which is, figuratively speaking, perfectly empty—virgin, immaculate, and pure—since not a trace of "I" remains in it. This is not literal empty-mindedness, but the equivalent of the Chinese *wu-hsin* ("no-mind") or *wu-nien* ("no-thought"= *nirvikalpa*), and of the Christian *agnosia* ("unknowing") whereby God is truly known. In this state the mind is "emptied of the past" and of all "things" in the sense that it perceives the world of abstract construction for what it is—*māyā*, measurements upon the Void. Instead, it perceives the world *yathabhutam*, i.e. just as it is in reality—existing undivided and undifferentiated in this eternal moment.

[2] "Person" is *hypostasis*, that which "under" (*hypo*) "stands" (*stasis*), i.e. the "ground" or "basis" of the being—in other words, the Self, which in Sanskrit is the *purusa* (person) or *ātman*.

all that pertains to it, so that he is not only true God but also true—that is, complete and perfect—Man. But he is *not*, as the Nestorians believed, a human person. He is *man*, but not *a* man. The inference is obviously that personality does not belong to the perfection of human nature, being essentially a divine and not a human property.[1]

But the importance of the truth that the Christ is Man and not *a* man is that the Incarnation of God is not something which comes to pass in a single, particular individual alone. Theological, as distinct from mythological, Christianity has always wanted to insist that such an Incarnation ocurred only with respect to the historical individual called Jesus of Nazareth. It has confused the true uniqueness of the Incarnation with mere historical abnormality. For the Incarnation is unique in the sense that it is the only real event, the only ocurrence which is Now, which is not past and abstract. It is thus the one creative and living act as distinct from dead fact, eternally happening in *this* moment. One would readily agree with the theologians that the Birth at Bethlehem is not simply—indeed not at all—the symbol of God incarnate as each and every man. There never was any question of God becoming each, a, or this particular man in the sense of any individual human personality. For there *are* no human personalities; at most one can say that there *were* such personalities, every ego being a construct of memory only. But He-Who-Is is never at any time That-Which-Was. "Before Abraham was, I am."

It is true that the Birth of Christ is told as a history—that it happened in that particular place and that particular time, but history has an eternal significance only when it is also myth,

[1] Human nature has personality (i.e. creative life and originality) only to the extent that it manifests the Creator and the Origin, the Person of the Eternal Word. While every such manifestation is outwardly unique, the words "personality" and "originality" are utterly misused when applied to the superficial idiosyncracies of purely abstract egos. "Human personality" is thus a contradiction in terms.

when the past fact symbolizes the timeless, present reality. Otherwise, its significance is merely temporal, since it is nothing but a past event whose effects must in time wear off, and pass into oblivion. To say that this historical event was the Incarnation of *God* is, quite necessarily, to say that its significance is eternal rather than temporal since God, the Eternal, is what it signifies. But it is almost nonsense to say that it is the only historical event which has this significance.

This "historical abnormality" version of the Incarnation was doubtless based, in the beginning, on the extreme insularity of the culture in which Christianity arose, since it knew of other cultures only as vague and legendary places from which merchant-adventurers brought such luxuries as silk and spices. It was thus unaware of the other Incarnation-myths of a stature equivalent to its own.¹ Furthermore, what had become, after the fourth century B.C., the extreme racial exclusivism of the Old Israel, became in turn the extreme spiritual exclusivism of the New Israel—the inferiority complex of a repressed nation becoming that of a repressed religion. In part, the notion of Jesus as the sole historical Incarnation was due to such a simple confusion as the application of the term "only-begotten Son" to Jesus as man, whereas it refers strictly to the Eternal Word "begotten before all ages".²

¹ St. Jerome, *adv. Jovinianum* i. 42, mentions the Virgin Birth of the Buddha, but of course knows nothing of Buddhism, of the cultural and spiritual context which would give this myth a stature equivalent to the story of Christ. The Buddha was born miraculously though not, expressly, virginally, though this may be presumed in that he descended from the Tushita heaven, entered the womb of his mother Māyā in the form of a glorious white elephant, and was delivered painlessly from her side. According to Ashvaghosha's life of the Buddha, *Fo-Sho-Hing-Tsan-King*, his mother Māyā "was beautiful as the water-lily and pure in mind as the lotus. As the Queen of Heaven, she lived on earth, untainted by desire, and immaculate." At the Buddha's birth, "the child came forth from the womb like the rising sun. . . . Celestial music rang through the air and the angels rejoiced with gladness."

² Cf. *John* 1: 14. Even if one were to take a literal and legal view of the authority of Scripture, this notion could not even be justified by *Acts* 4: 12,

In later times the theory that God has been incarnate but once in history has been defended for the curious reason that it illumines the special value of history, stressing the eternal value of unique and particular facts. It is felt that incarnations which came to pass more or less regularly—Krishna, the Buddha, Jesus, Ramakrishna—would render the act of incarnation almost "non-historical", like the recurrent cycle of the seasons. But if one wishes to advocate this special respect for history, it is hardly proper to base one's version of the facts upon one's theory of the value of history. Besides being a begging of the question, it is also a profound disrespect for scientific historical study to argue from the theory to the event, saying that *because* history is deeply significant *therefore* there must have been but one historical incarnation. Furthermore, this point of view involves the principle that cyclic and repetitive events are without historical significance, which is only to say that the Western view of time and history is linear— that the course of events is a series of significant steps towards God. Repetitions are not significant because they lack linear direction. But this is again to determine one's version of history by a particular philosophy of history and theory of time.

Yet here is another example of the marvelous way in which myth continues to be revealing even when distorted. The very insistence on the one historical incarnation as a unique step in a course of temporal events leading to the future Kingdom of God reveals the psychology of Western culture most clearly. It shows a mentality for which the present, real world is, in itself, joyless and barren, without value. The present can have value only in terms of meaning—if, like a word, it points to something beyond itself. This "beyond" which past and present events "mean" is the future. Thus the Western intellectual, as well as the literate common man, finds his life meaningless

since the *Name* of Jesus is always to be understood as the "spirit" of Jesus, which would, of course, be that Eternal Word which is embodied in every Incarnation or *avatar*.

except in terms of a promising future. But the future is a "tomorrow which never comes", and for this reason Western culture has a "frantic" character. It is a desperate rush in pursuit of an ever-receding "meaning", because the promising future is precisely the famous carrot which the clever rider dangles before his donkey's nose from the end of his whip. Tragically enough, this frantic search for God, for the ideal life, in the future renders the course of history anything but a series of unique steps towards a goal. Its real result is to make history repeat itself faster and more furiously, confusing "progress" with increased agitation.

But the Western disillusion with past and present events— excluding the Incarnation—is based on a sound intuition. We said that it seeks for the meaning of events, as if they were words: and, indeed, this is exactly what they are. In so far as we are aware of life as history only, as a series of facts, the life that we know is an abstraction without real value or joy. This will include our specious "present", which is not the true present but a memory of the immediate past—the so-called *nunc fluens* as distinct from the *nunc stans*, the present which is always flying away as distinct from that which is eternal. Our plight is that in failing to be aware of the true present we look for the meaning of events in the future, and it disappoints us perpetually because it is as abstract as the past. This is the folly of "laying up treasure upon earth", that is to say, in time, and of "being anxious for the morrow", for the Kingdom of Heaven is not future, within time, but now, above time.[1]

[1] St. Paul's "redeeming the time" is often understood to mean that, through Christ, the course of time is redeemed so that it leads to God, and not just on and on. This is not quite the sense of the passage in *Ephesians* 5: 14–16, "Awake thou that sleepest, and arise from the dead, and Christ shall give thee light. See, then, that ye walk circumspectly, not as fools but as wise, redeeming the time, because the days are evil." Arising from the dead is ceasing to identify the Self with the past—as a result of which time "leads to" or "ends in" Christ, not in the future, but now. Cf. Lynn White, "Christian Myth and Christian History," in *Journal of the History of Ideas*, iii. 2 (New York, 1942), p. 145—an excellent discussion of this whole problem of "the course of time" in Christian thought.

When, therefore, man awakens to the true present he finds his true Self, that wherein the reality of his life actually consists, as distinct from the "old man", the self that *was* and *is not*. He is then "no longer I, but Christ", and this "Christening" of mankind is the clear sense of the whole symbolism of the Incarnation, apart from which it is difficult to see how there can be any meaning in the important conception of Christ as the Second Adam. "For as in Adam all die, *even so* in Christ shall all be made alive."[1] If the First Adam communicates sin to all, the Second must communicate divinity to all—a point which was clear even to the earlier theologians.

> But we hold that to the whole of human nature the whole essence of the Godhead was united. . . . He in his fulness took upon himself me in my fulness, and was united whole to whole that he might in his grace bestow salvation on the whole man. . . . Further, the mind has become the seat of the divinity united with it in subsistence, just as is evidently the case with the body too.[2]

Patristic literature is, indeed, rich in its testimony to the truth that in the Incarnation God "so united himself to us and us to him, that the descent of God to the human level was at the same time the ascent of man to the divine level."[3] St. Cyril of Alexandria explains the symbolism of the New Adam thus:

> We are all in Christ, and the totality of mankind comes to life again in him. For he is called the new Adam because by sharing in our nature he has enriched all unto happiness and glory, as the first Adam filled all with

---

[1] I *Corinthians* 15: 22. Cf. also 15: 45, "The first man Adam was made a living soul (*psyche*), the last Adam a life-giving spirit (*pneuma*)." Note the contrast between *psyche* and *pneuma*, *nefesh* and *ruach*, ego and true Self.

[2] St. John of Damascus, *De Fide Orthodoxa* iii. 6.

[3] St. Leo, *Serm. VII de Nativitate Domini*, ii. Cf. also his *Serm. LXXIII*, iv: "We have been made one Body with the Son of God, and by him placed at the right hand of the Father."

corruption and ignominy. Thus by dwelling in one, the Word dwelt in all, so that, the one being constituted the Son of God in power, the same dignity might pass to the whole human race.[1]

Perhaps the point could hardly be put more strongly than in the words of St. Maximus of Turin:

> In the Saviour we have all risen, we have all been restored to life, we have all ascended into heaven. For a portion of the flesh and blood of each one of us is in the man Christ. Therefore, where a portion of me reigns, I believe that I reign; where my blood rules, I conceive that I rule; where my flesh is glorified, I know that I am glorious.[2]

Likewise St. Gregory of Nazianzus maintains that God became man "to sanctify man, and to be, as it were, a leaven for the entire mass; and by joining himself to what has been condemned, to free the whole from damnation."[3] For "from the whole of human nature, to which was joined divinity, arose, as the first fruit of the common mass, the man who is in Christ, by whom all humanity was united to divinity."[4]

Naclantus even goes so far as to stress the still deeper truth that, by virtue of the Incarnation, we have become not only of one nature but also of one Person with Christ:

> He not only is clothed, sheltered, and fed in us: "As long as you did it unto one of the least of these my brethren, you did it unto me"; but we are reputed to be one and the same Person as he, and we receive his

[1] In *Ioan. Evang.*, i. 9. 24. St. Cyril returns constantly to this theme: "We were crucified with him when his flesh was crucified; for in a sense it contained all nature, just as when Adam incurred condemnation the whole of nature contracted the disease of his curse in him." (In *Epist. ad Rom.*, vi.)

[2] *Hom. VI in Pascha.*

[3] *Or. XXX*, xxi. in *MPG* xxxvi, p. 132.

[4] *Or. de verbis 1 Cor. 15*, in *MPG* xliv, p. 1313.

throne. . . . And thus at last, from having been adopted sons, we become in a sense natural sons, and we call to the Father not alone by grace but, as it were, by natural right.[1]

For "he that is joined unto the Lord is one spirit,"[2] that is, one and the same Self or Person, and it is with this union of the divine and the human in mind that wine and water are together poured into the chalice at Mass, with the prayer—

> Grant that, by the mystery of this water and wine, we may be made partakers of his divinity who vouch‑safed to become partaker of our humanity.

The feeling that the Incarnation has, in principle, already achieved this union is the clearest indication of its mythological character—of the fact that, as a story, it is the outward and visible symbol of a perennial truth about man. For upon the historical figure of Jesus the "common man" has projected symbols referring to the inmost, unconscious depths of his own nature. For this reason the Christ of Catholic dogma is a far more powerful conception than the rationalized "Jesus of history". The latter is a mere preacher and exemplar of morals who, like all such, can only suggest superficial transformations of conduct which do not affect the inner core of our being. But the transforming power of the myth depends upon a full and effective realization of its meaning, which is something very much more than a devout fascination for the numinous quality of its symbols.

Yet the full sense of the myth comes to light only as it is seen

---

[1] *De Regno Christi*, from Thomassinus, *De Incarnatione* viii. 9. 18. To "call to the Father by natural right" means to have the same relationship to the Father which is enjoyed by God the Son as the Second Person of the Trinity. Some modern theologians have argued that so substantial an identity between man and God would destroy the possibility of love between the two, reducing all to a "meaningless monism". But by the same argument it would have to follow that there could be no love between the Persons of the Trinity, since all Three are One God! [2] 1 *Corinthians* 6: 17.

in the spirit of a true catholicity—*quod semper, quod ubique, quod ab omnibus*, of the truth held always, everywhere, and by all—which is neither the official ideology of a "party religion" nor the lowest-common-denominator faith of a statistical demo-cracy. That which has been held "always, everywhere, and by all" is the one common realization, doctrine, and myth which has appeared with consistent unanimity in every great culture, without benefit of "historical contacts" between the various traditions. It was even obvious to St. Augustine, though he later retracted the statement, that "the very thing now called the Christian religion was not wanting among the ancients from the beginning of the human race, until Christ came in the flesh, after which the true religion, which already existed, began to be called 'Christian'." In the light of such a catholicity the Virgin-born One, who is both God and Man, is that uncaused Reality which is both the timeless and the present, which is simultaneously the true life of man and of all. Every *avatar*, every incarnation of the "only-begotten Son" speaks in the name of this "one-and-only" Self who is YHVH, I am.

> I am the way, the truth, and the life. . . . I am the resurrection and the life. . . . I am the door. . . . Before Abraham was, I am.[1]

> I am the Self in the heart of all beings; I am the beginning, the middle, and the very end of beings. . . . I am the origin of all. . . . I am the father of this world. . . . I am light in moon and sun. . . . I am the insight of the wise.[2]

> I was in many a guise before I was disenchanted, I was the hero in trouble, I am old and I am young. . . . I am universal.[3]

[1] *John* 14: 6, 11: 25, 10: 7, 8: 58.
[2] Sri Krishna in *Bhagavad-Gita* 10: 20, 10: 8, 9: 17, 7: 8, 10.
[3] Taliesin, from Coomaraswamy, *On the One and Only Transmigrant*, in *JAOS*, vol. 64, No. 2, supplement, p. 33 n.

I am the wind which blows o'er the sea, I am the wave of the ocean . . . a beam of the sun . . . the God who creates in the head the fire.[1]

I am in heaven and on earth, in water and in air; I am in beasts and plants; I am a babe in the womb, and one that is not yet conceived, and one that has been born; I am present everywhere.[2]

[1] Amergin, from Coomaraswamy, *ibid*. "Wind" and "wave of ocean" are the Spirit and Water of *Genesis* 1: 2.
[2] Hermes Trismegistus, *Lib*., xiii. 11b.

CHAPTER V

The Passion

IN the cycle of the Christian Year we move very swiftly from the Birth of Christ to his Passion, Death, and Resurrection, for the great feasts and fasts of the calendar commemorate the mythological aspects of the life of Christ—his great, world‑saving actions rather than his teachings or miracles for the healing of individuals. However, the season of Christmas and Epiphany is separated from that of the Passion by the fast‑time of Lent.[1] The purpose of Lent is not primarily to commemorate the forty‑day fast of Christ in the wilderness which immediately followed his baptism; in the ancient Church Lent was, above all things, the period of spiritual

[1] Lent is actually divided from Epiphany by the so‑called Pre‑Lenten season, the three Sundays of Septuagesima, Sexagesima, and Quinquagesima. These names are derived from the fact that the First Sunday in Lent was originally called Quadragesima—the fortieth day before Easter—and the three Sundays preceding take these names by analogy, and not because they are respectively the fiftieth, sixtieth, and seventieth days before Easter.

training and instruction which preceded initiation into the
Christian Mysteries by the Sacrament of Baptism. The proper
time for initiation was Easter Eve, because the Sunday of the
Resurrection is the greatest feast of the whole year—representing the fulfilment of the Incarnation, whereas Christmas is
only the beginning.

Prior to the general practice of infant baptism, initiation into
the Christian Mysteries was a tremendous solemnity involving
preliminary disciplines, tests, and exorcisms of a most serious
kind. For in this respect, as in many others, Christianity was
following the pattern of the other great Mystery cults of the
Graeco-Roman world. In those days the inner Mystery of the
Mass was by no means a public rite which anyone might
attend. It was a true *mystery*, and the actual rite was divided
into two parts—the Mass of the Catechumens and the Mass
of the Faithful. The Catechumens were those undergoing
preparation for baptism—being catechized—and because they
had not yet received initiation were permitted to attend only
the introductory part of the Mass. After the reading of the
Gospel for the day, the Deacon of the Mass would turn to the
people and say, "Let the catechumens depart", whereafter it
was the duty of the Door-keepers to see that no uninitiated
person remained in the church. This custom prevailed so long
as Christians were a minority in their society, but disappeared
when Christianity had been adopted as a state-religion, and
when whole societies were nominally Christian.

While the primary purpose of the Quadragesima or Lent
was, therefore, the preparation of the Catechumens, the fast
was also kept by the Initiated Faithful as a matter of annual
participation in the labours of Christ. Thus with the third
Sunday before Lent—Septuagesima—the Church changes
its vestments to the purple of penitence, and goes with Christ,
as Christ, into the cycle of darkness. From now until Easter
the *Gloria in excelsis* is not sung, nor is the triumphal cry
"Alleluia!" heard in the liturgy. The Mass of Septuagesima

opens with an introit from Psalm 17, appropriate to the entry of Christ in the darkness which he is to redeem:

> The groans of death surrounded me; the sorrows of hell encompassed me: and in my affliction I called upon the Lord.

Lent[1] itself begins on the Wednesday before Quadragesima Sunday—a day called Ash Wednesday because of the rite of imposing blessed ashes on the foreheads of the faithful. Before the Mass, the priest takes ashes which have been made from palm leaves used on Palm Sunday of the year before, and solemnly blesses them at the altar with holy water and the sign of the Cross. Thereafter the faithful come to the altar, and the priest traces the sign of the Cross with the ashes upon their foreheads, saying to each: "Remember, O man, that dust thou art, and unto dust thou shalt return", while the choir sings:

> Let us change our garments for ashes and sack-cloth: let us fast and lament before the Lord: for our God is plenteous in mercy to forgive our sins. . . . Attend, O Lord, and have mercy: for we have sinned against thee.

The fast itself consists in special acts of piety carried on throughout the forty days, as well as abstention from "flesh" food—that is to say, from "blood". For both Hebrew and Christian symbolism identify blood with the life-principle, and abstention from blood is in recollection of the shedding of the Blood of Christ—that is, of the pouring out of the Divine Life into human nature.

Generally speaking, the penitential observances of the Church have, in practice, a sentimental rather than a spiritual atmosphere because they express the feeling of remorse rather

---

[1] "Lent" is an Anglo-Saxon word meaning "spring" (*lencten*). In France the season is known as *Carême*, in Italy as *Quaresima*, both from the Latin Quadragesima.

than "metaphysical conversion" or *metanoia*. From the earliest times they have dwelt upon the extreme "horror" of sin, and upon how deeply it "wounds the feelings" of Christ, and "grieves" the Holy Spirit. While it is all too true that the "missing of the mark" called egocentricity underlies all the enormities of human behaviour, Christians have seldom recognized that the inculcation of shame, horror, and guilt is in no sense a cure for sin. It is merely the opposite of misconduct, the automatic reaction of the ego to social rejection, and, like every mere opposite or reaction, it is nothing more than a swing of the pendulum. The pendulum will continue to swing between good and evil until the weight is raised to the fulcrum, the Centre above and beyond the opposites. For sentimental guilt by no means destroys egocentricity, being nothing other than the sensation of its wounded pride—a pride which it then labours to restore by acts of penitence and piety.

> When the Devil was ill,
> The Devil a monk would be;
> But when the Devil was well,
> The Devil the Devil was he!

In the sentimental sphere of "morals" both good and evil are sin, because the weight is away from the Centre, and thus "off the mark". The Church recognizes this in principle, but nct in practice, in the doctrine that, lacking the divine Grace, even moral actions are done "under sin". In effect, however, this has come to mean that only those "good" actions performed under the auspices of the Church are "really" good. The state of Grace has been confused with a permanent swing of the pendulum in one direction—an impossibility so long as the end, the ego, remains weighted.

After five weeks of Lent the Church comes to the week in which it celebrates the central mystery of the entire Christian myth—the Mystery of the Atonement, of the "at-one-ment" of God and man achieved by the Incarnation. The rites of the

Birth and of the Labours of Christ have been enacted, and the Church now turns to that phase of the Incarnation wherein God the Son descends into man's suffering and death as well as into his life and labour, thereby raising the most finite level of human experience to the infinite.

The Sacrificial Victim enters the temple for the final act of the Mystery with a triumphal procession, commemorating the entry of Jesus into Jerusalem for that Passover Sacrifice which was to be his own crucifixion.[1] Thus the first day of

[1] Here again, I suggest that the reader refresh his memory of the Gospel narrative—if necessary—before proceeding further with this chapter. The rites of the Church follow the order of events as described in *John*, and the relevant sections of this Gospel are *John* 12: 12 to 13: 38, and 18: 1 to the end of the Gospel. *John*, however, has no complete account of the Last Supper, and to fill in the full details of this and other events one should read also the accounts of both *Matthew* and *Luke*, at least. For these, see *Matthew* 21: 1–20, and 26: 1 to the end of the Gospel, and *Luke* 19: 28–48, and 22: 1 to the end of the Gospel. To clarify the order of events in the second part of the week, I append the parallel Jewish and Christian calendars, inserting the events of the Christ-story as *John* places them:

CHURCH CALENDAR		JEWISH CALENDAR	CHRIST STORY
Weds. in Holy Week			
	Sunset:	Nisan 13th	
		First Day of	
		Unleavened Bread	
Thurs. (Maundy)			
	Sunset:	Nisan 14th	
		The Parasceve	Last Supper
			Gethsemane
Fri. of Preparation			Peter's Denial
			Trial by Pilate
			Crucifixion
	3 p.m.	Paschal Lamb	Death of Christ
		slain	Burial of Christ
	Sunset:	The Sabbath	
		Passover meal	
		eaten	
Sat. (Easter Eve)			
	Sunset:	First Day of	
		the Week	
Sun. (Easter Day)	*Dawn:*		Resurrection

Note that in the Jewish Calendar days are reckoned from sunset to sunset.

Holy Week is Palm Sunday—a day upon which the rites of the Church assume, and retain throughout the week, the definite character of a Mystery Drama in which the actual events of the Passion are re-enacted year after year, in witness to the fact that what is done here, in time, is the *anamnesis* or re-presentation of a truth which, at the metaphysical level, ever *is*. Jerusalem, the City of God and of the Temple, is Heaven when considered as the Jerusalem Above, but as the Jerusalem on earth it is the type of the human body, the material Temple of the Holy Spirit. To this shrine the Christ comes in triumph, the Word assuming the flesh to be crucified in the flesh, and "the children of the Hebrews" honour him by strewing their garments in his path and waving branches of palm and olive about his head, crying, "Hosanna! Blessed is he that cometh in the Name of the Lord! Hosanna in the highest!"[1]

The Mass of Palm Sunday is therefore preceded by a rite of peculiar interest and solemnity, having itself the form of a mass, save that the elements to be consecrated are not bread and wine but branches of palm and olive. As the procession of the priest and his ministers enters the church, the choir chants:

> Hosanna to the Son of David; blessed is he that cometh in the Name of the Lord. O King of Israel: Hosanna in the Highest.

They repair to the altar for the intoning of a Collect, Lesson, and Gospel after the usual manner of the Mass, and thereafter chant the Preface and Sanctus to the music of the Mass for the Dead. The priest then blesses the branches with incense and holy water, recalling in his prayer not only the palms with

[1] It should be noted, too, that in entering the City of the Body he rides upon the animal—"Brother Ass" as St. Francis called the body. Many of the *avatars* are thus pictured, Lao-tzu upon the water-buffalo, the Buddha entering Māyā upon the elephant, and Feng-kan riding the tiger. Krishna as the Charioteer has the same sense, for ultimately it is always the real Self who holds the reins and "rides the beast" and not this "I".

which Christ was greeted at Jerusalem, but also the olive-branch which the dove brought to Noah as a sign of the ending of the Flood and of peace between God and man. For the Flood is ever the symbol of that unconsciousness of the Spirit, the true Self, into which the Divine—as the Sun—descends at night, and from which it arises at dawn, since these are the same waters from which the world was made in the beginning. The essential meaning of the Atonement is that it is the representation in time of the Sacrifice which was made "before time", of the voluntary sacrifice wherein and whereby the One seems to become the Many. By the spell of the Word the true Self is enchanted, and appears to be this, that, and the other "I", unconscious of its original Identity as, by night, the sun is lost in "the waters beneath the earth".

After the blessing, the palms are distributed to the people, a procession is formed, and the clergy with the choir leave the church, gathering outside the great West Door which stands at the opposite end of the church from the altar. At this point a group of cantors re-enters the church, and, facing the closed Door, begin the hymn *Gloria, laus et honor*:

> All glory, laud and honour
> To thee, Redeemer King,
> To whom the lips of children
> Made sweet Hosannas ring.

And at the close of each verse the choir outside repeats the refrain, echoing back and forth, until with the last verse the Subdeacon strikes upon the door with the foot of the processional cross. At this, the Gate of Jerusalem, the Door of Christ's Body the Church, is opened and the whole procession makes its triumphal entry, singing:

> As the Lord entered the holy city, the children of
> the Hebrews, declaring the resurrection of life, with
> palm branches cried out: Hosanna in the highest.

During the Mass, at the time for the chanting of the Gospel, the clergy and the choir sing the whole story of the Passion according to *Matthew* in a dramatic form, wherein members of the clergy take the parts of Christ, Pilate, Judas, and the Narrator, while the choir sings the words of the Hebrew multitude. The same rite is repeated on Tuesday, Wednesday, and Good Friday with the Passion stories according to *Mark, Luke* and *John.*

Thursday is an exception, because it is the feast *Caena Domini*, of the Lord's Supper, commemorating the institution of the Mass itself, and for a moment the purple of mourning is exchanged for the white of gladness. On the night before he was crucified Christ and his Twelve Disciples partook of a last meal together. This, according to *John*, was not the Passover meal itself, which would have been eaten after sunset on Friday; it was possibly a *chaburah*, a type of solemn fraternal banquet held from time to time among Hebrew religious societies. At this supper Christ instituted the Sacrament or Mystery which was thereafter to be the very centre of Christian life and worship, and to be known by such names as the Holy Sacrifice of the Mass, the Eucharist, and the Divine Liturgy.[1]

The action of Christ at the Last Supper may best be described in the words of the Mass itself, taken from the *Quam oblationem*—the Prayer of Consecration in the Canon or Order of the Roman Mass. Having given thanks, and having called

[1] The word "mass" is supposedly derived from the final salutation of the priest to the people, *Ite missa est*—"Go, it has been sent forth"—in other words, the mission of the Incarnation has been completed. "Eucharist" is the Greek word for "thanksgiving", and is used because Christ "gave thanks" before he took the Bread and the Cup to perform the Mystery. The priest does the same before repeating the Act, beginning the Preface with the words, "It is very meet, right, and our bounden duty that we should at all times and in all places give thanks unto thee, O Holy Lord, Almighty Father, Eternal God". The word "liturgy" is from the Greek *leitourgos*, that is, "public" *leitos* "work" *ourgos*—a term applied to the rites of the Church as a whole, but to the Mass in particular as the Great Work performed by the Church as the Body of Christ, the company of all faithful people.

upon the Father to accept the Bread and Wine offered upon the altar, the priest continues:

> Which offering do thou, O God, vouchsafe in all things to bless ✠, consecrate ✠, approve ✠, make reasonable and acceptable: that it may become for us the Body ✠ and Blood ✠ of thy most beloved Son our Lord Jesus Christ. Who the day before he suffered took bread into his holy and venerable hands, and with his eyes lifted up to heaven, unto thee, God, his almighty Father, giving thanks to thee, he blessed ✠, brake, and gave to his disciples, saying: Take and eat this all of you, FOR THIS IS MY BODY.
>
> In like manner, after he had supped, taking also this excellent Chalice into his holy and venerable hands; also giving thanks to thee, he blessed ✠, and gave it to his disciples, saying: Take and drink this all of you, FOR THIS IS THE CHALICE OF MY BLOOD, OF THE NEW AND ETERNAL TESTAMENT; THE MYSTERY OF FAITH: WHICH SHALL BE SHED FOR YOU AND FOR MANY UNTO THE REMISSION OF SINS. As often as ye shall do these things, ye shall do them in memory of me.

At these words, spoken first by Christ, and thereafter by any duly ordered priest of the Apostolic Succession, that which was bread and wine becomes, in substance, the veritable Body and Blood of Christ. Thus the frail Host, the round wafer of bread, which the priest holds in his hands, becomes effectively the Eternal Word, God and Man, Creator and Ruler of the universe. Lifting it above his head, the priest shows it to be adored by all amid the rising smoke of incense and to the solemn ringing of bells.

Bread and wine are respectively the staple food and drink

of men, and thus the substance of human life. Yet before they become food, the wheat and the grapes undergo a transformation: they are ground and crushed, baked and fermented, and in this they typify the strangest and most problematic aspect of life itself. For every form of life exists at the expense of some other form, the whole living world constituting a colossal cannibalism, a holocaust in which life continues only at the cost of death. Man lives because of the sacrifice of the wheat and the vine, and he, in his own turn, is a sacrifice to the birds and the worms, or to the bacilli which effect his death. This is the inescapably grim fact of being alive, and which most civilized peoples do their best to conceal.

From the relative standpoint of time and space this mutual slaughter is hardly a sacrifice in the accepted sense; for every true sacrifice is voluntary, whereas the wheat which was ground for our bread, and the lamb which was slain for our roast could not exactly be called the willing victims of their fate. On the other hand, the Mass represents a true sacrifice, in that Christ submitted deliberately and willingly to his crucifixion, which took place at the very moment when the Jews were sacrificing the Passover Lamb at the Temple. The reason why the new Christ-Sacrifice redeems and the old Passover-Sacrifice does not is that the Victim of the former is *willing*, the performer of a self-sacrifice, at once Priest and Offering.[1]

Now the voluntary sacrifice redeems man from the curse of sin and death because there is but One who can actually perform self-sacrifice—namely God, the true Self. That other self called "I" is utterly unable to end itself, for it can only think in terms of its own continuity. Even ordinary suicide is not a true self-ending because, like every desire for a future, it is an

---

[1] Naturally, the Jews have to play the part of "villain" in this story, but if one were to consider Hebrew Mythology in its own right, it would be found to express the same *philosophia perennis* as the Christian, more especially in that complete form known as the Kabala.

attempt to retain something out of the past, out of memory—in this instance the memory of sleep, but sleep to continue for ever. But "I" comes to an end when, in the light of immediate "now-consciousness", of the true Self, it is seen to be unreal, abstract, and incapable of creative action. This actual Self alone, being of eternity and not time, is free from the wish to continue, and is able to come to an end—the "end" here signifying the "mark" which sin misses, the point of the needle on which the angels stand, the One Moment of eternity.

The marvelous symbolism of the Mass, as of the Crucifixion itself, has to be understood in relation to the mysterious "Lamb sacrificed from the foundation of the world" which is mentioned in the *Apocalypse*.[1] Seen from the temporal standpoint of "I", life is founded on the grim holocaust of mutual slaughter unwillingly endured, since "I" must ever wish to continue. But from the standpoint of *the* Point, of eternity, this holocaust is the outward expression of the eternal self-ending of the Creator. Hindu mythology puts it rather more directly by saying that each form of life is the disguise of God, and that life exists because it ever offers itself to itself, since the food which is eaten is the disguised God giving himself to be eaten. Hence the formula, *Annam Brahman*—food is God—and the verse:

> Who gives me away verily helps me!
> I—the food—eat the eater of food!
> I overcome the world![2]

All of which is to say, with Christ, of the Bread, "Take and eat this all of you, for this is my Body. . . . Be of good cheer, for I have overcome the world."

The "death" from which we are redeemed is always the past, and salvation is release from the enchantment of time. At once this deprives physical death, so essential to life, of its peculiar horror because the mind is no more obsessed with the wish to

---

[1] *Revelation* 13: 8.   [2] *Taittiriya Upanishad*, iii. 10. 6.

continue, to go on piling up memories indefinitely. Physical death is then understood as the instrument of eternal renewal. It is not only the transformation of life into food; it is also the wiping away of memory, of the past, which, if it continued to accummulate indefinitely, would strangle all creative life with a sense of unutterable monotony. Physical death is the in-voluntary end of the memory-system called myself—the end of my time. But the real and eternal Self does not die at death—for the paradoxical reason that it *wills* to "die", to "end", eternally, and is therefore "new" at every moment.

> Behold, I make all things new. . . . It is done.
> I am Alpha and Omega, the beginning and the
> end. . . . Behold, I come quickly, and my reward
> is with me.[1]

To put it less symbolically—the world of reality is ever-present, always at an end because it has no future, and always new because it has no past.[2]

In the Mass, then, we represent the crux of the whole Myth: the bread and wine which we are, because we eat it, becomes by Sacrifice the Body and Blood (i.e. Life) of Christ. And this, in turn, we eat again so that it becomes us, making our body and blood Christ's. This is why the myth so properly insists that the Mass is much more than a *mere* symbol: the bread and wine become in actuality and not alone in figure the very Christ. It is precisely in the almost magical character of the Catholic Mass that its whole truth lies, and all attempts to rationalize the Mystery deprive it of its real point. For in every

[1] *Revelation* 21: 5, 6; 22: 12.

[2] Cf. Jami, *Lawā'ih*, xxvi: "The universe consists of accidents pertaining to a single substance, which is the Reality underlying all existences. This universe is changed and renewed unceasingly at every moment and every breath. Every instant one universe is annihilated and another resembling it takes its place. . . . In consequence of this rapid succession, the spectator is deceived into the belief that the universe is a permanent existence." Trs. Whinfield and Kazwini (London, 1906).

way the rite of the Mass concentrates upon a point—the point of time at which the priest utters the solemn words, *Hoc est enim Corpus meum, Hoc est enim Calix Sanguinis mei*, and the point of space, the altar, where the attention of the whole congregation is focused in its worship of the Sacramental Presence. Yet because the Mass is *also* a symbol as well as an actual Mystery, this one point is the temporal and spatial "focus" of the point of the Eternal Now, in which and at which the very universe is Christ's Body. In the language of time and space the miracle of transubstantiation is limited to a particular point of time and space—to that bread and wine ritually consecrated. But from the eternal point represented by the temporal point the miracle of transubstantiation does not *become* but *is*, from the foundation of the world, and includes the entire creation.[1]

The actual rite of the Mass is, as we saw, divided into two parts—the Mass of the Catechumens and the Mass of the Faithful. The former is a re-adaptation of the Jewish synagogue service, consisting of prayers and readings. The actual action of the Mass does not begin until the Mass of the Faithful. It is

[1] It should hardly be necessary to labour this point, for the symbolism of the Mass is so clear and obvious—the transformation of the substance of life into the divine nature. However, official theology in its peculiar horror of anything that might possibly suggest "pantheism"—the doctrine that all "things" are God—has very much discouraged any interpretation of the Mass which fails to confuse the language of myth with that of science. But, as a matter of fact, pantheism has never been a part of the *philosophia perennis*, since it would be absurd to identify with God those "things" which, as we have seen, exist in a verbal and conventional sense alone. This deeper significance of the Mass is beginning to appear again in the contemporary Liturgical Reform movement within the Church, whereas during the whole period of the transubstantiation controversies with Protestantism a very narrow view of the Mass prevailed. Its essential work was, as it were, stopped short at the altar, and the communicant remained in actual touch with the True Body only for so long as the sacred species continued undissolved in his stomach! However, Patristic views were quite otherwise, as St. Leo, in *Sermo* 63 (*MPL*, liv, 357), "Nothing else is aimed at in our partaking of the Body and Blood of Christ than that we change into what we consume, and ever bear in spirit and in flesh him in whom we have died, been buried, and have risen."

divided into three main phases—Offertory, Consecration, and Communion. The Offertory is the presentation of the bread and wine at the altar, and represents the offering of ourselves, the laying open of humanity to Godhead in the spirit of the Virgin's "Be it unto me according to thy word". In the Consecration the priest assumes the part of Christ and repeats the actions of the Last Supper, as described above, performing with his hands what he also says in words—concluding with the solemn breaking of the Host, called the Fraction, because an essential part of the Mystery is that the Body of Christ is broken and divided and yet remains entire in every fragment. The "natural" world of separate "things" is always the seeming division of the supernatural, which, however, remains One and undifferentiated. In the final act of Communion all the clergy and people gather at the altar and consume the sacred elements, brought to them by the priest and his attendant ministers.[1]

The Mass which is celebrated on the Thursday of Holy Week is, then, a very special commemoration in honour of Christ's first celebration of this Mystery. The *Gloria in excelsis*, ordinarily omitted in Lent, is sung, and at this time the bells of the church ring out for the last time until Easter. During the Mass the priest consecrates a special Host which, when the Mass is over, is placed in the Chalice, veiled, and, attended with lights, is carried in solemn procession to a side-altar radiant with candles and flowers. In this fashion the Church accompanies

---

[1] In the Roman Catholic rite the Chalice is not received by any but the priest himself, a restriction dating from early mediaeval times when, because of the prevalence of shaggy moustaches and beards which might catch drops of the consecrated wine, precautions were taken to preserve the Blood of Christ from profanation. Not all of the consecrated bread is consumed in the Communion, and that which remains is "reserved" in a tabernacle upon the altar which is ceremoniously veiled and attended by an ever-burning light. This "reservation of the Sacrament" is for the purpose of having the Host ready at all times for the Communion of the sick and dying, and to constitute the perpetual centre of devotion for the faithful who visit the church outside the time of Mass.

Christ to the Garden of Gethsemane, singing as it goes the great hymn of St. Thomas Aquinas, *Pange lingua:*

> Now, my tongue, the mystery telling
> Of the glorious Body, sing,
> And the Blood, all price excelling,
> Which the nations' Lord and King,
> In a Virgin's womb once dwelling,
> Shed for this world's ransoming.

At the side-altar the Host is reserved throughout the remaining hours of the day and night until the morning of Good Friday, and during this time groups of the faithful take turns at the altar to keep the vigil with Christ in the Garden.

After Vespers have been sung, the priest and his ministers go to the high altar and strip off its fine cloths of linen and silk while the choir sings:

> They parted my garments among them;
> And upon my vesture they cast lots—

remembering how Christ was stripped of his clothes before crucifixion. This done, the priest puts aside his purple cope (i.e. cloak), girds himself with a linen towel and, taking a vessel of water, goes and washes the feet of the faithful. He pours a little water on the right foot of each person, wipes it with a towel, and kisses it, and, while he re-enacts the humility of Christ in washing the feet of his disciples after the Supper, there is chanted the antiphon:

> *Mandatum novum do vobis*—A new commandment
> I give you: that you love one another, as I have loved
> you, saith the Lord.

And thus in English-speaking lands this day is called Maundy Thursday from the first word of this antiphon—*mandatum,* a commandment.

In a monastic church where the Divine Office is regularly

sung in choir, the ensuing hours of the night are observed with
the marvelous rite of *Tenebrae* or "Darkness", consisting of the
special version of Matins and Lauds appropriate to Holy
Week. By the altar there is set a triangular stand upon which
there burn fifteen unbleached candles, one of which is extinguished at the end of each psalm composing the Office—in
representation of the desertion of Christ by his disciples. The
psalms are interspersed with various anthems and lections from
the scriptures and the Fathers, so that the whole rite may last
for two or more hours.

The profound psychological effect of *Tenebrae* is largely
dependent upon the "contemplative" tone of the endlessly
flowing Gregorian chant to which the words are sung. Unlike
modern, and like most types of "traditional" music, it has no
fixed rhythm, so that it follows the natural rhythm of the
spoken word. Furthermore, it has a peculiarly impersonal
quality. That is to say, it is not at all suggestive of strong
individual emotions, and lacks the "personal style" which
post-Renaissance composers have worked so assiduously to
cultivate. It is therefore a music possessed of a universal and
supra-individual character wholly suited to the words of the
Divine Office, and likewise of the Mass itself, since these are
understood to be the words of God and not of man. Indeed,
the entire principle of worship is that man speaks, not words,
but the Word, in expression of the fact that he is "no longer I
but Christ".[1]

As *Tenebrae* proceeds into the night the church grows darker
and darker. Psalm by psalm the candles at the altar are put out,
and towards the end all other lights in the church are extinguished too, until one solitary light remains at the apex of the
stand. This is Christ alone, surrounded by the "forces of
darkness" when all his disciples have fled. At a deeper level

---

[1] *Galatians* 2: 20. Strictly speaking, then, Christianity knows of no such
thing as "private prayer", which is actually a contradiction in terms. Man is
related to God only *as* Christ, and never as "I".

Tenebrae is a representation of the spiritual journey into the "Dark Night of the Soul", the disappearance of light symboliz, ing the progressive realization that "I am nothing". After the singing of the Canticle of Zacharias, the *Benedictus*, the one light remaining is taken out and concealed behind the altar so that the church is plunged into total darkness.

Even Christ has gone—"crucified, dead, and buried". There is nothing whatsoever left to which "I" can cling. Every belief and hope, even in God, which seemed to offer life to the "I" has been taken away, for as Christ said to his disciples, "It is expedient for you that I go away, for if I go not away the Paraclete (the Holy Spirit) cannot come unto you."[1] This is, then, the "cloud of unknowing", the "divine darkness", of St. Dionysius in which it is discovered that because all "knowledge" is memory, knowledge of that which was, all our knowledge amounts to nothing in so far as it fails entirely to grasp That which *is*. But in the now total darkness and silence of the church there is a sudden, sharp noise, and the one candle is brought back to its place on the stand—whereupon all leave the church in silence. This *strepitus* or sudden noise, heralding the return of the light, of the "one point" of fire, is the promised Resurrection into Life—always "sudden" in representation of the timeless and instant nature of eternity.

The day of the Crucifixion, known as Good Friday or the Friday of the Preparation (for the Passover), is observed with the sombre splendour of the Mass of the Presanctified. The clergy, vested in black, come to the bare altar and celebrate the ritual drama of the Passion according to *John*, singing the 18th and 19th chapters of the Gospel, from the Agony in the Garden to the Burial in the tomb of St. Joseph of Arimathaea. This done, the priest chants some sixteen prayers of intercession for the Church and for the whole human race. When these are ended, he receives from the deacon of the mass a great wooden crucifix veiled in black. He holds it up

[1] *John* 16: 7.

FIG. 8 THE CRUCIFIXION

This extraordinary woodcut was made in Rennes, France, about 1830. It shows almost the full symbolism of the Cross as the Tree of Life, surmounted by the figure of God the Father and the Dove of the Holy Spirit. To the left and right are the sun and moon, the sponge and the spear. Below, the Skull of Golgotha is clearly associated with the sphere of the world, encircled by the Serpent. I am unable to account for the peculiar symbolism of the dismembered heads and limbs, except by association with other traditions in which the divine sacrifice is more explicitly a dismemberment than a crucifixion.

before the people, and, unveiling the top part, sings upon a
low note—

> *Ecce lignum crucis*—Behold the wood of the cross,
> on which hung the Saviour of the world.

And the choir responds:

> *Venite adoremus*—Come let us adore.

Unveiling the right arm of the crucifix, the same words are
sung again louder and a little higher. Finally the whole
crucifix is laid bare, and the words are cried out once more
upon a note higher still. The "wood of the cross" is placed
before the altar upon a cushion, where the priest removes his
shoes, kneels before it and kisses it, all the people following
him in turn.

As the adoration of the Wood of the Cross proceeds, the
choir sings the Reproaches:

> O my people, what have I done unto thee?
> or in what have I afflicted thee? answer me.

> Because I led thee out of the land of Egypt,
> thou hast prepared a Cross for thy Saviour.

The Reproaches are interspersed with an ancient Greek
litany—the use of Greek rather than Latin indicating the
great antiquity of this rite.

> *Agios o Theos*—O holy God,

to which are echoed the same words in Latin—

> *Sanctus Deus!*

And the Litany proceeds:

> *Agios ischyros*—O holy mighty One!

> *Sanctus fortis!*

Agios athanatos, eleison imas—O holy
immortal One, have mercy upon us!

Sanctus immortalis, miserere nobis!

The Reproaches call to mind all the "types" of salvation
bestowed upon the Chosen People in the *Old Testament*—the
manna in the desert, the opening of the Red Sea, the pillar of
fire, the water from the rock, and the sceptre of the Throne of
David—the while reproaching the People for crucifying the
Substance of which these types were the shadows.

> I gave thee a royal sceptre, and thou hast given
> me a crown of thorns.

Yet it is just here that the rite brings out the marvelous
paradox of the whole Crucifixion Mystery. On the one hand,
the wood of the Cross is the entire summation of man's
ignorance and sin, being the instrument of torture which it
prepared for the Man who is God. On the other hand, the
Reproaches close with the antiphon:

> We adore thy Cross, O Lord: and we praise and
> glorify thy holy Resurrection: for by the wood of the
> Cross the whole world is filled with joy.

Whereupon there is immediately sung the extraordinary hymn,
Crux fidelis, in which the instrument of execution appears as
the very Tree of Life:

> *Crux fidelis, inter omnes*
> *Arbor una nobilis:*
> *Nulla silva tamen profert*
> *Fronde, flore, germine.*

> Faithful Cross, the one Tree noble above all:
> no forest affords the like of this in leaf, or
> flower, or seed.

De parentis protoplasti
Fraude factor condolens,
Quando pomi noxialis
In necem morsu ruit:
Ipse lignum tunc notavit,
Damna ligni ut solveret.

The Creator pitying the sin of our first parent,
wherefrom he fell into death by the bite of the
poisoned apple, did himself forthwith signify
wood for his healing of the hurts of wood.

It is obvious that the Wood or Tree of the Cross is of the
highest mythological significance, and that its relation to the
actual *stauros* (stake) upon which the historical Jesus was hung
is relatively small. Many modern Christian historians think
it most unlikely that Jesus was actually crucified upon a
wooden cross of the type familiar in crucifixes, whether of the
Latin †, Greek ✚, or Egyptian Tau-cross T forms. It was
more probably a simple stake, such that the actual symbol of
the Cross was shaped according to mythological rather than
historical considerations. As is well known, the Cross and
the Sacrificial Tree are symbols far more ancient than Christianity, and had a significance of such importance that it is not
at all inappropriate for the hymn to say:

Sola digna tu fuisti
Ferre mundi victimam.

Thou alone (the Tree) wert found *worthy*
to bear the Victim of the world.

So many of the hero-gods and *avatars* are associated with the
Tree that the central symbol of Christianity is of a truly universal
nature, and by no means a historical abnormality. In the myth
of Osiris, "he who springs from the returning waters", the
body of the God—slain by Set the Evil One—is found within

a giant tamarisk or pine-tree which had been cut down and used for the *central pillar* of the Palace of Byblos. Attis, son of the virgin Nana, died by self-sacrifice under a pine-tree. Gautama the Buddha, son of Māyā, attained his supreme Awakening as he sat in meditation beneath the Bo Tree. Odin learned the wisdom of the runes by immolating himself upon the World-Tree, Yggdrasil, with a spear cut from the same Tree:

> I know that I hung
> On a wind-rocked tree
> Nine whole nights,
> With a spear wounded,
> And to Odin offered
> Myself to myself;
> On that tree
> Of which no one knows
> From what root it springs.[1]

In like manner, Adonis (=*Adonai*, the Lord) was born of Myrrha the myrtle, and the Babylonian god Tammuz was associated in his death with the cedar, the tamarisk, and the willow.[2]

In almost all the mythological traditions this Tree is the *Axis Mundi*, the Centre of the World, growing in the "navel of the world" as, in mediaeval drawings, the Tree of Jesse is shown growing from the navel of Jesse. In the myth of Eden the Tree stands in the *centre* of the Garden, at the source of *four* rivers which "go out to water the garden".[3] For obvious reasons, Christianity regards the Cross as the centre of the

[1] *Odin's Rune Song,* trs. Benjamin Thorpe in *The Edda of Saemund the Learned* (London, 1866).

[2] In the Babylonian hymn called *The Lament of the Flutes for Tammuz,* a so-called "fertility" god taken to represent the death and resurrection of the crops, he is described as "a tamarisk that in the garden has drunk no water, . . . a willow that rejoiced not by the water-course."

[3] The clear identity of the Cross with this central Tree of Eden is shown, not only in the legends of the Holy Rood which assert that the Cross of Christ

world, and likewise places it upon the altar as the ritual centre of the church. The World-Ash, Yggdrasil, had its roots in Niflheim, the uttermost depths, and its topmost branch, Lerad, reached to the palace of the Allfather Odin in heaven. Similarly the world-tree of the Siberian Yakuts grows at "the central point, the World Navel, where the moon does not wane, nor the sun go down."[1] Conversely, the Axle-Tree of the *Upanishads* and the *Bhagavad-Gītā* grows out of Brahma and, like the Sephiroth Tree of the Kabala, has roots above and branches below.

The symbolism of the Tree is quite clearly that the Tree is the world—Life itself—having its stem rooted in the unknown. Its branches, leaves, flowers, and fruit form the multiplicity of creatures—"I am the vine; ye are the branches"—which blossom from the ever-fertile source of life. The *wood* of the Tree is matter, *prima materia*, out of which all things are made, so that it is not unfitting that, in his earthly incarnation, the Son of God should be also the Son of the Carpenter—Joseph. For this reason the Gnostics distinguished between three types of men, the pneumatic, the psychic, and the hylic—the

was made from the wood of that Tree, but also in the famous Great Cross of the Lateran, a mosaic dating, perhaps, from the time of Constantine, and restored by Nicolas IV. It shows an ornate Cross of the Latin form, having at its head the descending Dove of the Holy Spirit. From its foot there flow four rivers named Gihon, Pison, Tigris, and Euphrates, which were the four rivers of Eden. Between these rivers stands the City of God, guarded by the Archangel Michael, and behind him, in the midst of the City, stands a palm-tree surmounted by a phoenix. (The phoenix was commonly associated with Christ because it was supposed to rise eternally from the ashes of the fire in which it perished.) Two stags stand upon either side of the Cross, and at the bottom of the whole mosaic six sheep are standing in the waters of the four rivers. The parallel with Yggdrasil is extraordinary, for its topmost branch, Lerad, bears the falcon Vedfolnir whose piercing eye sees all things in the universe, and the four stags Dain, Dvalin, Duneyr, and Durathor feed upon its leaves. Honey-dew drops down from their horns, and supplies water for all the rivers of the earth.

[1] From Joseph Campbell, *The Hero With a Thousand Faces* (New York, 1949), pp. 334-5. Many representations of the crucified Christ likewise show the sun and moon on either side of the Cross.

last-named being those unfitted for supreme knowledge because of their total involvement in materiality, in *hylē*, which in Greek is "wood". Furthermore, the Tree is cruciform because the Cross is the "shape of the world", since the earth has four directions or quarters, and the very universe itself—ringed by the Zodiac—has four fixed, four cardinal, and four mutable points. Christ with his Twelve Apostles is in clear correspondence with the Sun in its twelve zodiacal signs, and the crucifix is very frequently found with the four fixed signs Taurus, Leo, Scorpio (interchangeable with the phoenix-eagle), and Aquarius at its extremities, standing for the Four Evangelists who, with the Four Archangels, do duty in Christianity for the Four Regents of Hindu-Buddhist mythology—the caryatidal kings who support the dome of heaven.[1]

To this Tree, image of the finite world, the Son of God is nailed by his hands and feet, and a spear is thrust in his side. And because the finite world is manifested by the contrast of opposites, left and right, high and low, before and behind, day and night, good and evil, the image of the world is cruciform. On the right hand is the sun, and on the left the moon. At the head is the fiery Dove, and at the foot the serpent or the skull—contrasting figures of life and death, liberation and bondage. The whole is, in short, a revelation of what human life is—in so far as our life is the identification of the true Self with time and space, past and future, pleasure and pain. This identification is the nailing, in consequence of which we are "dead and buried"—absorbed and confused in a past which "is not".

[1] Fanciful as these correspondences may seem to the modern mind, we must not forget that the Christian myth was formulated by people for whom they were immensely significant. Christianity was not elaborated from the scriptures by the rational and historical methods of its modern apologists. The tremendous importance of the four directions and of astrological symbolism in general is well treated in Dr. Austin Farrer's study of the *Apocalypse* entitled *A Rebirth of Images* (London, 1949).

This is why the Son of God is impaled with Five Wounds, for the world of time and space with which the Self is identified is based on the five senses—strictly speaking, on the *memory* of what comes to us through the five senses, for this is the sense of being "stuck" or nailed. In reality the past drops away, but in the mind it "sticks" and so impales us that we are in bondage to the past and to death. By the sticking, the memory, of the five senses we are helplessly attached to a world which we simul-taneously love and hate, which is pain to the degree that it is irresistible pleasure. In the *Jataka Tales* the Buddha, as Prince Five Weapons, is found in a similar predicament with the Giant Sticky-Hair—a monstrous ogre whom no man could defeat because all weapons became stuck in the clinging hairs which covered his body. The Prince fared no better than others, for he fought with the giant until he was glued to its hair by both hands, both feet, and even by his head. But just as the giant was about to devour him, the Prince said, "Monster, why should I fear? For in one life one death is quite certain. Moreover, I have in my stomach a thunderbolt—a weapon which you will be unable to digest if you eat me. It will tear your insides to pieces!"[1] At this, Sticky-Hair let go, and the Prince was free.

The thunderbolt, the lightning-flash, in the future Buddha's stomach was the *vajra*, otherwise known as the Diamond Body, which is equivalent to the Godhead in Christ—the eternal Self which is never actually in time. So long, then, as man thinks of himself as this "I", he finds that there is absolutely nothing he can do to release himself from the bondage of time; indeed, the more he struggles to be free, to be unselfish, just, and good, the more he is stuck in the entanglements of pride. "I-consciousness" is a vicious circle such that every attempt to

---

[1] *Jataka*, 55: 1. Cf. A. K. Coomaraswamy, "A Note on the Stickfast Motif", in *Journal of American Folklore*, vol. 57, pp. 128–31 (1944). This is, of course, a version of the universal motif which appears in American folklore as the Tar-Baby story.

FIG. 9 THE CRUCIFIXION

From a Spanish woodcut in the British Museum, *c.* 15th century. The Virgin
and St. John the Evangelist stand upon either side

stop or escape from it makes it whirl the more. Every move,
whether towards self-assertion or self-denial, is like the plight
of the fly in honey—for one loves oneself only to hate oneself,
and then the struggle to be free imprisons every limb. In such
an *impasse* "I" must at last give up.

My God, my God, why hast thou forsaken me?

Father, into thy hands I commend my spirit.

It is finished.

And he gave up the ghost.

This is the universal testimony of the "knowers of God"
—that the spiritual life of man dawns in the moment when,

in a profound and special sense, he does nothing. "I do nothing of myself." This is no ordinary inactivity, for to be idle with the express intention of attaining sanctity, as in formal "quietism", is still activity in so far as it is a method, a means to discover God. But the true state of divine union is "without means", and comes to pass when man "gives up" not as a means to get, but because he knows with certainty that he has no other alternative. In the ordinary way, such certainty comes only through a struggle to be free by all available means, leading to the conviction of their futility. To put it in another way, the mind does not become free from the illusion of ego by the way of unconsciousness— by any attempted reversion to "nature", or to primitive innocence, and still less by any kind of forgetful inebriation in ecstatic sensations, whether induced by drugs or selfhypnosis. The ego is dissolved only through the way of consciousness, through becoming so conscious of what "I" is that it has no more power to enthrall.

This "giving up" is the Sacrifice by which the Cross is transformed from the instrument of torture to the "medicine of the world", so that the Tree of Death becomes the Tree of Life. By the same alchemy the cruciform symbol of the earth, of conflict and opposition, is also the symbol of the sun, of lifegiving radiation.

> *Fulget crucis mysterium;*
> *Qua vita mortem pertulit,*
> *Et morte vitam protulit.*

> Shines forth the mystery of the Cross;
> whereby life suffered death, and by
> death brought forth life.

For this reason Christian art fashions the crucifix in two ways— the Cross of Christ suffering and the Cross of Christ in triumph, the latter showing him crowned and vested as King and Priest amid a full aureole radiating from the centre of the Cross. Properly, the first type of crucifix hangs or stands at the Rood Beam above the entrance to the choir or sanctuary, while the second type belongs upon the altar.

Thus the Tree standing at the axis, the cross-roads of the world, at the central point of time and space, is at once the Now out of which time and space, past and future, are exfoliated to the crucifixion of the Self, and the Now into which the Self "returns" when it "takes up the Cross" and no longer "misses the mark"—the "target" into which the spear of attention is at last thrust, releasing the river of blood and water which cleanses the world.

> *Spina, clavi, lancea,*
> *Mite corpus perforarunt:*
> *Unda manat et cruor:*
> *Terra, pontus, astra, mundus,*
> *Quo lavantur flumine!*

> Thorns, nails, and spear pierce that gentle
> Body: water flows forth, and blood: in which
> stream are cleansed the earth, the ocean, the
> stars, and the world![1]

The Mass of the Presanctified moves on to its climax with the solemn procession which, after the adoration of the Wood

---

[1] From the hymn *Crux fidelis.* Cf. *Mundaka Upanishad*, ii. 2. 3:

> "Using for a bow the great weapon of the Upanishad,
> One should set thereon an arrow made sharp by meditation.
> Stretching it with a mind pointed to the essence of That,
> Penetrate as the mark that Imperishable."

Note also that the cross of the Aztec saviour, Quetzalcoatl, was formed when the hero shot a *pochotl* tree through with another *pochotl*, used as an arrow. Likewise, Love comes to birth when Cupid penetrates the Heart (of the world) with his dart, which Heart appears in Catholic symbolism as the Sacred Heart of Jesus pierced with a dagger or spear.

of the Cross, brings from the altar of repose—Gethsemane—the Host which was consecrated the previous day.[1] As the choir sings the *Vexilla Regis*, the hymn praising the Cross as the triumphal Banner of the King, the Host is brought to the high altar amid lights and incense. It is laid upon the corporal, the small square cloth which is always spread upon the altar for the Holy Sacrament, and solemnly the priest swings the censer of incense thrice around it, and once over it in the form of a cross. He washes his hands, and then, after singing the *Pater noster*, elevates the Host for the adoration of the people. Silently, he receives it in Communion, and the Mass ends without another word. All lights are extinguished; the doors of the Tabernacle are unveiled and thrown wide open; the church is deserted.[2]

When Christ had "given up the ghost" and the spear had been thrust into his side, his body was taken down from the Cross and taken to the garden of St. Joseph of Arimathaea. Just before sundown, the beginning of the Passover Sabbath, it was laid in St. Joseph's tomb to await embalming upon the first day of the week since this was a work which, according to Jewish law, might not be performed on the Sabbath. This was the St. Joseph who, according to the great tradition of Western Christianity, received the Holy Cup of the Last Supper and brought it to the Celtic lands of Western Europe —a tradition which is the legendary basis for the cult of the Holy Graal.[3]

While the Body of Christ remained in the tomb, his soul and spirit descended into Hades or Sheol, the place of imprisonment

[1] Hence the name Mass of the *Presanctified*.

[2] It is a relatively recent custom to follow the Mass of the Presanctified with the *Tre Hore*, the Three Hour service of meditation upon the Seven Last Words from the Cross, which is more of an instruction than a regular part of the Liturgy.

[3] Unfortunately the vast subject of the Graal myths cannot form a part of this book since it is our purpose to confine the subject to the central story of Christianity, excluding the many subsidiary myths which have accrued to it.

of all who had departed this world from Adam until that very day. This tradition is only once mentioned in the canonical scriptures, but is preserved in detail in the apocryphal *Acts of John*. Catholic art, taking this text as its source, represents Hades or Hell as a monstrous dragon with a vast mouth lined with terrible teeth. At the approach of Christ, carrying a Cross which is now transformed into a spear and pennant, the dragon of Hades yawns wide to release Adam and Eve, Noah, Abraham, Isaac, and Jacob, Moses, Aaron, and all those who had lived justly under the Old Dispensation of the ages before the Incarnation. After this "harrowing of Hell" only those remain in prison who are in the following of Lucifer and his angels—chief among them the traitor Judas who betrayed Christ and then hanged himself—there to stay until the Day of the Last Judgement.

The importance of the "harrowing of Hell" is that the power of the Incarnation is retroactive or, to put it in another way, timeless. The coming of Christ is not a truly historical event—a step in a temporal process which is effective only for those who follow. It is equally effective for those who came before, and thus the Descent into Hades is a feature of the Christ-story which particularly suggests the timeless and mythological character of the whole. From another point of view, the descent into the depths is almost invariably one of the great tasks of "the Hero with a Thousand Faces", of the Christ in his many forms. Hades or Hell may here be understood as the Valley of the Shadow, the experience of impotence and despair in which "I" die and Christ comes to life. The descent is likewise a figure of the descent of consciousness into the unconscious, of the necessity of knowing one's very depths. For so long as the unconscious remains unexplored it is possible to retain the naïve feeling of the insularity and separateness of the conscious ego. Its actions are still taken to be free and spontaneous movements of the "will", and it can congratulate itself upon having motivations which are purely "good", unaware of the "dark" and hidden forces of conditioning which actually guide them.[1]

Down in Hades the work of Christ is to bring Adam through the jaws of the dragon into Paradise. It will be remembered that when Adam was expelled from the Paradise Garden, the way back was guarded by a Cherub with a flaming sword which "turned every way". The gnashing jaws of the dragon and the whirling sword are forms of the important mytho/logical motif which also appears as Symplegades, the Clashing Rocks, the task of the hero being to leap through before he is cut or crushed. But this "Active Door" opens and shuts with such incredible rapidity or suddenness that the hero has to get through in "no time at all". His only chance is to leap without hesitation, for the slightest wavering or indecision will be his undoing. Obviously, the Active Door is the same as the "needle's eye" and the "strait and narrow gate", through which one can enter into heaven only on the condition of having become nothing and nobody. Adam can pass through the Jaws of Hades into Paradise because now that he has been "crucified with Christ" who took upon himself the flesh of Adam, he is no more Adam but Christ. He goes forth into Paradise *as* Christ, as the New Adam. The reason is that Christ is the only one who can pass through the Active Door, being the Real Man who has no past and does not exist in time. Living entirely in the eternal Moment, it is no problem for him to move between the jaws of past and future where all others are trapped.

In many of the myths of the Active Door, the hero gets

---

[1] Jung has admirably demonstrated the compensatory relationship between the conscious and the unconscious, whereby the unconscious is identified with "evil" to the extent that the conscious is identified with "good", and *vice versa*. In other words, the relationship between good and evil is polar, and the only means of holding to the one and rejecting the other is by unconsciousness—by forgetting the rejected pole. Liberation from this vicious circle is possible only from a standpoint which is "beyond good and evil"—i.e. a standpoint which is strictly un/self/ish.

through at the cost of leaving something behind. A European folk-story tells of the Hare who wrests the Herb of Immortality from the Guardian Dog, leaving, however, his tail in the Dog's jaws. In the Christian version, the one left behind is Lucifer. Obviously, the Hare's tail is his past, that which is behind him, being the only thing which Time the Devourer can actually devour. Similarly, Lucifer is the "dead man", the ego abstracted from memory. So long as the mind is identified with it the gate of heaven is closed. Past and future clash together in a present which is exasperatingly brief, giving the sense that we have "no time" for anything. But when it is seen that the true Self is not the self we remember, the tail is "docked" and the Hare is "through".[1]

In the Old Testament the analogous situation is Moses' passage of the Red Sea, where the waters roll back to let "Israel" go through but rush together to trap "Egypt" in the flood. Very properly, then, Christ's passage through Death and Hades is likened by the Church to the Crossing of the Red Sea, for in the "harrowing of Hell" the jaws of the dragon yawn wide to give passage to those that are "in Christ", but close again upon Lucifer and his hosts. Beyond the rolling waters, the perilous gates or jaws of Hell, past and future, good and evil, life and death, and the whole gamut of opposites wherein man as ego is inescapably trapped, there lies the Risen Life— always open to him who leaps without hesitation, who moves with the Moment and does not linger in the past.

[1] Cf. *Wu-men Kwan*, xxxviii. "A cow passes through a gate. Its head, horns, and the four legs pass through easily, but only the tail cannot pass. Why can't it?" For the entire treatment of this motif I am indebted to A. K. Coomaraswamy's essay "Symplegades" in *Essays in the History of Science and Learning*, ed. M. F. Ashley Montagu (New York, 1947), pp. 463–88.

CHAPTER VI

From Easter to Pentecost

DESPITE the greater popularity of Christmas, Easter is the most important feast of the annual cycle. Known in Latin countries as the Pascha, its English name "Easter" is said to be derived from an Anglo-Saxon goddess of dawn, Eostre, whose rites were celebrated at the Vernal Equinox.[1] Be this as it may, its importance for the Christian myth is that it represents the fulfilment of the work of Christ—the Resurrection of his Body from death, seen as the very result of his voluntary sacrifice upon the Cross. The myth makes it clear that this is not merely the return of a ghost from the dead, nor even a simple resuscitation of the corpse. The Body which was nailed to the Cross and pierced with the Spear rises again into life, but so transformed that it can pass through closed doors, and appear and

[1] A folk-lorist "legend" for which I have been able to find no really sound authority, though one uses it for lack of any good alternative explanation! The original source of this supposition is the *Historia Ecclesiastica* of the Venerable Bede, and we have it on his authority alone.

disappear out of all conformity to the ordinary physical laws. It can even be touched and handled by the doubting Thomas, but Mary Magdalene is forbidden to cling to it when she recognizes Christ in the garden.[1]

The stress upon bodily resurrection, though problematic for rationalists, is of great mythological importance. For the resurrection of man from death, from self-identification with the past, involves an utterly different view of what was hitherto known as the "physical" world and the "material" body. What were formerly "things" are now seen as "That" which neither dies nor is born, neither comes nor goes, and to which it is simply impossible to "cling" with the memory, or to confine within the walls of conventional concepts and categories. From this standpoint bodily existence is no longer felt as an intolerable restriction upon the spirit; on the contrary, the body is "spiritualized"—becoming a member of the Risen Body, of the world as it really is beyond the conventions of time, space, multiplicity, and duality. Obviously this cannot be described, for that which is described—by the "compass upon the face of the deep"—is of necessity the conventional world. The Risen Body of the Word is no longer bound by its own spell.

In the Church, the rites of the Resurrection began anciently at midnight between Holy Saturday and Easter Sunday.[2] Because this was also the time of initiation into the Christian Mystery, the candidates (i.e. white-robed ones) for Baptism were assembled in the church before midnight for the final scrutiny, exorcism, and examination of their faith. Just before the midnight hour the church was put into complete darkness, lacking even the light which was left burning at the close of

[1] The usual translation of *John* 20: 17 is "Touch me not—*Noli me tangere*", but the Greek ἅπτω has rather the sense of "fasten" or "cling", and sometimes "to embrace carnally".

[2] For some centuries now it has been the custom of the Roman Church to observe these rites on the morning of Holy Saturday—a concession to secular routine!

Tenebrae. In the narthex, or porch, at the West Door there gathered the priest or bishop, with his deacon, subdeacon, and attendant acolytes. Equipped with the special ritual objects for these ceremonies—flint and steel, holy water, five grains of incense imbedded in wax nails, a triple-candle shaped like a trident and mounted upon a reed, and the processional cross— they made ready for the rite which announces the first moment of the Resurrection, the Blessing of Fire.

Remaining still in the narthex, the priest strikes a spark from the flint and blows it into a flame upon tinder. Over this newly kindled fire he utters the following prayer:

> O God who by thy Son, the Cornerstone, hast bestowed upon the faithful the fire of thy brightness; sanctify this new fire produced from a stone for our use: and grant that, during this Paschal festival, we may be so inflamed with heavenly desires, that with pure minds we may come to the solemnity of eternal glory.[1]

Having blessed the New Fire, he blesses the five nails of incense—

> that not only the sacrifice which is offered this night may shine by thy mysterious light; but also into whatever place anything of this mystical sanctifica- tion shall be brought, there, by the power of thy majesty, all the malicious artifices of the devil may be defeated.

He sprinkles both with holy water, and, when the coals in a censer have been lighted from the flame, they move a little into the church. Here they kneel for a moment while fire is brought

---

[1] "Eternal glory" is *perpetua claritas*, more literally "perpetual clarity", the quality of a "pure mind" which is "empty" of any clinging to the past. Thus, "Happy are the pure in heart, for they shall see God". Note again the symbolism of Christ as the Cornerstone "who maketh both one", who overcomes the opposites.

FIG. 10 TRIPLE CANDLE FOR HOLY SATURDAY

to one of the branches of the triple-candle, carried by the deacon, who, as it catches, sings on a quiet, low note:

Lumen Christi! The light of Christ!

And on the same note the choir replies:

Deo gratias! Thanks be to God!

The procession moves to the middle of the church, where a second branch of the candle is lighted, and upon a note higher and louder the deacon sings again, "The light of Christ!" Again the choir responds, "Thanks be to God!" When they arrive at the sanctuary, close to the high altar, the third branch is lighted, and the voice of the deacon calls out with full force, "The light of Christ!" And now the choir roars back, "Thanks be to God!"

Beside the high altar, at the "Gospel corner" which is to the left as one faces it, there stands a great candle known as the Paschal Taper, which is to burn throughout the Great Forty Days from Easter to the Ascension as witness of the Risen Christ upon earth. To this the deacon now carries the triple-candle with its three branches alight, and begins to sing the Paschal Praeconium for the blessing of the Paschal Taper. This prayer is chanted to what is perhaps the most ancient music in Christendom, and constitutes one of the most extraordinary passages in the whole Liturgy, sometimes known as the *Exsultet* from its first words—

> *Exsultet iam angelica turba caelorum*—Rejoice now all ye heavenly legions of angels! Celebrate with joy the divine mysteries, and for the King that cometh with victory let the trumpet proclaim salva/ tion. Rejoice, O earth, illumined by this celestial radiancy: and may the whole world know itself to be delivered from darkness, brightened by the glory of the Eternal King.

Having called upon the whole Church, and upon all those present to rejoice with him, he sings the versicles and responses which normally introduce the Canon of the Mass:

V. The Lord be with you.
R. And with thy spirit.
V. Hearts on high!
R. We lift them up to the Lord.
V. Let us give thanks to the Lord our God.
R. It is meet and just.

And the Praeconium continues:

> It is truly meet and just to proclaim with the whole affection of heart and mind, and with the service of our voice, God the invisible almighty Father, and his only/begotten Son, our Lord Jesus Christ. Who paid for us to the eternal Father the debt of Adam; and by his precious Blood put away the bond of the ancient sin. For this is the Paschal feast in which that true Lamb was slain, by whose Blood the door/posts of the faithful were consecrated.[1] This

---

[1] Throughout the Praeconium the *Old Testament* types, especially those connected with the Passover, are rehearsed. Most missals for the laity translate

is the night wherein formerly thou didst bring forth our forefathers the sons of Israel from Egypt, leading them with dry feet through the Red Sea. This, therefore, is the night which purified the darkness of sin by the light of the Pillar (of Fire). This is the night which today delivers throughout the whole world those who trust in Christ from the vices of the world, and from the darkness of sin, restores to grace, and clothes with sanctity. This is the night in which, breaking the chains of death, Christ ascended conqueror from the depths. For it availed us nothing to be born, unless it had availed us to be redeemed. O how wondrous is thy faithfulness towards us! O how inestimable is thy loving kindness: in that thou hast delivered up thy Son to redeem a slave! O truly necessary sin of Adam, which the death of Christ has blotted out! O happy fault, that merited such and so great a Redeemer!

O truly blessed night, which alone deserves to know the time and the hour, in which Christ rose from the depths. This is the night of which it is written: And the night shall be as light as the day, and the night is my illumination in my delights.[1]

veteris piaculi cautionem as "the guilt of the ancient (or original) sin"—which is somewhat misleading in that the modern equivalent of *cautio* is a bond given in bail. In the *Exodus* narrative the Destroying Angel "passed over" the houses of the Hebrews whose door-posts were sprinkled with the blood of the sacrificial lamb. Presumably the door-posts are the gates (*ayatana*) of the senses, which, when purified from the past, do not involve the mind in death.

[1] Step by step the Praeconium builds up "the praise of night", including even the darkness of sin, to conclude with the phrase from *Psalm* 138 (*Vulg.*) or 139 (AV) which St. Dionysius applied to that "divine darkness" which is the highest degree of mystical contemplation—because the light of God is to be seen only in the moment when it is realized that all other knowledge is by comparison darkness and ignorance. In yet another sense the immediate knowledge of God is "dark", because metaphysical reality is always denoted by negations. Thus it is only in the Dark Night of the Soul, the "despair" of finding that one has neither past nor future, that it is possible to "know the

Therefore the sanctification of this night puts crime to flight, washes away blame, and restores innocence to the fallen and joy to the sorrowful. It banishes enmities, brings concord, and humbles empires.

At this point the deacon inserts the five wax nails with their grains of incense into the side of the Taper in the form of a cross—marking the Five Wounds and the five senses whereby Christ is crucified to the world. He then continues:

Therefore in this sacred night, receive, O holy Father, this evening sacrifice of incense, which thy holy Church presents to thee in the solemn offering of this wax candle made by the labour of bees. But now we know the excellence of this pillar, which the shining fire sets alight in the honour of God.

With these words he lifts up the triple-candle and with one of its branches lights the great Taper.

Which (fire), though now divided, suffers no loss from the communication of its light.[1] Because it is fed by the melted wax, which the mother bee brought forth for the substance of this precious lamp.

Acolytes now take lights from the flame, carrying them to the altar candles and other candles in the church, multiplying the fire to flood the whole church in light.

O truly blessed night which despoiled the Egyptians and enriched the Hebrews: night in which

time and the hour" which is the One Moment of Eternity. The startling "O truly necessary sin of Adam, etc." so disturbed the Abbot Hugh of Cluny that he forbade it to be sung in the monastery. It remains the sole explicit mention, in the Liturgy, of the necessary part of Lucifer in the "play" of God.

[1] And similarly the Bread is broken, but the Body of Christ remains entire in every fragment. By the power of the Word, God divides and dismembers himself into the whole universe of "things"; yet in truth he remains undivided and ever One.

heaven is united with earth, and humanity with divinity.[1] We beseech thee therefore, O Lord, that this candle, consecrated in the honour of thy Name, may continue to dispel the darkness of this night. And being accepted as a sweet savour, may it be united with the lights supernal. May the morning star find it burning: that morning star, I say, which knows no setting.[2] That (star) which being returned from the depths, shineth serene upon the human race.

After the Praeconium comes the solemn chanting of the Prophecies, consisting of twelve passages from the *Old Testament* prefiguring the mystery of the Resurrection. This done, the Paschal Taper is taken down from its stand and carried in procession to the Baptismal Font as the choir sings:

Like as the hart panteth after the fountains of water, so longeth my soul after thee, O God. My soul hath thirsted for the living God: when shall I come and appear before the face of God!

Arrived at the Font, the priest or bishop proceeds to the solemn consecration of the baptismal waters, singing an invocation similar in both form and chant to the Praeconium:

O God, whose Spirit in the very beginning of the world moved over the waters, that even then the

[1] On the whole theme of the luminous night, cf. Apuleius in *Metamorphoses*, "Understand that I approached the bounds of death; I trod the threshold of Persephone; and after that I was ravished through all the elements, I returned to my proper place. About midnight I saw the sun brightly shine"—a description of his initiation into the Mysteries of Osiris.

[2] The "morning star" is, of course, *lucifer*—in Greek *phosphorus*—and is the planet Venus, representing that love which is from one standpoint divine charity, and from another venereal. This is a wonderful "riddle" of the divine ambivalence, manifesting itself in duality as that star which is both Lucifer and Christ. Cf. 2 *Peter* 1: 19, "We have also a more sure word of prophecy; whereunto ye do well that ye take heed, as unto a light that shineth in a dark place, until the day dawn, and the day star (*phosphorus*) arise in your hearts".

nature of water might receive the virtue of sanctification. O God, who by water didst wash away the
crimes of an evil world, and in the overflowing of
the Flood didst give a figure of regeneration: that one
and the same element might, in a mystery, be the end
of vice and the origin of virtue. . . .

As God with his "compass" divided the waters of Chaos in
the beginning of time, the priest now with his hand divides
the water of the Font in the form of a cross, singing:

Who makes this water fruitful for the regeneration
of men by the arcane admixture of his Divine Power,
to the end that those who have been conceived in
sanctity in the immaculate womb of this divine
Font, may be born a new creature, and come forth a
heavenly offspring:[1] and that all who are distinguished either in sex or in body, or by age in time,
may be born into one infancy by grace, their
mother.

Here is the process in reverse of the one Body or the one Light
which, however much divided, suffers no loss. Those who
were "distinguished" are now brought into "one infancy"—the
infant signifying the ever-newness of eternal life, which, like
the new-born babe, has no past.

After an exorcism of the water from the secret artifices of the
powers of darkness, the priest utters the blessing itself:

Wherefore I bless thee, O creature of water, by
God ✠ the living, God ✠ the true, God ✠ the holy,
by that God who in the beginning separated thee
by his Word from the dry land; whose Spirit
moved over thee.

---

[1] Baptism, as the Sacrament of Initiation, identifies the Christian with
Christ—conceived by the "arcane admixture" of the divine power of the Holy
Spirit with the humanity of the Immaculate Mother, and born as first-fruit of
the New Creation.

Dividing the water again with his hands, he scatters some of it towards each of the four quarters of the world, singing:

> Who made thee to flow forth from the fountain of Paradise, and commanded thee to water the whole earth in four rivers. Who, changing thy bitterness in the desert into sweetness, made thee fit to drink, and produced thee out of the Rock to quench the thirst of the people. I bless ✠ thee also by Jesus Christ his only Son, our Lord, who in Cana of Galilee, in a wonderful figure, changed thee by his power into wine. . . . Who made thee to flow together with blood out of his side.[1]

As the blessing proceeds, he stoops to breathe thrice upon the water as God in the beginning breathed upon it with his Spirit.

> Do thou with thy mouth bless these clear (*simplices*) waters: that besides their natural virtue of cleansing the body, they may also be effectual for the purification of minds.

And then he takes the Paschal Taper and plunges it thrice into the Font, singing each time on a higher note:

> May the power of the Holy Spirit descend into the fulness of this Font.

And breathing thrice upon it once more, he goes on:

> And make the whole substance of this water fruitful for the effecting of regeneration.

And the Taper is finally lifted out of the water.[2]

---

[1] Water and wine are symbols of the human and the divine, the union of the two being signified in the mixture or transformation of the one into the other.

[2] The symbolism of the immersion of the Taper in the "immaculate womb" of the Font is very obviously phallic, though, just as obviously, this is the form

The chant continues:

> Here may the stains of all sins be washed out: here
> may human nature, created in thine image, and
> reformed to the honour of its Principle, be cleansed
> from the entire squalor of the old man: that every
> one who enters into this sacrament of regeneration
> may be reborn into the new childhood of true
> innocence. Through our Lord Jesus Christ thy Son:
> who shall come to judge the living and the dead
> and the world by fire. Amen.

When the consecrated water has been sprinkled over the
congregation, the priest takes vessels of the two holy oils called
the Oil of Catechumens and the Oil of Chrism—one for the
anointing of catechumens and the other for conferring the
power of the Holy Spirit—oil being a symbol of healing and
mercy. These he pours into the Font in the form of a cross,
and finally spreads the oil over the whole surface of the
water.[1]

All is now ready for the initiation of the catechumens, for
whom the whole liturgy has thus far been a kind of final
instruction in the *arcana* of the Faith. The rite of the Blessing
of the Font has sufficiently explained the mystery of Baptism

rather than the content of the symbol. Mediaeval artists were not afraid to
represent the conception of Christ by the Spirit in the figure of the Dove with
its beak in a tube which passed under the skirts of the Virgin. Once again,
mythology is not sexual, but sexuality is mythological, since the union of the
sexes prefigures the transcending of duality, of the schism whereby man's
experience is divided into subject and object, self and other.

[1] Thereby, incidentally, insulating the water from air, as it is to remain in
the Font for the whole succeeding year. It was usually necessary in the Middle
Ages to keep the lid of the Font locked, since the water was frequently stolen
for magical purposes. The same precaution was observed in regard to the Host
kept in the tabernacle of the altar, so as to preserve the Body of Christ from the
desecration of the Black Mass offered in honour of the Devil. This diabolical
rite was celebrated with a stolen Host by an unfrocked priest upon the body of a
naked woman. The text of the Mass was read backwards, and the Host ritually
defiled.

that little more needs to be said of it. Clearly, it involves the most extraordinary complex of symbols, since the water is all in one the Womb of the Virgin, the stuff of the world, the emblem of Purity or Voidness in which the past leaves no stain, and the depths into which the neophyte descends with Christ in his death, and from which he rises with Christ in his Resurrection. All in all, Baptism represents the involution and evolution of the Spirit, the descent into and ascent from the waters being the whole "play" of God in dis-membering and re-membering himself, in dying into multiplicity and rising into Unity.

Fully celebrated, the rite of Baptism is an impressive cere-mony, involving not only the actual immersion of the candi-dates but also a preliminary anointing upon the "gates of the senses"—the eyes, ears, nose, lips, hands and feet—and the placing of "the salt of wisdom" upon the tongue. Strictly speaking, the candidates should be thrice immersed in the Font so that the water covers their heads, and at the same time the priest gives them the new Name, which is "in Christ", conjoining it with the Name of the Holy Trinity, saying, "N, I baptize thee in the Name of the Father and of the Son and of the Holy Spirit."[1] After immersion the "new Christs" are again vested in white, and given candles lit from the New Fire.[2]

Official Catholicism takes the position that the reception of the physical sacrament, with certain exceptions, is the *sine qua non* of salvation and confers regeneration "automatically" (*ex opere operato*) whether the candidate actually understands

---

[1] However, it has long been considered ritually sufficient to pour the water thrice upon some part of the body, usually the forehead.

[2] Since ancient times this sacrament has suffered a great deal of curtailment in the richness of its symbolism. The inevitable prudery of the early Church soon made an end of the proper custom of plunging the candidates into the waters naked—signifying the casting-off of every possession to which the mind has clung, every device for the protection of the ego. For the ego is, as a matter of fact, nothing but "clothing"—that is, *habit*, the repeated meeting of the present and the "new" with a mind conditioned wholly by the past.

what is happening or not.[1] This doctrine is a strange twisting
of a marvelous insight—the insight that no man, no ego, can
possibly attain the Godhead by its own effort or accumulation
of knowledge. That the true Self of man is the divinity is an
"automatic truth"—which is to say that it is so, whether it is
realized or not. What is necessary for Baptism is not at all the
acquisition of knowledge but rather the getting rid of it—
"knowledge" in this sense meaning the taking seriously of the
conventional vision of life. It requires, too, not the making of
an effort, but the giving up of every effort—in the sense of effort
made to cling to the past, to hold on to death. But the tragedy
of merely formal Baptism is not that it is given to people without understanding, but that it is given without un-understand-
ing, and remains the empty enactment of a myth to which the
keys have been lost.

When the initiations have been completed, the priest and his
ministers return to the high altar, and, prostrating themselves
before it, begin the Litanies—

> *Kyrie eleison*
> *Christe eleison*
> *Kyrie eleison*

calling upon the Holy Trinity for its mercy, and upon all the
angels and saints for their prayers of intercession. About
half-way through the Litanies, the sacred ministers leave the
sanctuary to vest themselves in white for the celebration of the
Mass. Since the ceremonies began a little before midnight,

---

[1] The exceptions being the Baptism of Blood (i.e. the martyrdom of an
unbaptized person on behalf of the Faith) and the Baptism of Desire, said to
have been received by such as would have accepted Baptism had they ever had
the opportunity of receiving it, or of being exposed to the teaching of the Faith.
A sacrament is said to be effective and valid *ex opere operato*, by the deed done,
as distinct from *ex opere operantis*, by the deed of the doer. Thus the validity of
the sacrament depends neither upon the personal sanctity of the priest nor upon
the full comprehension of the recipient. This is, of course, a shadow of the
metaphysical principle that however much the universe may seem to be divided
into parts, its Reality remains undivided.

FIG. II THE RESURRECTION
Spanish woodcut, *c.* 15th century

it would now be close to dawn, and the rising sun would be greeted by the bells of the church pealing out once more, as the priest begins the Mass intoning—

Gloria in excelsis Deo!

For the newly initiated this is the first Mass in which they have ever participated. Having descended with Christ into the dark waters and risen again from them, they are now ready to partake of the mystery which represents their identity with the Risen Body—projected out of eternity into time as the Bread and Wine forming human flesh and blood.

In the Eastern Orthodox Church the solemnity and glory of Easter is stressed even more than in the West, though the Liturgy lacks the formal and structural interest of the Roman rite. However, what it lacks in this respect is made up in the sheer splendour of a celebration which turns night into day, converting the church into a veritable image of heaven by the brilliance of gold vestments and icons shining in the light of innumerable candles. As in the ancient West, the rite begins at midnight. It starts with the symbolic act of opening the Holy Door which, in the Eastern Church, closes off the entrance to the sanctuary and the altar. For in the Eastern Rite it is still very clear that the Mass is a mystery; it is not, as in the West, celebrated in open view but behind the *iconostasis*, the screen which divides the sanctuary from the main body of the church. The Holy Door stands at the centre of this screen as a type of the *janua coeli*, the Gate of Heaven which, viewed from the opposite direction, is also the Jaws of Death and Hades, and thus the Active Door of the entrance to Paradise, guarded by the Cherubim, as well as the Narrow Gate of the needle's eye.

At the moment of the Resurrection it is thrown open, and remains open throughout the whole week of Easter. Thereupon a procession of the priest and people, all carrying lighted candles, passes out of the church, makes a circuit of the building, and returns to the porch outside the main entrance doors. The priest censes the doors in the form of a cross, singing with the choir:

> Christ is risen from the dead, trampling down death by death, and bestowing life upon those in the tomb.
> Like as the smoke vanisheth, so shall they vanish, and like as wax that melteth at the fire.
> Even so let the ungodly perish at the presence of God, but let the righteous rejoice.
> This is the day which the Lord hath made: we will rejoice and be glad in it.

Upon *this* day those who are in the tomb, in the past, vanish like smoke and melt like wax—a dissolution which, to the ungodly, is "perishing" but to the "righteous" life and joy.

The doors are then opened, and all return into the church for some hours of continuous singing and rejoicing before the actual commencement of the Mass.

> Let us purify our senses and we shall behold Christ, radiant with the light ineffable of the Resurrection. . . .

> *Now* are all things filled with light: heaven and earth, and the places under the earth. All creation doth celebrate the Resurrection of Christ, on whom also it is founded.

> Yesterday, O Christ, I was buried with thee, and today I rise again with thy rising. Yesterday I was crucified with thee: do thou thyself glorify me, O Saviour, in thy kingdom.

> O Christ, who didst not break the Virgin's gate by thy birth, having kept intact the seals; thou hast opened unto us the gates of Paradise.

> O . . . sacrifice living and unslain! When, as God, thou hadst of thine own will offered up thyself unto the Father, thou didst raise up with thee also Adam, the father of our race, in that thou thyself didst rise from the grave.

> We celebrate the death of death, the annihilation of Hades, the beginning of a life new and eternal.[1]

As Easter is preceded by forty days of sorrow—Lent—it is followed by forty days of rejoicing, leading up to the Feast of the Ascension. Christmas and Ascension mark the beginning and the end of the appearance of Christ on earth, and as the former is the mystery of the birth of God in man,

[1] From the Canon of the Easter Liturgy, attributed to St. John of Damascus. For a translation of the full text, see Hapgood, *Service Book of the Holy Orthodox-Catholic Apostolic Church* (New York, 1922), pp. 226–41.

the latter is the mystery of the birth of man in God—for the point of the Ascension is always that Christ carries back into heaven the human body which he received from the Virgin. The myth also makes the point that the further purpose of the Ascension is the sending of the Holy Spirit, which is to be celebrated ten days later at Pentecost, an event which cannot occur until Christ himself has "gone away". For this reason Ascension and Pentecost are so closely related that the two must be understood together, for they illumine one another mutually.[1]

The *Old Testament* "antitype" of these events is really the building of the Tower of Babel, the story in *Genesis* of the attempt of men to build a tower whose top would ascend to heaven—an arrogance which the Lord God punished by the "confusion of tongues", which is ordinarily held to be the origin of the fact that men speak different languages. Contrariwise, when Christ truly ascends to heaven he sends upon his Apostles the Holy Spirit with the "gift of tongues"—the power to speak a language which all men will understand. The first three gifts of the Holy Spirit are traditionally said to be Wisdom, Understanding, and Counsel, and in general the reception of the Holy Spirit is connected with the actual realization, the inward experiencing, of all that the myth signifies in an external and figurative way. Babel is *hybris*—pride—the futile attempt of the ego to reach heaven, to comprehend reality, by its own efforts and in its own terms, which is to say by verbal knowledge. The attempt to define reality conceptually and verbally leads, then, to nothing but confusion, since whatever is described or conceived is "by definition"—that is, finite and conventional.

The Ascension of Christ and the carrying of manhood into heaven with his own Body involves, of course, an extension of the truth already signified in the Resurrection—that what has hitherto been known as the material, bodily universe of

[1] For the consecutive story, see *Acts* 1: 1 to 2: 21.

FIG. 12 THE ASCENSION
Spanish woodcut, *c.* 15th century

"things", is, in the light of the Eternal Now, divinity itself. But this transfiguration of the world is not realized while it remains "in symbol" only—that is to say, so long as the myth is not realized, so long as the Resurrection and Ascension seem to have happened only to Jesus of Nazareth. It is for this reason that the Spirit, the real understanding, cannot come until Jesus departs. The mission of Christ is not, therefore, fulfilled until the historical Jesus has vanished into eternity, until man finds God supremely revealed in the Now, and no more in the mere record of the Gospels. It is really astonishing that official theology should have failed to see this point when the myth itself points it out with such marvelous clarity, telling that the Apostles receive Wisdom and Understanding, and the gift of interpretation, only in the moment when the historical Jesus has disappeared.

This may explain the fact that to this day the Holy Spirit has played a very minor part in Christian symbolism as compared with the Father and the Son, remaining, as it were, the submerged and occluded Person of the Trinity. Patristic writers speak frequently of the "divine economy" whereby the Three Persons of the Trinity have different functions—as that the Father is God "above" us, the Son is God "with" us, and the Spirit is God "in" us. For the Third Person of the Trinity is precisely that "breath of God", the *ruach Adonai*, which was breathed into the mouth of Adam, so that to be enlightened by the Holy Spirit is to realize the divinity and eternity of the true Self, of that which one *is*, as distinct from that which one was. But before such an understanding comes to pass God is apprehended in the letter rather than the spirit, in the mythical image rather than the actuality.[1]

Pentecost, coming fifty days after the Passover, was the Jewish Feast of Weeks, the celebration of fruition, of the harvest. Now the Passover celebrated not only the deliverance from Egypt, but also the first-fruits of the harvest, for which reason Christian imagery refers constantly to Christ as the "first-fruit" of the New Creation. The first to rise from death rises in the very season when the buried grain first rises again into fruition. "But now is Christ risen from the dead, and become the first-fruits of those that slept."[2] At Pentecost all the fruits are gathered in, and the work of Christ is complete because the Resurrection is now inclusive of all men and of the total universe. Ascended into heaven, Christ is no more Jesus but "all-in-all", for

> when he ascended up on high, he led captivity
> captive, and gave gifts unto men. Now that he

[1] For the more strictly theological aspects of the identification of the Holy Spirit with that *ruach* or *pneuma* which is the third component of the Pauline trichotomy of man, see my *Supreme Identity* (London and New York, 1950), esp. pp. 79-84.

[2] 1 *Corinthians* 15: 20.

ascended, what is it but that he also descended first into the lowest parts of the earth? He that descended is the same also that ascended up far above all heavens, that he might fill all things.[1]

Since, then, Pentecost is the time of "gathering in" we may well expect to find that "when the day of Pentecost was fully come" the Apostles "were all with one accord in one place", because "I, if I be lifted up, will draw all men unto me". And then, because the great awakening is always "in a moment, in the twinkling of an eye",—"*suddenly* there came a sound from heaven as of a rushing, mighty wind; and it filled all the house where they were sitting. And there appeared unto them cloven tongues like as of fire, and it sat upon each of them.[2] And they were all filled with the Holy Spirit."[3] The immediate result was that there descended upon them the "gift of tongues" —*glossolalia*—so that when they spoke every man heard them in his own native language. This gift is the sign that all which has hitherto come to pass, the entire mystery of Incarnation and Atonement, is now no more understood "in the letter" but "in the Spirit". For when the mind is no longer spell-bound, the confusion of tongues gives place to the gift of tongues—the power to use the Word without being enthralled by it. But, of course, this power belongs only to him who *is* the Word, so that the sending of the Spirit is the realization of Christ not merely *with* us but *in* us. His Ascension into Heaven is his "withdrawal" from the circumference of things, from the external world, to the centre—to be the inmost reality of all.

It is for this reason that Pentecost is regarded as the origin,

[1] *Ephesians* 4: 8–10.
[2] The tongue of flame just above the head is immediately recognizable to anyone familiar with the symbolism of Kundalini-Yoga as the final liberation in which the spirit *ascends* out through the Sun-door in the dome of the skull—architecturally represented in East and West alike as the point, spire, or other ornament surmounting the dome. See Coomaraswamy, art. "Symbolism of the Dome" in *Indian Historical Quarterly*, vol. xiv, 3 (1938).
[3] *Acts* 2: 1–4.

the birthday, of the Church—*Ecclesia*—those "called forth" from the world by the Word and "gathered together" in union with him to be "one Body" with Christ. For the proper sense of the word "Church" is not a building or institution: it is the "comm⁄union of saints", of those who realize themselves to be the One Christ in present truth, and "many selves" in past seeming only. Thus the Church is also known as the Mystical Body of Christ, for which reason Catholicism has always insisted that spiritual authority resides in the living Church rather than in the "dead letter" of Scripture. But the Church has authority only in so far as it remains truly the Church, the company of those who realize effectively that they are one with the Author by whose Word the universe of time, space, and duality is exfoliated from eternity. Apart from this, the Church remains no more than a myth, a form or image of a truth which is unrealized, so that its authority becomes conventional rather than actual.

Because the Church is a Body it has members, which is to say a structure or organic form. It is a confusion to speak of the members of Christ's Body as the mere individuals who "belong" to the Church, for, strictly speaking, one cannot belong to the Church and remain an individual. The members of the Body are therefore the various "orders" of the Church. These orders are the various "vocations" or "callings" of men, which, in the Church, become so many different works performed by the hands of Christ. Basically there are two types of Order—Holy and Secular, clerical and lay, for whether priest or artisan every Christened person regards his work as that which he does *as* Christ, so that the work must always be worthy of its Author. It is in this sense that, on the one hand, the priest is said to have authority and, on the other, the artist is said to have originality, since the work of both is to be done by the Author and Origin of the world.

The primitive Church existed in a non⁄Christian society, and it was not until after the time of Constantine that the full structure of a Christian society could be developed clearly. For when Church and State are united, it appears that the Order of the Church is threefold rather than twofold. For the Secular Order is then further separated into Rulers and People, so that three groups formed the structure of mediaeval Christian societies—Lords Spiritual, Lords Temporal, and Commons—corresponding precisely to the three castes of Hindu society, Brahmana, Kshatriya, and Vaishya, as well as to the threefold nature of man—spirit, soul, and body. The Christian rites for the coronation of kings make it very clear that the temporal monarch is in some sense being ordained, for he is sacramentally anointed and has the hands of the bishop laid upon him in the same manner as at the ordination of a priest. Thus the office of a "Most Christian King, ruling by Divine Right under God" is to be an instrument of the divine ordering of the natural world.

In the full concept of a Christian society there is, therefore, no real division of Church and State. The whole society is incorporated within the Church, and its visible structure is conceived as an earthly image of the Holy Trinity, or—perhaps more correctly—of the Incarnate Word. For, as we saw, the Christ has two natures, divine and human, the latter being further divided into soul and body. From still another point of view the Second Person of the Trinity is threefold in that his divine nature comprises male Logos and female Sophia, in which case the human nature would count as a single element —the Flesh. Thus it is not uncommon in mythology to find conceptions of the Spiritual and Temporal powers as respect-ively male and female, with the union of Church and State regarded as a marriage.[1]

As to the Holy Order of the Church, it consisted from

[1] On this whole theme see Coomaraswamy's *Spiritual Authority and Temporal Power*, American Oriental Series XXII (New Haven, 1942). Also René Guénon, *Autorité spirituelle et Pouvoir temporelle* (Paris, 1930). On the threefold structure of society compare, too, E. J. Urwick, *The Message of Plato* (London, 1920).

ancient times of seven distinct offices, generally held to comprise the following:

Major Orders:	1.	Bishops
	2.	Priests
	3.	Deacons
Minor Orders:	4.	Subdeacons
	5.	Exorcists
	6.	Readers
	7.	Doorkeepers

For many centuries, however, the last three have fallen into abeyance, and in the Roman Catholic Church both the Diaconate and Subdiaconate are usually no more than stepping-stones to the Priesthood. Each order is held to include the powers of every lower order, and the whole hierarchy constitutes a series of steps corresponding, like the courts of a temple, to various levels of insight or degrees of initiation. Thus the Doorkeeper protects the Church from the profane, and admits only those who sincerely desire that preliminary instruction represented by the office of Reader. The Doorkeeper has his "type", *in divinis*, in the Keeper of the Gate of Heaven—St. Peter—who opens the "needle's eye" only to those small enough to enter, to those who are "no longer anyone". When, upon seeking admittance, St. Peter asks *who* it is that applies for entrance, the answer must always be, "No more I, but Christ".

Having made up his mind, on the basis of preliminary instruction, to enter the mystery, the applicant must next be purified—so that the office of Exorcist stands for the cutting off of his past, of his devil with its barbed tail which is still caught in the narrow door. Thus initiated, he may ascend the steps to the altar. At Solemn Mass the Subdeacon stands upon the floor of the Sanctuary, at the foot of the altar steps, while the Deacon stands above him on the first step itself. Their office is to serve the Priest, standing on the top step or pavement, in his offering of the Sacrifice. The Subdeacon sings the Lesson and pours the water into the Chalice; the Deacon sings the Gospel and pours in the wine.

The Priest's order represents identity with Christ himself, since it is the Priest alone who may actually celebrate the Mass and grant Absolution from sin. Lastly the Bishop is a sort of Chief Priest, who has the special function of conferring the several orders and of ruling the Church as a whole. In the Sanctuary, his proper place is the throne behind the altar, facing the people.[1]

In common and loose speech "the Church" often refers to the Holy Orders or to the actual church building, which is understandable, since both have a structure symbolizing the Church in its proper sense as the whole Body of Christ. The earlier Christian temples were built in the style of a *basilica*, or court of a king—usually a wide, rectangular hall terminating at the East end in an apse. The bishop's throne was placed at the extreme end of the apse, against its semicircular wall, with the seats of the assisting clergy upon either side. They faced the people across the altar, which stood at the entrance or chord of the apse, whose entire floor was raised above that of the main court of the temple. The altar itself was usually a stone table or a cubic block, raised on steps, and before it and to either side towards the people stood two lecterns, one for the book of Lessons and the other for the book of Gospels. This remains the essential ground-plan of Eastern Orthodox churches, save that the altar within the apse is screened off from the main body

[1] Since mediaeval times, however, the altar has been pushed to the extreme East end of the Church, so that the Episcopal Throne is more usually found to one side of the Sanctuary. The English word "bishop" is derived from *biscop*, a sloppy way of saying the Graeco-Latin *episcopus*, lit. "over-seer". While an *episcopus* was normally understood, in ancient Greek speech, to be a guardian, overseer, or ruler, it is of considerable interest that the word has also the precise opposite sense of *hamartanein*, to sin or "miss the mark". It means a "hitting of the mark", or a "being on the mark"—a sense which is far more appropriate to the highest of the Holy Orders, though I am not aware that anyone has ever called attention to this.

of the church by the *iconostasis*, the screen adorned with icons, while two smaller apses stand on either side of the main apse. One is a sacristy for the vestments and vessels of the Liturgy, and the other is for the *prothesis*—the table at which the bread and wine are prepared before being brought to the altar.

In the West, churches have undergone a far more complex development, reaching its height in the superb Romanesque and Gothic cathedrals of Europe. The usual plan of such churches is cruciform, after the pattern of the Latin Cross with the long descending arm, and the main body of the church is within the central "upright" of the cross—divided into three sections, the Sanctuary, the Choir, and the Nave. If one enters such a church by the main door, at the West end or "foot" of the cross, there will be found within the porch or narthex a small fountain or stoup for holy water—blessed for the special purpose of defeating the arts of the Devil. As the faithful enter, they dip their fingers in the stoup and make the sign of the Cross upon themselves, repeating in figure the Baptism by which they enter the Body of Christ. Beyond the narthex, and extending as far as the centre of the whole cross, is the Nave. This term is of doubtful etymology, and may be derived simply from the Greek *naos*, a temple, or from the Latin *navis*, a ship, and in the latter case it would be by association of the Church with the Ship or Ark of Salvation. Be this as it may, the Nave is that part of the church proper to the laity, and at its extreme West end there stands the Baptismal Font, that "immaculate womb" out of which man is born into the divine life.

The East end of the Nave is usually the "crossing", the physical centre of the church above which stands the central tower or dome. To either side stand the two arms of the cross, the North and South Transepts, which are normally chapels with altars dedicated to certain saints—such as the Mother of God or the Patron Saint of the church. Beyond the crossing, steps ascend to the Choir (or Chancel), often divided from the

Nave by a screen corresponding to the *iconostasis*—a barrier shielding the mystery of the inner courts.

Passing through the Choir Screen, one enters the "upper arm" of the cross, occupied by the Choir and Sanctuary. In most Western churches the Choir is set out according to the monastic plan—that is to say, with rows of stalls running lengthwise so that the monks face one another across the church. A second flight of steps divides the Choir from the Sanctuary, and above these steps and between the flanking pillars one will normally find the Rood Beam, supporting a huge Crucifix, so named because the Cross is the Holy Rood, Rod, or Stem of the Tree of Life. To the centre and back of the Sanctuary stands the high altar, two steps higher than the floor of the Sanctuary itself. Usually it is a rectangular stone block, incised on the *mensa* or top with five Greek crosses, one at the centre and one in each corner. Upon it, and to the back, stands a crucifix flanked by six candlesticks. Immediately in front of the crucifix is the Tabernacle, often a short, hollowed out "pillar" of stone with bronze doors in which the Sacrament of Christ's Body is kept at all times. Lamps hang from the roof before the altar, one white lamp in honour of the Host within the Tabernacle, and seven red lamps—following the words of the *Apocalypse*, "And there were seven lamps of fire burning before the Throne, which are the seven Spirits of God".[1]

Because the altar is the "point of passage" between time and eternity it is very properly regarded as a tomb. While it is not altogether true, as is generally supposed, that the first Christian altars were the tombs of the martyrs in the Catacombs, it has for centuries been customary to lay the altar stone over a repository containing relics of the saints. The attribution of

[1] *Revelation* 4: 5. Presumably the Seven Gifts of the Holy Spirit—Wisdom, Understanding, Counsel, Might, Knowledge, Holy Fear, and True God likeness. Based on *Isaiah* 11: 2, this is, however, a purely homiletic invention, and it might seem more reasonable to equate the Seven Spirits of God with the Seven Rays of the Sun. See above, p. 50.

miraculous power to such relics reflects the truth that what has departed from "this" life has become divinized, though here, as elsewhere, the death is that of "self" rather than of the physical body. In the Eastern Church the altar is expressly identified with the Sepulchre of Christ and the Throne of God —simultaneously—with the lower linen altar-cloth representing the winding-sheet, and the upper brocaded cloth the glory of the Throne.

This material house of Christ's Body exhibits the essential elements of the Axle-Tree motif which we have already noted in connection with the Tree of Eden, the Cross, and the Kundalini symbolism of Indian Yoga. For if one looks at the ground-plan of such a church (as in the accompanying figure), it is immediately obvious that here is the outline of a cross, tree, or human figure, stretched between the Waters, at the feet, and the Heavens, at the head, suggested by the dome-shape of the apse. The path from the Font to the Altar represents the whole course of the spirit's ascent into liberation—from the material waters into which it descended at Creation and Incarnation. Rising from the Waters, it passes by the Way of the Cross—marked by representations of the "Stations of the Cross" on the pillars of the Nave—to the Sanctuary within the "head", answering to the symbolism of the "lotus in the skull" or the "sun in the firmament", the point at which the union of humanity with divinity is fully realized. In the church this point is the Altar, the place of the miracle of transubstantiation where the elements of material life—bread and wine—become God. Indian and Christian mythology again reveal their common structure, for as the Serpent Power (Kundalini) of human consciousness ascends the spinal-tree to the sun-lotus in the head, where it realizes its divinity, so the faithful in the Church ascend from Baptism to the Mass—the sacrament of Union celebrated in the 'head" of the church towards the East, where the sun rises. This confluence of symbols is further emphasized by the fact that when the consecrated Host is

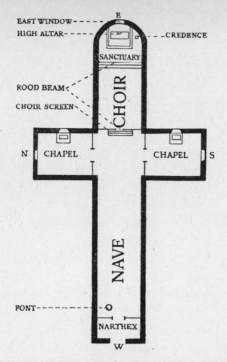

FIG. 13 TYPICAL GROUND-PLAN OF A CHURCH

exposed for adoration, it is set upon the altar in a monstrance—
a golden image of the sun raised upon a pedestal.

It is unimportant that these two mythological traditions may
have obscure origins in primitive sun-worship, for the Christian
and the Hindu alike recognize that the astronomical sun is
used as a figure. The yogis who stare for hours at the actual sun,
or at their navels, are just as much victims of the "mere letter"
as Christians who gaze in adoration at the Host in the monstrance. In both traditions, the sun, the navel, the altar, and the
monstrance are figures of the *central point*, the Eternal Now,
in which man's consciousness must come to rest if he is to be
liberated from time. In this sense, the focal point is the "sun-
door" through which one passes from time into eternity, having

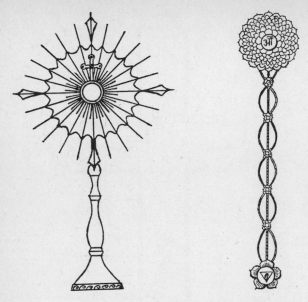

FIG. 14   FIG. 15

FIG. 14 MONSTRANCE FOR BENEDICTION AND EXPOSITION OF THE
SACRAMENT. FIG. 15 THE "SPINAL-TREE" OF KUNDALINI YOGA SYMBOLISM,
showing the seven *chakras*, with the thousand-petalled lotus at the head
(inscribed with the *pranava* AUM, the Supreme Name) and the sleeping
serpent coiled about the phallus at the base

its numerous images in the aperture in the crown of the skull
through which, in Hindu mythology, the spirit is liberated at
"death", the lantern at the crown of the dome, the Tabernacle
Door upon the altar, and the East window in the apse which
should properly carry the figure of Christ ascending or reigning
in glory.

By a common convention the East window is of the lancet
form, high and narrow and thus "male", corresponding to
spirit, while the West window is of the rose form, circular

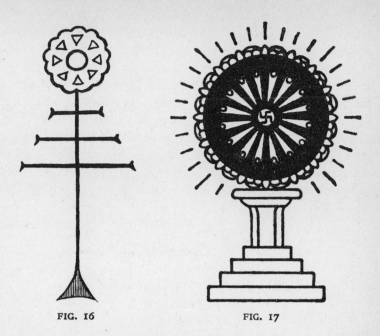

FIG. 16   FIG. 17

FIG. 16 CROSS FROM THE CEMETERY OF ST. AGNES IN ROME. (Early
Christian.) FIG. 17 BUDDHIST WHEEL OF THE LAW (*Dharmachakra*) from
Sanchi, India. A single glance will show the obvious similarity between
the four figures, showing the perennial motif of the Axle-Tree ascending
from the earth to the sun, and through the heart of the sun—the Sun-
Door—into the World beyond

and "female", corresponding to Prima Materia, the womb of
creation. Thus the whole edifice of the church is the image of
Christus Pontifex, Christ the Bridgemaker, between heaven
and earth, Creator and creation, the spirit and the flesh, the
airy heights and the watery depths—of the "one and only noble
Tree" planted in Golgotha, the Place of the Skull, which is
again the dome of the firmament, *this* world, and ascending
by the Sun-Door—"I am the Door"—to the "world without
end".

We have considered the Church as the Mystical Body, the Communion of Saints, the Secular and Holy Orders, and the Temple. It remains to say that the Church is not only a structure, an organism, but also an action; for that which is done by the Communion of Saints in the Temple is the work of Sacrifice—*sacer*, holy, *facere*, to make—the work of hallowing the world. This is why the Church is sometimes called "the extension of the Incarnation", for its work is to be and do what the Christ is and does—the reconciliation of God and the world, the infinite and the finite, the eternal and the temporal. The operation by which this is achieved is the system of the Seven Sacraments:

1. Baptism
2. Holy Chrism or Confirmation
3. The Mass
4. Penance or Absolution
5. Holy Matrimony
6. Holy Order
7. Extreme Unction

The concept of a sacrament is of special importance because it is an almost perfect definition of a mythological symbol. For a sacrament is no mere sign, no mere figure for a known reality which exists in our experience quite apart from its sign. A "known reality" is, in this sense, something remembered, a fact or an idea, which, because of its complexity, is conveniently indicated by a sign of greater simplicity. Thus a sacrament is not an allegorical action, a way of representing something which the participants "understand" in some other and more direct manner. The "material part" of a sacrament, the "matter" which it employs and the "form" in which it is employed, always signifies what is otherwise *unknown*. That is to say, it signifies the real and present world which cannot be remembered and is never, therefore, an object of knowledge. Apart from the sacrament, it is only possible to "know" this

Reality, God, by "becoming" it. But since "no man can see God and live", it is possible to dispense with the sacrament only "after death". Theologically, this is confused with physical death, but from the metaphysical standpoint, "after death" is the point—*now*—at which there is no "I".

There is a certain order or gradation in the Seven Sacraments, such as one finds in the hierarchy of the Holy Orders and in the courts of the Temple, for they mark the essential steps or stages of the Christian life. By Baptism one is initiated or incorporated into the Mystical Body and made "no more I, but Christ", since, as we have seen, to be born of the Font is to be born of the Virgin. Technically, Chrism or Confirmation should accompany Baptism, but with the growth of infant Baptism it became customary to defer it until a child had reached the "age of reason". Consisting in the anointing with the Oil of Chrism and the laying-on of hands by the bishop, it represents the other half of the mystery of incorporation into Christ, for he was not only born of the Virgin but also conceived by the Holy Spirit. To be en-Christed, a man must be born again of "water and the Spirit", and Chrism is being born of the Spirit. The fact that it is deferred until the "age of reason" suggests that its inward sense is the conscious realization of what Baptism means—not the mere verbal comprehension, but the effective experiencing of regeneration.

Because Baptism and Chrism, washing and anointing, transform man into Christ, he enters into that Communion-by-Sacrifice of the divine and the human which involves union with both God and humanity. He is thus ready to participate in the Mass, so that after Chrism he is admitted to First Communion.

The Sacrament of Penance or Absolution exists in the scheme as a sort of renewal of Baptism for those upon whom the original initiation did not altogether "take". Baptism was always understood to involve the total "forgiveness of sins", but because the Christian consciousness has so persistently confused an event which happens in eternity with a merely temporal occurrence, it has seemed possible to commit sin "after" Baptism. This is only to say that the Sacraments do not work while they remain myths alone, and are taken to signify happenings in time. Nor do they work when misapplied, when their power is expected to join forces with relative good against relative evil—a battle which is inconclusive by definition. Obviously, then, Baptism does not "take" when it is expected to take sides, and when the "sin" from which it delivers is confused with relative evil, and the grace which it confers with relative good. So long as this confusion prevails, the effects of Baptism will seem to be disappointing. Penance will continue to exist to reinforce Baptism in its misapplied role, and, incidentally, to increase the confusion.

Commonly called "Confession", the Sacrament of Penance consists in making a confession of one's "sins" to a priest or bishop, involving the expression of a sincere intention not to commit them again, and in receiving from him—as from Christ —the authoritative Absolution, "I absolve thee from all thy sins in the Name of the Father, and of the Son, and of the Holy Spirit". No Catholic Christian, feeling himself to have committed "mortal" sin, will dare to receive the Host without first seeking Absolution.[1] With a certain practical wisdom of the "boys will be boys" type, the Church has made Absolution extraordinarily easy to obtain, and priests are carefully schooled to be loving and understanding rather than scolding in their treatment of penitents. This is, indeed, "worldly wisdom" in the very best sense, but it has no relation at all to

---

[1] "Mortal" sin is theologically defined as that which involves the death of the soul, in the sense that it immediately incurs the penalty of eternal damnation. The characteristics of such sin are: (1) that it constitute deliberate disobedience to the known will of God; (2) that it be committed in full freedom of choice; and (3) that the actual matter of the sin be of grave import—lacking which the sin is regarded as "venial". Yet when mortal sin is identified with "evil actions" in their relative sense, there will always remain the astonishing contradiction of rewarding a temporal sin with an eternal punishment.

metaphysical sin—deliverance from which is so clearly the meaning of the other Sacraments, as of the entire Catholic myth.

In the Western Church, the sacraments of Matrimony and Holy Order are alternatives, representing what in other traditions are the active and contemplative lives, or the vocations of householder and ascetic. They follow Baptism, Chrism, and the Mass as the sacraments of vocation, of the hallowing of the work to be done by the members of the Body. There are, however, some differences here between the Christian and other traditions, for if Holy Order is to be regarded—as in practice it was—as one of the three "estates" of the social order, it must not be confused with the vocation to the homeless life of the ascetic, who is beyond caste and outside society. It would seem that in a healthy society the vocation to the homeless life should *follow* the vocation to the life of householder, and not be an alternative. The Eastern Church observes this principle, at least in token, by permitting priests to marry if they do so before ordination. But when the Western Church demands celibacy of its priesthood, it confuses the Sacerdotium, the Brahmana Caste, with the vocation to Religion, in its strict sense of the ascetic rule and the homeless life of poverty, chastity, and obedience. The Roman Church prohibits the priesthood to marry on the ostensible ground that it would constitute a distraction from the vocation, but the same objection could be made with equal force to the vocation of physician or artist. The real reason is rather that the hands which consecrate the Host must not be "defiled" by contact with "Woman".

Modern Christian apologists tend to "tone down" this objection to the marriage of priests, and at the same time to stress the fact that Holy Matrimony "ennobles" the mystery of sex and procreation. But if one studies the writings of Early Christian and Mediaeval theologians, there can be no doubt whatsoever that historical Christianity regards sexuality with unanimous disgust, and permits the sacrament of Holy Matrimony as a concession to the weakness of human nature. As St. Paul said, "It is better to marry than to burn". Other traditions, too, have perhaps made the same mistake of blaming Māyā for enthralling men's minds when, as a matter of fact, she is only the "screen" upon which the spell is projected by the Word. A man who bruises his nose by trying to walk into a picture should blame, not the picture, but his ignorance of the convention of perspective. But so long as the convention "fools" him, he blames the *materia* against which he banged his nose rather than the "Word", the concept, which beguiled his mind. Thus man's attitude to woman is always a measure of his self-understanding: the less he understands, the more he projects upon her the contents of his own unconscious.

The Christian mentality has been so peculiarly hostile to the Flesh—despite the fact that "the Word was made Flesh", and "God so loved the world"—because the Western mind has been so unconscious of its own depths. This is why Christianity is taken more literally than the other great mythological traditions, and why even sophisticated Christian philosophers will insist upon the eternal reality of the ego-soul, and tend to project both God and Satan into the world of external objects.

But it is to the credit of Christianity that it has never regarded woman as not having *even* a soul, and that, whatever its attitude to sexuality, the concept of Holy Matrimony has protected women and children alike from the extremes of callousness and cruelty which were so common in the Graeco-Roman world. For this, our culture must be grateful indeed, even though this compassionate concern for woman was moved by love for the soul rather than for the body, for woman in so far as she is the same as man, rather than in the respect in which she differs from him.[1]

[1] This is, of course, a problem of immense subtlety—such that even to begin to discuss it adequately would require a separate volume! Modern theologians make a good deal of the point of Christian "materialism", of reverence for the

Of the seventh Sacrament, Extreme Unction, we shall have more to say when, in the following chapter, we come to the Four Last Things—Death, Judgement, Hell and Heaven— and follow the Christian soul in its departure from this world. It is enough to say here that Unction is in one way the crown of the Sacraments, in that it is held to confer immediate admission, upon death, to the Beatific Vision and the life of Heaven. In other words, the sacramental grace of Unction is such a powerful incorporation of manhood into God that in many cases those who have received it and then recovered from sickness have felt it necessary to spend the rest of their lives in the cloister—or at least in daily attendance in the church.

In a more general sense, however, the principal sacrament is the Mass—not only because it embodies the Sacrifice of Christ, but also because it is the regular, diurnal sacrament which is independent of special occasions, the perpetual action of worship whereby the Church identifies itself with the Son and sacrifices itself to the Father. In this sense, the Mass involves all that the Church "does"; it is *the* action of the Church, since the transformation of bread and wine into Christ is the whole work of realizing the unity of creation with its Creator. For it is the *anamnesis*, the re-membering, of the One whose dismemberment is the formation of the world.

body, and insist that the Christian attitude to sexuality is a part of this reverence —adducing the sound reason that "lust" is often a mere exploitation of the body to find escape from feelings of spiritual and psychological disquiet. An appetite for food may be exploited in just the same way, not to mention a thirst for wine, and both eating and drinking are quite as essential to human continuity as reproduction. The unwisdom of exploiting the appetites does not, therefore, explain the very special antagonism of the Church to "lust". Certainly other spiritual traditions have manifested a similar prudery, but they have not attempted to force it upon society as a whole, or to regard it as anything more than a strictly voluntary discipline for those of the ascetic vocation, who have abandoned the life of householder. It should be added that the special attitude to woman involved in the cult of Chivalry is of Manichaean rather than Christian origin.

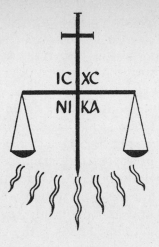

CHAPTER VII

The Four Last Things

AFTER the long summer season of Pentecost is over, the cycle of the year returns again to Advent, which, like Janus whose month begins the secular year, looks backwards and forwards at once—back to the First Advent of Christ in the cave of Bethlehem, and forward to the Second Advent when he is to come again with glory, "to judge the living and the dead and the world by fire". Advent is, then, the season of the Four Last Things in which the Church turns its mind to the contemplation of Death and Judgement, Hell and Heaven, to the mysteries of what is called Eschatology —the science of ends. For although the Christian myth is presented as history, as the narrative of the "mighty acts of God", the fact that it is by no means a merely "historical" religion is most plainly shown in its constant expectation of the end of the world. Christianity is an eschatological, not a historical, religion—for its whole hope is directed towards

Dies illa, "that Day", upon which time and history will come to an end.

It is well known that the first Christians lived in almost daily anticipation of the Second Advent and the End of the World, for, if one takes the words of the Gospels literally, Christ made it plain that it was to be expected in the immediate future. But as the years and centuries passed and a *temporal* "Last Day" failed to arrive, the expectancy which had been directed towards it was gradually shifted to the event of physical death. In the first century the Christian was in constant watchfulness for the Son of Man in the clouds of heaven, but by the Middle Ages he was watchful against the possibility of sudden death, lest it should find him, like the ghost in *Hamlet,* "unshrived, unhouseled, unaneled"—without the last rites of Confession, Communion, and Unction. And now that, with liberal Protestantism, the very life after death has become shadowy and doubtful, Christianity has become a historical religion of *this* world, finding the significance of life in time rather than beyond time.

Because of his literal understanding of the Christian myth, Western man has an attitude to death which other cultures find puzzling. The Christian way of thought has made so deep an impression upon our culture that this attitude prevails even when the intellectual assent to Christian dogma exists no more. For it is no easy matter to cast off the influence of our history, to be rid of a habit of thought and emotion which has prevailed for close to two thousand years. Western man has learned a peculiarly exaggerated dread of death, because he has seen it as the event which will precipitate him *for ever* into either unspeakable joy or unimaginable misery. Few have dared to be quite certain as to the outcome, for though one might *hope* for the mercy of God, it was a very serious sin to *presume* upon it. The sense of uncertainty was, furthermore, part and parcel of Christian feeling for the insidious subtlety of evil, so that the more one approached sanctity, the more one

was aware of diabolical motivations, and of the near impossibility of a pure intent. Many sold their souls to the Devil just
because this very uncertainty seemed more insupportable than
damnation itself.

For it has always seemed that there is a certain and simple
way to be damned. But the way of salvation is as narrow as a
tight-rope, and the balance always in doubt. However easy of
access the Sacraments, however simple to say, "Lord, I believe,
help thou mine unbelief!"—there always remained the problem of sincerity, and of the pure intent, since if one failed to
receive the Sacraments "worthily" they imparted damnation
instead of salvation. Thus, if I ask myself *why* I believe,
why I receive the Sacraments, and if I think by a logic which
must answer the question "why" in terms of past causes, what
I am and what I do is ever the fruit of what I was and
what I did. Thus I never escape the Old Adam, nor succeed
in being more than a wolf in sheep's clothing. I can believe
that I repent sincerely and that I love genuinely upon the sole
condition of not asking questions too persistently, of not
examining my conscience too clearly. It was thus that Luther
saw the impossibility of obtaining salvation through works. It
is interesting to wonder what would have happened if he had
asked himself as persistently *why* he had faith.

Historical Christianity is thus a religion in which anxiety
plays a far greater part than faith, and in which this anxiety is
even valued as a virtue because it is a constant check to presumption and pride. Our culture has thus evolved a species
which might be called *homo sollicitus*, "anxious man", always
remembering that *sollicitus* means oscillating, wobbling, or
trembling. "Work out your own salvation with fear and
trembling."[1] It is thus of special importance that this agitation
or oscillation is the characteristic behaviour of an organism
confused by logical paradox.[2] In our case this is precisely the

---

[1] *Philippians* 2: 12.
[2] See the excellent essay on the psychological significance of logical paradox

paradox of self-consciousness, which we have shown to be analogous to the "I am lying" paradox of Eubulides. Anxiety stands as a virtue between the two opposed sins of presumption and despair—even though Christ said, "Be not anxious— *Nolite solliciti*", knowing, perhaps, that the illusion of self-consciousness and its attendant anxiety is the whole significance of Lucifer.[1] For Lucifer is the Dark Christ—Anti-Christ—which is to say, the divine nature under the thrall of its own spell, wobbling, oscillating, or trembling between the pairs of opposites. And Lucifer's anxiety must impress the Christian mind as a virtue so long as it seems that salvation is a matter of choice between mutually related opposites, such as good and evil, and so long as it seems that the Man to be saved is the ego-soul.

From one point of view the Catholic rites of death are the most eloquent expression of this anxiety. From another, they contain the whole mystery of overcoming anxiety. This double interpretation is possible because of the very nature of the opposites—good and evil, life and death, Heaven and Hell. In reality, in Christ the Cornerstone "who maketh both one", the opposites are reconciled. But in seeming, in the situation where there seems to be a real distinction and a real choice between them, the equivalent of reconciliation is oscillation, so that while above there is peace, below there is trembling. Similarly, the rites of death convey peace when understood inwardly, but anxiety when taken in the letter.

When, therefore, a Christian comes to the point of death, he sends an urgent request to the priest to come to him with the Viaticum, the Rites of Passage, between this world and the

by Gregory Bateson in Ruesch and Bateson, *Communication* (New York, 1951), ch. 8.

[1] Cf. *James* 2: 19, "The devils also believe, and tremble"—since trembling is the necessary consequence of sin, of missing the mark and confusing the present Self which is alive and free with the past self which is dead and determined. One trembles, oscillates, because of the irresolvable paradox created by the necessity of performing a free act with determined motives.

"next". Whereupon the priest goes to the Tabernacle of the Altar, attended by an acolyte carrying bell and candle. He removes a Host from the ciborium, the cup in which the Sacrament of Christ's Body is reserved, and places it in a small gold vessel called a pyx. This he ceremoniously veils, and with the bell and the light proceeding him goes to the house of the dying person. Upon entering he says, "Peace be to this house", and sprinkles holy water around with the words of the psalm, "Thou shalt purge me with hyssop and I shall be clean; thou shalt wash me and I shall be whiter than snow".

By the bed of the dying person there has been set a small table with crucifix and candles. Here the priest lays down the pyx, and, putting a purple stole about his neck, prepares to hear the last confession of the departing soul—for which purpose all others are bidden to withdraw. And when the sick man has fully unburdened himself to "God Almighty, to the Blessed Virgin Mary, Blessed Michael the Archangel, Blessed John the Baptist, the Holy Apostles Peter and Paul, to all the Saints, and to you, my Father", confessing that he has sinned in thought, word, and deed "by my fault, by my fault, by my most great fault", the priest wipes out the spiritual stain with the formula of Absolution—"By the authority of our Lord Jesus Christ committed to me, I absolve thee from all thy sins in the Name ✠ of the Father and of the Son and of the Holy Spirit."

This done, the priest removes the Host from the pyx and holds it up before the dying man, saying, "Behold the Lamb of God, behold him who taketh away the sins of the world! Lord I am not worthy that thou shouldest come under my roof, but speak the word only and my soul shall be healed". He then lays it upon the tongue of the departing, with the solemn words, "Receive, brother, the Viaticum of the Body of our Lord Jesus Christ, who shall guard thee from the malign Enemy, and bring thee unto life eternal".

After the Viaticum there follows Extreme Unction. The

priest makes the sign of the cross thrice upon the departing, with the words:

> In the Name of the Father ✠, and of the Son ✠, and of the Holy Spirit ✠, may there be extinguished in thee every power of the Devil by the imposition of our hands, and by the invocation of all the holy Angels, Archangels, Patriarchs, Prophets, Apostles, Martyrs, Confessors, Virgins, and all the Saints.

He then moistens his thumb in the vessel of the *Oleum Infirmorum*, of olive oil consecrated by the bishop for the healing of physical and spiritual disease, and makes the sign of the cross with the oil on seven parts of the body, namely, the eyes, ears, nose, mouth, hands, feet, and thighs, saying each time—for example—"By this holy Unction ✠, and by his most tender compassion, may the Lord forgive thee in whatsoever way thou hast sinned by sight." If the miracle of physical healing, which is sometimes to be expected from this Sacra-ment, does not occur, and if the person is clearly at the very point of death, the priest begins the Litany for the dying, calling on the Mother of God, the Angels, Patriarchs, and Saints to pray for him. And then, as his eyes begin to close in death, the priest says:

> Go forth, Christian soul, from this world in the Name of God the Father Almighty, who created thee; in the Name of Jesus Christ, the Son of the living God, who suffered for thee; in the Name of the Holy Spirit, who was poured out upon thee; in the Name of the holy and glorious Mother of God, the Virgin Mary—

and so on, through the whole shining hierarchy of Angels, Archangels, Thrones, Dominions, Principalities, Powers, Cherubim, Seraphim, Patriarchs, Prophets, Apostles,

Evangelists, Martyrs, Confessors, Monks, Hermits, Virgins, and Saints, concluding—

> today let thy place be in peace, and thine abode in holy Sion. Through the same Christ our Lord.[1]

At the moment of expiration the departing is urged to repeat the Name of Jesus, and to say, "Into thy hands, O Lord, I commend my spirit". And when the light of life has gone out at last, and the soul gone on its way to the Centre of the Universe, those remaining at the bed sing together:

> Make speed to aid him, ye Saints of God; come forth to meet him, ye Angels of the Lord; receiving his soul, presenting him before the face of the Most Highest. . . . Rest eternal grant unto him, O Lord; and let light perpetual shine upon him.

As it fades from the light of day into the intense brightness of the "Day all days illumining", the soul is immediately faced with its Particular Judgement. For Judgement comes in two stages—first, the Particular Judgement of the individual soul, and second, upon the Last Day when, at the sound of the Trumpet, all the bodies of the dead rise from their graves, the General or Last Judgement.

As soon, then, as the soul has left this world it goes with its guardian angel and its appointed devil of temptation before the Throne of Heaven. Hardly visible for light, there sits in the centre the white and radiant figure of the Father Almighty, surrounded by the eyed wings of the Cherubim and Seraphim. Hovering above him is the Dove of Fire, the Holy Spirit, with his seven descending flames. To his right is enthroned Jesus the Christ, and to his left the Virgin Mother, while lower thrones on either side seat the Holy Apostles and Martyrs. In the centre, before the Throne of God, stands the

[1] The entire Order for the Commendation of the Soul will be found in the *Rituale Romanum*, which provides much more than this should the agony of dying be prolonged.

Archangel Michael, armoured and golden-winged, with the sword of divine wrath in his right hand, and the scales of divine judgement in his left. Here the virtues of the soul are weighed against anything that remains of unrepented and unforgiven sin. Mediaeval portrayals of the weighing vary in their symbolism, sometimes representing the soul as a vessel to be balanced against a bat-like demon,[1] and sometimes making the guardian angel at one end of the balance struggle against the attendant demon at the other.[2]

The object of the weighing is to decide whether the soul shall be sent immediately to Heaven or Hell, or delayed in Purgatory. When the soul has died in a state of "perfect contrition" for all sins it goes straight to Heaven, because the fire of contrition is said to have burned away not only the possibility of everlasting damnation but also the temporal penalties due to each sin. When the contrition has been imperfect, or when the soul—although forgiven—has not made adequate penance and satisfaction for its sins, the temporal penalties still remain to be exacted. For the Roman Church teaches that sin incurs both an eternal and a temporal punishment. The eternal punishment is wiped out by the Sacrifice of Christ, provided, of course, that its effects have been mediated to the particular soul through the sacraments. But the temporal punishment remains, and this must be remitted either by suffering in Purgatory or by works of piety and charity performed by the soul during its lifetime, or by others on its behalf after it has died. Masses and prayers offered for the departed have, then, the effect of shortening their sojourn in Purgatory.

---

[1] As on the tympanum of Bourges Cathedral, where the vessel of the soul is strangely like the vessel of the Ab, or Heart, shown in ancient Egyptian versions of the Judgement. In the latter, the Heart is weighed against the Feather of Truth, and must *balance* with it, presumably because the heart is expected to be without weight. But, as might be expected, the Christian versions of the balancing suppose that the good must outweigh the evil.

[2] As on the tympanum of Autun Cathedral, where the soul in the pan of the scales is the upper part of a human figure.

If the weighing shows that the soul must be consigned to Purgatory, it is delivered *temporarily* to the tortures of the demons, or to the fires which burn upon the mountain of Purgatory standing above Hell on the other side of the earth. Purgatory, as its name implies, is primarily a place of burning, where a fire unbelievably hotter than anything known on earth consumes the remaining imperfections of the soul. The *Golden Legend* says that a single drop of sweat from a person suffering in Purgatory will instantly burn its way through a living hand, as if it had been shot through with an arrow. Yet the punishments of Purgatory are not always by fire. Some souls are sent to haunt the scenes of their crimes upon earth, or to undertake various labours symbolically connected with their misdeeds. Although their tortures are of an agony far more extreme than we can imagine, they nevertheless enjoy the consolations and ministrations of the angels, as well as the clear certainty of eventual Heaven. But as to those consigned to Hell we shall have more to say later.

The mitigation of the punishments in Purgatory is the immediate purpose of the obsequies now to be offered for the soul by the Church on earth, consisting primarily of the Requiem or Mass for the Dead. If the soul has actually been committed to Hell or Heaven, the effects of the Mass will, of course, redound to others able to profit from them. For the merits of piety and charity are transferable, and it is taught that there is a Treasury of Merits accummulated by the saints far in excess of their own personal needs. Such surplus merits may be applied by the Church for the remission of temporal punishments due to the less holy, and are known as Indulgences. Thus the Church may authorize Indulgences involving the remission of so many days' punishment in Purgatory in return for the saying of certain prayers or visiting certain shrines.[1]

---

[1] This incredibly legal and commercial trade in rewards and punishments is not recognized in the Eastern Orthodox Church, and would seem to be a

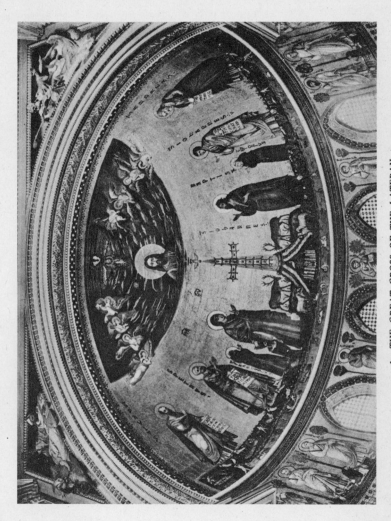

5. THE GREAT CROSS OF THE LATERAN

Apsidal mosaic in the Basilica of St. John Lateran, at Rome. Description in the text, p. 159, footnote 3.

6. THE LAST JUDGEMENT

Engraving from the painting by Breughel the Elder, 1558. Description in the text, p. 223.

After death, then, the body of the deceased is laid in its coffin and taken to the church. Here it is set upon a bier before the altar, and covered with a black or purple pall, six large candles being placed around it. If the deceased is a priest, the head is pointed towards the altar, and away from the altar if a layman. Here the body rests until the time of Mass, and it may be that the faithful come to offer their prayers or to recite the Breviary Office for the Dead on the soul's behalf. For the Mass, the clergy come vested in black, and during the procession to the altar the choir sings the *Subvenite*—

> Make speed to aid him, ye Saints of God; come
> forth to meet him, ye Angels of the Lord. . . .

The Mass itself begins with the singing of the beautiful introit *Requiem aeternam*—

> Rest eternal grant unto them, O Lord; and let
> light perpetual shine upon them—

a refrain which is repeated again and again throughout the rites. For the Sequence Hymn, between the Lesson and the Gospel, they sing the celebrated *Dies irae*, the hymn which incarnates the whole mood of Christian dread in the face of the Last Things:

> *Dies irae, dies illa*
> *Solvet saeclum in favilla,*
> *Teste David cum Sibylla.*

> Day of wrath, that day, when the world
> dissolves in glowing ashes, as witness
> David with the Sibyl.

rather late development in the West. It is difficult not to be rather cynical about it, and to see it as a clever way of ruling people and keeping up their interest in and dependence upon an established priesthood. An institution which flourishes through the mediation of salvation, or any other desideratum, will not flourish for very long if it gives results too quickly. To remain *necessary* to the public, the process of attainment must be drawn out for as long as possible. Otherwise the Church will be (what it really should be) a bridge over which men will pass without building a house upon it.

> *Quantus tremor est futurus,*
> *Quando judex est venturus,*
> *Cuncta stricte discussurus.*

How great shall be the trembling when
the Judge shall come to try all things
exactly.

> *Tuba mirum spargens sonum*
> *Per sepulcra regionum,*
> *Coget omnes ante thronum.*

The Trumpet swelling its wondrous
sound through the place of the tombs,
will gather all before the Throne.

Death, it continues, and the whole world of nature will be
struck aghast when all creatures arise to plead before the Final
Judgement. The Book will be brought forth, containing the
exact record of all things meet for the world's judgement, and
the Judge from his Throne will bring to light every hidden
secret so that nothing remains unavenged. And the remainder
of the hymn is taken up with what is doubtless the most
fervently abject plea for mercy in all the poetry of the world.

It is difficult, if not impossible, to convey the peculiar
atmosphere of this hymn in an English translation and without
its traditional music, which suggests not so much an apocalyptic
and sensational shaking of the universe as a quietly contemplative awe. For the *Dies irae* conveys the mood of the Church
rather than of the individual. The quality of personal terror
comes out more strongly in, say, Isaac Watts's hymn on *The
Day of Judgement*:

> Such shall the noise be, and the wild disorder
> (If things eternal may be like these earthly),
> Such the dire terror when the great Archangel
> 　　　　Shakes the creation;

Tears the strong pillars of the vault of Heaven,
Breaks up old marble, the repose of princes,
Sees the graves open, and the bones arising,
    Flames all around them.

Hark, the shrill outcries of the guilty wretches!
Lively bright horror and amazing anguish
Stare through their eyelids, while the living worm lies
    Gnawing within them.

Thoughts, like old vultures, prey upon their heart-strings,
And the smart twinges, when the eye beholds the
Lofty Judge frowning, and a flood of vengeance
    Rolling before Him.

Hopeless immortals, how they scream and shiver,
While devils push them to the pit wide-yawning,
Hideous and gloomy, to receive them headlong
    Down to the centre!

The Requiem continues with its strange alternation of hope and dread, and yet somehow manages, in the end, to overcome anxiety with a mood of total serenity. At the Offertory, while the ministers prepare the holy elements, the choir continues the mood of dread:

> O Lord Jesus Christ, King of glory, deliver the souls of all the faithful departed from the pains of Hell, and from the deep pit. Deliver them from the mouth of the lion, that Tartarus may not swallow them, and that they fall not into darkness; but let Michael, the holy standard-bearer, bring them into the holy light.

But at the Communion the smoke of Tartarus has cleared away to reveal the brightness of the Eternal Day—

> May light eternal shine upon them, O Lord, with thy saints for evermore, for thou art gracious.

> Rest eternal grant unto them, O Lord; and let light
> perpetual shine upon them, with thy saints for ever-
> more, for thou art gracious.

When the Mass proper has ended, the ministers come down
from the altar to the bier, and all the choir and clergy gather
about the body carrying lighted candles for the ceremony
called the Absolution of the Dead. The priest stands at the end
of the bier towards the altar, and at the other end the subdeacon
takes his place with the processional cross. Incense is prepared
while the choir sings the responsory *Libera me*:

> Deliver me, O Lord, from everlasting death in
> that dreadful day when heaven and earth shall quake,
> when thou shalt come to judge the world by fire.
> I tremble and am sore afraid, at the judgement and
> the wrath to come; when heaven and earth shall
> quake. O that day, that day of wrath, of calamity
> and woe, a great day and exceeding bitter! When
> thou shalt come to judge the world by fire. Rest
> eternal grant unto him, O Lord; and let light
> perpetual shine upon him.

And then the priest walks around the bier, sprinkling it with
holy water and swinging over it the thurible of incense. After
some final prayers, the body is taken to its resting-place, to the
accompaniment of the serenely joyous anthem *In Paradisum*:

> May the Angels lead thee into Paradise; may the
> Martyrs receive thee at thy coming, and bring thee
> into the Holy City, Jerusalem. May the choir of
> Angels receive thee, and with Lazarus, once a
> pauper, mayest thou have rest eternal.

And the body is at last put to rest in its sepulchre to the
words of the Canticle of Zacharias, the *Benedictus*, with the
antiphon:

I am the Resurrection and the Life; whosoever believeth in me, though he were dead, yet shall he live; and whosoever liveth, and believeth in me, shall not die in eternity.

While the soul has gone to its destiny—Heaven, Purgatory, or Hell—the corruptible body waits through the centuries in its grave for the dawn of the Last Day, which is to come at a time known only within the most secret counsels of the Holy Trinity—perhaps tomorrow, perhaps a thousand or ten thousand years away. Yet—sometime—there will come a day when there rises in the East, not the familiar sun, but the Sun of Justice, the Lord Christ, riding upon the clouds of heaven with myriads of angels. As he appears, the whole firmament will be shattered like glass by the shrilling Trumpeter of Heaven, and its sound, ringing through all the sepulchres of the earth and the very depths of the sea, will lift every body from its grave, reassemble corrupt and scattered members, and cause each one, reunited with its soul, to stand up and face the Judge of the World. Priests, buried with their heads to the East, will stand up and face their flocks along with Christ, and yet be judged with them as to whether they have faithfully fulfilled their ministry.

From the presence of the Terrible Judge there will go forth a fire of such heat that the whole earth will be reduced to ashes and the oceans dissolved in steam. The sun and the moon will be darkened, and the stars will fall from heaven. And then the Recording Angel will open the Book of Life wherein are written the names of all those to be saved and called to stand upon the Right Hand of the Judge. But all those not found in the Book shall be made to stand upon his Left Hand. To those upon the right he will say, "Enter thou into the joy of thy Lord!" But to those upon the left he will say, "Depart from me, for I know you not!" In that moment every secret of all hearts will be made utterly plain, for the resurrected shall be naked in body and soul, and utterly defenceless before that Refining Fire which, to the pure in heart, is glory, but to the impure the most unspeakable torment.

By now the earth and the former heavens will have altogether dissolved, and out of the burning blue on high there will appear the Bejeweled City of the Mystical Rose, the New Jerusalem, "coming down from God out of heaven, prepared as a bride adorned for her husband". At the same time, the fathomless abyss below will reveal a lake of fire and sulphur. With the support of the old earth withdrawn, the swarming and blackened bodies of the damned will plunge down and down endlessly into that pit where they must writhe and shriek in unmitigated torture for ever and ever. Far above the smoke and stench of the inferno, Michael and his legions will fling Lucifer and his diabolic host into the uttermost depths of the pit to eat and be eaten, to torment and be tormented, on and on for the ages that will never end.

The Mediaeval mind exercised its most lively and creative imagination in conceiving the horrors and abominations of what is, thus far, the most dreadful product of the human mind. By comparison, its imaginative descriptions of the delights of Heaven were extraordinarily tame. In contemplating Hell, however, the Christian consciousness has indulged itself in a sado-masochistic orgy which makes all other hells, hot or cold, relatively cosy. One must remember that other traditions, such as the Buddhist and Hindu, have never contemplated an abode of *everlasting* punishment, so that their so-called "hells" are in fact purgatories. While the symbol of everlasting torment has its special mythological significance if it be understood in the sense of *saṃsara*, a circle from which there is no exit so long as one takes the path of its circumference, the Christian imagination has not conceived it in this way. It has considered Hell as torment in a dimension of linear time without end, from which there is no possibility whatsoever of deliverance. It is true that some of the Fathers, in particular Origen and St. Gregory of Nyssa, taught the doc⁄ trine of "apocatastasis", of the ultimate restoration of all souls to the state of blessedness after many aeons of time. But this doctrine has been condemned in both the Eastern and Western Churches.

This profoundly sinister conception is by no means "merely Mediaeval". It remains, in all its literal horror, the explicit doctrine of the Catholic Church to this day, and has been defended by one who is, in other respects, among the most inspired and perceptive theologians of modern times, Matthias Scheeben. His great work, *The Mysteries of Christianity*, which is so obviously the production of a highly subtle, reasonable, and sensitive mind, nevertheless contains the following remarkable passage:

> As concerns the punishment itself, it must be clearly conceived . . . as a state which is inversely proportionate to the glorification of the bodies of the blessed; it must be a punishment that qualitatively and quantitatively is so great and terrible that it immeasurably surpasses all the forebodings and concepts of natural reason. It must be the result of a supernatural force which penetrates and devours the body without destroying it, and through the body dreadfully racks and tortures the soul fettered to it.

He adds that the physical fire of Hell

> differs from natural fire in this respect, that its flame is not the result of a natural, chemical process, but is sustained by divine power, and therefore does not dissolve the body which it envelops, but preserves it forever in the condition of burning agony.[1]

Such is the measured philosophical language which justifies the hideous fantasies of Matthew Paris, St. Salvius, Cranach,

[1] Scheeben, *Mysteries of Christianity*. Trs. Cyril Vollert, S.J. (London and St. Louis, 1947), pp. 692–3.

Bosch, and Breughel in every respect save their insufficiency of realism and the grotesque humour of the Flemings. For the imagination may descend to what depths of sadistic fantasy it will, yet always fail to portray the ultimate and concrete ghastliness of the reality. With Cranach the Elder one may visualize the damned in their fits of convulsion upon flaming rocks, being gnawed and lusted upon by dog-like fiends. Or with Bosch and Breughel one may simply suggest outrages of unimaginable depravity by depicting the damned half-transformed into the obscene gargoyles which infest them—bat-winged bladders with barbed spines for noses, cross-breeds of ape and horseshoe crab, reptilian birds with suckers in place of beaks, armed fish with rotting sides and drooling mandibles, writhing deformities of misplaced limbs with mouths between the buttocks—a whole world of animated slime and orgiastic cruelty as yet, I believe, unplumbed even by modern Surrealism. One may go this far and, if possible, farther, yet still hardly begin to suggest a state of punishment both spiritual and physical which highly intellectual and cultured people even now believe to be a certain reality.

This conception, with which the Western mind has tormented itself for many centuries, is admitted by most theologians to be the necessary consequence of its opposite—the everlasting and supernal bliss of the saints.[1] The justice, the logic, of a God who is absolute and eternal Goodness and Love *requires* that there should be the visitation of a proportionably absolute and eternal Wrath upon those who are not on his side with the fullest sincerity and enthusiasm. Nothing of a middle way is contemplated, since "he who is not with us is against us". This is, indeed, straight and realistic thinking in comparison with the strictly sentimental conception of the

---

[1] This is the view of Scheeben, *ibid.*, p. 692, "The miraculous resuscitation of the body and its permanent conservation for eternal punishment is inseparably related to the resurrection and conservation of the body for the reception of everlasting reward. *If the latter did not occur, the former would not occur either.*" (Italics mine)

Last End as a state of pure Goodness which simply annihilates its opposite, or includes all souls in its bliss.

For the whole significance of this part of the myth is that Absolute Goodness of necessity implies Absolute Evil, not merely logically but psychologically. This is the law of "enantiodromia" whereby every extreme turns into its opposite, whereby Satanism is actually created by Puritanism and deviltry by sanctity. Thus the conception of the everlasting Heaven of goodness, love, and delight is no less monstrous than that of Hell. For it is essentially the *same* conception. We should not, then, be surprised to find theologians admitting that the sufferings of the damned in Hell are contemplated with delight by the blessed in Heaven, who see all things in the mirror of God's omniscience. Of course—because psychologically the sterile monotony of unalloyed pleasure or of unremitting saintliness must have its compensation. This is why the conception of Hell had to be invented by men who bent the full force of their conscious energies towards "being good". Not in Heaven, but here on earth, the inhumanly "good" already regard the torments of the damned with secret delight— a fact which comes out so clearly in Mediaeval art where the depiction of Hell shows far more creative imagination and life than that of Heaven.

An instructive example is the painting of the Last Judgement by Breughel the Elder (1558). To the right of the Judging Christ goes a procession of the blessed which is for the most part a multitude of heads as characterless as an army at drill and as dead as a cobbled street. But to the left, where the damned are shoveled into the gulping maw of Hell the picture is alive in rather the same sense as the earth beneath a large stone: it crawls and swarms with strange organisms. One may admit that Breughel may have had satirical intentions. One may invoke the glowing mosaics of Monreale and the luminous glory of Chartres to protest the real triumph of Mediaeval man's depiction of the Absolute Good. But the triumph, like the permanent bliss of Heaven, could not be sustained. By the end of the Middle Ages the "beautiful" art of the Church—of Michelangelo, Fra Angelico, and Rafael—was concerning itself with the beauty of a world relative and natural rather than a world absolute and eternal. So far as the Christian imagination produced truly iconographic and devotional images at this time, they were not the marvelously anatomical studies of Michelangelo but the tortured Christs of Grunewald and the Baroque.

For piety could not sustain itself at the level of the formally sublime. By the time of the Renaissance and the Catholic Counter-Reformation Christian devotion was less and less inspired by the radiant, unearthly images of Christ and the Saints in glory. It turned to feast itself upon vivid, realistic images of the Passion. It produced the Spiritual Exercises of St. Ignatius, with their concentration of the imagination upon the horrors of Hell and the sufferings of the Saviour. It turned from the sublimely intellectual mysticism of the Victorines and St. Bonaventure to the mysticism of desolation typified in St. John of the Cross. It let loose the full fury of the Inquisition. And the turnabout was not only Catholic, for the Protestant piety of the same period was just as preoccupied with morbidity, and its inquisitions upon Papists no less cruel. For this was also the period of Calvin's damnation by predestination, of the fascination with death in the piety of Tudor and Stuart England, of *Paradise Lost*, and of the Puritans' unprecedented revel in spiritual gloom.

As an historical movement this was really an exaggeration, a breaking-loose, of a tendency which had existed throughout the Middle Ages, where there is already sufficient illustration of the truth of the ambivalence of psychic energy, of the fact that the perfectly good God necessarily creates the perfectly evil Devil by way of unconscious compensation, which, just because it is unconscious, is the one thing that theology cannot admit. Thus we may return, for example, to the end of the thirteenth century and consider the sculptured Last Judgement on the tympanum of Bourges Cathedral as a peculiarly vivid illustration of this ambivalence. One must bear it in mind that, to a very considerable extent, the attainment of perfect sanctity was identified with a suppression of lust. However, this does not go along with a simple avoidance of or indifference to lust and its objects. It requires a positive and energetic opposition to so great a natural force, leading to a kind of fury, of divine wrath, against everything that incites to lust. Yet as this increases it *becomes* lust. The blessed delight in the punishments of the damned because the infliction of pain is the symbolic, "unconscious" substitution for sexual conquest.[1] Thus the sculptor of Bourges can outwardly edify but secretly delight, because convention permits him to show the bodies of the damned naked. What is ostensibly a scene of the punishment of the lost by devils is *in fact* a portrayal of satyrs about to begin a sadistic orgy with a group of nymphs. By such a roundabout course a sculpture which might have adorned one of the more depraved Roman brothels turns up in the guise of ecclesiastical art.

Taken literally, the state of the blessed in Heaven is actually no less frightful than that of the damned in Hell. Here again we must remember that really profound theological minds have taken it literally, expecting in all seriousness a future resuscitation of the decomposed body to be the instrument of the soul's enjoyment of perpetual bliss. They maintain that the life of the soul-and-body in Heaven will be at once eternal, in the strict sense, and everlasting. For the supreme delight of Heaven is to be the Beatific Vision of God himself. Looking into the immeasurable depths of this Vision, the soul will see time as God sees it—all at once, past, present, and future embraced in a single moment of perception. Yet because the

[1] It should be added—not *necessarily* an unconscious substitute, for it is sometimes just another form of the same thing, a conscious exaggeration of sexual activity.

soul-and-body remains by nature finite and creaturely it will continue to dwell in the dimension of time, though by reason of its intimate union with the supernatural power of God it will not perish in time. It will contemplate the "moment" of eternity for an everlasting time. The body, with its senses inconceivably sharpened and amplified, will experience thrills of ecstasy and rapture beyond the wildest dreams of imagination, and will remain thus transported for always and always and always.

It will enjoy not only the infinitely satisfying Vision of God itself, but also the loving companionship and the incomparably varied beauties of the Saints and Angels, as well as everlasting fellowship with those whom it has loved upon earth.

> And I saw a new heaven and a new earth: for the first heaven and the first earth were passed away; and there was no more sea. . . . Behold, the tabernacle of God is with men, and he will dwell with them, and they shall be his people, and God himself shall be with them, and be their God. And God shall wipe away all tears from their eyes; and there shall be no more death, neither sorrow, nor crying, neither shall there be any more pain; for the former things are passed away.[1]

For the life of Heaven is by no means to be that of a disem-bodied soul floating through a radiant sky. There is to be "a new heaven and a new earth", a re-creation of the original Paradise Garden—the Rose Garden of Our Lady—a world of skies and landscapes, of intensities of light and colour, scent and texture, beyond anything yet seen under the fantastic spell of hemp and poppy. For out of his inexhaustible omnipotence God will create beauty upon beauty, wonder upon wonder, playing for ever with his children around the Tree of Life as if it were perpetually Christmas Day.

This is a beautiful conception—so long as one does not

[1] *Revelation* 21: 1, 3-4.

think or feel about it too deeply, so long as one takes it just as a glimpse and then turns away. It can, perhaps, be supposed that the divine omnipotence will arrange some miracle to prevent the terrible monotony of everlasting pleasure, and to make it possible for the mind to accumulate memories indefinitely without going mad. Yet it would seem that such miracles belong in the class of creating square circles, a class of *jeux d'omnipotence* of which the better theologians have never approved. In fact the delightful shock of wonder and the possibility of everlasting newness depend upon the miracle of forgetfulness. To be entranced eternally the blessed would have to forget eternally, so that the dance of omnipotence would not wear out the floor of memory with its tracks, so that the writing would not become illegible by reason of the crowded page. Now to forget is to die, since what we call physical death is above all else the destruction of a system of memories, of an "I". Such considerations lead us to a profounder under-standing of the myth of the Four Last Things.

The everlasting Heaven turns out to be no more than another form of Hell for the very reason that it is everlasting and is constituted by one of a pair of opposites. It never attains to God, to the Hand which holds the Dividers at the Pivot. Endless, it never reaches man's True End. The farther those on the Right are separated from those on the Left, the sooner they swing around the Pivot to find Hell beyond Heaven. For the End lies nowhere on the circle, nowhere in time, but only at the Pivot itself. Because we speak in figures of time and space it must seem that beyond the duality of Right and Left there is a further duality of Pivot and Circumference, Eternity and Time. Yet this is the illusion of language, for whatever is described is of the Circumference, described about the Centre. Some angel has taught us to use the circle for zero, for apart from, away from, its Centre the Circumference is nothing. And perhaps the same angel has led us to see that the Point of the Centre is no mere infinitesimal abstraction of a position without magnitude, but the very concrete necessity of an undefined Principle—without which nothing can ever be defined. Hence St. Bonaventure's inspired notion of God as the "circle whose centre is everywhere and whose circumference is nowhere".

The difficulty of geometrical mythology is that its abstract quality seems to deprive its meaning of rich reality, for it is hard to feel that a mere *point* can be creative. The living myths say more because they say it with living, concrete images; yet they say the same thing. Consider St. John's vision of the Heavenly City:

> Her light was like unto a stone most precious, even like a jasper stone, clear as crystal;[1] and had a wall great and high, and had twelve gates, and at the gates twelve angels, and names written thereon, which are the names of the twelve tribes of the children of Israel. On the East three gates; on the North three gates; on the South three gates; and on the West three gates. And the wall of the city had twelve foundations, and in them the names of the Twelve Apostles of the Lamb.[2] And he that talked with me had a golden reed to measure the city, and the gates thereof, and the wall thereof.[3] And the city lieth foursquare, and the length is as large as the breadth: and he measured the city with the reed,

[1] Austin Farrer in his *Rebirth of Images* relates the jasper stone to the Zodiacal sign of Virgo, so that the whole city ("*her* light") is an emblem of the Virgin Mother, who is also the Void ("clear as crystal") in which the past leaves no stain. Cf. *Rev.* 21: 27, "There shall in no wise enter into it any thing that defileth."

[2] Though, as we shall see, the city is conceived as a cube it is divided twelvefold as the circle. The common mythological motif of the *mandala* or "magic circle" very frequently combines circle and square.

[3] Again the measuring of the Mother with the Golden Rod of the Stem of Jesse. As life, creation, comes from the putting of the phallus to the womb, which is said to be "knowing" a woman, so, at the deeper level, the Void appears as the intelligible world of things by measurement, division, description —by the Word.

twelve thousand furlongs. The length and the breadth and the height of it are equal.[1] ... And the building of the wall of it was of jasper: and the city was pure gold, like unto clear glass. And the foundations of the wall of the city were garnished with all manner of precious stones. The first foundation was jasper; the second, sapphire; the third, a chalcedony; the fourth, an emerald; the fifth, sardonyx; the sixth, sardius; the seventh, chrysolyte; the eighth, beryl; the ninth, a topaz; the tenth, a chrysoprasus; the eleventh, a jacinth (hyacinth); the twelfth, an amethyst.[2]

And the twelve gates were twelve pearls; every several gate was of one pearl:[3] and the street of the city was pure gold, as it were transparent glass. And I saw no temple therein: for the Lord God Almighty and the Lamb are the temple of it.[4] And the city had no need of the sun, neither of the moon, to shine in it: for the glory of God did lighten it, and the Lamb is the light thereof.[5]

Perhaps the full force of this passage lies in the last lines, describing the disappearance of the luminaries marking the years and months and days. Time has gone. The opposites have likewise gone, for it is a common mythological image to

[1] Likewise the Holy of Holies was a cube, symbol of completion or perfection. Interestingly enough, the cube unfolded becomes the Latin Cross!

[2] With some variations these are the twelve stones of Aaron's breastplate, representing the twelve tribes and the twelve zodiacal signs. St. John's "jasper" is presumably a very clear amber—image of a void filled with light.

[3] A strange image indeed, unless one considers the gates as the minute holes through which pearls are strung. Thus we should have here another form of the "needle's eye". Hindu imagery likens the lives of men to pearls or beads upon a string, the string—which alone can pass the gate—being the *atman*, the true Self which is not this "I".

[4] For in the state of eternal life there is no further necessity of the Church, of the symbol communicating life to the dead.

[5] *Revelation* 21: 11–23.

let the sun and the moon stand for the right and left eyes,
whereby the ordinary man sees the world as dual. On the
other hand, the divine man sees life with the Third Eye,
revealing it to him as "non-dual". Thus, "if thine eye be
single, thy whole body shall be full of light".[1] Furthermore,
the whole image of the city is of the form of a *mandala*—that is,
of a foursquare circle or sphere, which, though a universal
symbol, appears most commonly in Buddhist art as a figure of
the reconciliation of all opposites in the "Void" (*sunyata*)—
symbolized in Buddhism by the *vajra* or diamond, and in the
Apocalypse by the jasper-stone.

The *mandala* form appears likewise in the vision of Dante, for
whom the company of the blessed is the Mystic Rose, imaging
the triple circle of light in which he finally beholds the Trinity
—the Point in the midst of the Rose, which seems to be embraced by what it embraces.[2] Visually as well as symbolically,
the obvious function of the *mandala* is to "frame" its own centre,
like the rings around the bull's-eye of a target, or to indicate a
centre sending forth effluence like the sun or a flower. The
streets from the twelve gates, the four arms of the Cross, and
the petals of the rose lead the eye to the centre at which they
meet, and from which they originate. Where it is not satisfied
with the human form itself, man's imagination everywhere
tends to represent the Ultimate End by this encircled Point,
this beginning and end of rays—*point* in that it endlessly
escapes definition, *circle* (or square, or cube) in that it embraces
the world in every direction.

This, then, is the image of the Centre of Heaven—the
Beatific Vision ringed about with the nine choirs of angels and
the transfixed hosts of Patriarchs and Prophets, Apostles and
Martyrs, Doctors and Confessors, and the whole company
of blessed ones—all together making up that Mystic Rose
which is, in turn, the Virgin of Virgins, Matrix of the World,
Māyā, radiating from and returning into its Origin. Imagery

[1] *Matthew* 6: 22.   [2] *Paradiso* xxx. 10.

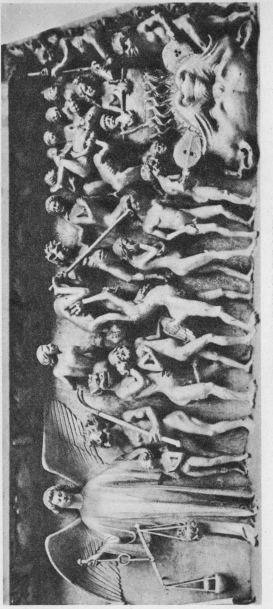

7. THE DAMNATION OF THE LOST

Scene from the tympanum of Bourges Cathedral, thirteenth century. Description in the text, p. 225.

8. CORONATION OF THE VIRGIN

("Die Krönung Mariae durch die Dreieinigkeit." French (?) Master J. M.
1457. Basel Museum.) A *mandala* representing the ultimate fulfilment of the
drama of creation. The crowning of the Virgin by the Holy Trinity is the
final divinization of Nature, of the created or manifested Universe, so that
the Trinity becomes in some sense a Quarternity. The central scene is surrounded by an inner ring of angels and an outer ring of Apostles, Prophets,
Martyrs, Virgins, and other Saints. The four corners are occupied by the
Tetramorph, the symbolic figures of the Four Evangelists and the Four Fixed
Signs of the Zodiac.

describes this Centre as a destination, an end, towards which man travels through time, and which lies beyond the Last Day of the future when the arrow of the soul will either plunge into its Mark, or miss it for ever. But we must not mistake that which is beyond the future for that which is in the future. Only Hell is in the future, for the more effectively man is able to prognosticate, the more he must be anxious and tremble. For the future has no other content than the disappearance of the past, which is what we think we are; it is by definition a time in which the past has no place. And thus the more accurately and realistically men consider the future, the more they are depressed.

> He that observeth the wind shall not sow; and he that regardeth the clouds shall not reap. . . . Truly the light is sweet, and a pleasant thing it is for the eyes to behold the sun: But if a man live many years, and rejoice in them all, yet let him remember the days of darkness, for they shall be many. All that cometh is vanity.[1]

Nevertheless popular Christianity has always been an expression of the hope that, in the future, beyond "the days of darkness" there will lie "the life of the world to come". In Heaven God is central, but on earth he is extreme—far out on the edges of time, the First Cause and the Last End. We have come from God in the forgotten past, and are on our way back to him in the distant future, so that here and now our life is one of exile and pilgrimage.

> To thee we exiles, children of Eve, lift our crying. To thee we are sighing, as mournful and weeping, we pass through this vale of sorrow. . . . Hereafter, when our earthly exile shall be ended, show us Jesus, the blessed fruit of thy womb, O gentle, O tender, O gracious Virgin Mary.[2]

[1] *Ecclesiastes* 11: 4, 7–8.   [2] Final Antiphon B.V.M., *Salve Regina*.

Whether in the poetry of the *Salve Regina* or the doggerel of
"There is a happy land, far, far away", this is the dominant
myth of Western culture both Christian and Humanist—the
myth of the impoverished present, empty of content. The
significance of life is felt to lie in its past history and its future
promise, so that the time in which we live seems almost to be
nothing—a hairline at most, fleeting, momentary, ever beyond
our grasp. As time goes on and, with the passing centuries,
Heaven recedes so far as to be implausible, we are forced
against every habit of will and imagination to see that time
takes us nowhere, so that—as always—the opposites change
places and hope becomes despair.

At the present time it is hard to say whether the Christian
myth is to stay with us as an effective power. Certain signs of
revival do not warrant hasty conclusions, for there is all the
difference in the world between genuine faith in God, on the
one hand, and the tormented intellectual's faith in faith, on
the other. As I have observed elsewhere,[1] much of the present
"return to religion" is based, not upon a veritable trust in God,
but upon the feeling that faith in the Christian God is a social
and psychological necessity. But Christianity cannot survive
in the role of a "therapeutic illusion", nor as a mere refuge of
authority and certainty for those who shrink from the bleak
consequences of logical thought, and still less as a nostalgic
self-indulgence for those who need it as a pretext for the
physical beauty of the Liturgy.

I do not feel that the Christian myth has anything left to tell
Western man unless he understands it outside-in. He must
discover that what seemed to be the far-off edges of time, where
God is Alpha and Omega, are the present, and that the
pilgrimage from earth to Heaven is not a journey into the future
but into the Centre. He must realize that the "death" through
which we must pass before God can be seen does not lie ahead
of us in time. "Death" is the point at which "I" come to an end,

[1] *The Wisdom of Insecurity* (New York, 1951), ch. 1.

and beyond which lies the unknown, and this point is not "on" but "in". "The kingdom of God is within you."[1] For if I explore myself a little way, I come to a point where I do not understand or recognize myself any more. The "I was" which I know becomes the "I am" which I never see. The roots of my consciousness disappear into an unknown region where I am as foreign to myself as to the pulse of my heart and the currents of my nerves. For what is most truly and inwardly myself is ever beyond that small area of knowledge and control which is called the ego. Paradoxically, the most central and fundamental region of my being seems to be most "other"—like the God of theistic imagery. Thus while I think of the ego as my actual *self*, I am off-centre. I am "beside myself", so that the coursing of my blood and all the deeper processes of body and mind seem to be the work of someone or something else, giving a sensation of strangeness and "the creeps" when I feel them.

This basic "shift" in the position of God from the periphery of the world to the centre requires also a shift of faith. We have to recognize that the totally undefinable and incomprehensible "something" which is our most inward self is—in all important respects—beyond our control. For the self which knows and controls is never, at the same time, the known and controlled.[2] This is the most important lesson in the world for a civilization which aspires to omnipotence, to the control of *everything*. For every attempt to establish total control on the part of the

---

[1] As one would expect, the "social-gospellers" interpret *Luke* 17: 21 as "The kingdom of God is *among* you"—in terms of the "fellowship" of the Church. This is in line with the current theological fashion for avoiding all "mystical" interpretations because of the inability to distinguish between what is truly inward and what is merely subjective and "psychological".

[2] "Self-control" is always a form of "feed-back" mechanism. But in every such mechanism there is a lag between the initial action and the return of information making it possible to correct the action, so that literally instantaneous control of the controller is ever impossible. Furthermore, the feed-back mechanism is self-correcting in relation to its environment rather than in relation to itself.

conscious ego starts a vicious circle. Thus our culture becomes
a system of controls in which the solution of each problem
simply multiplies the number of problems to be solved, as in
the myth of the Hydra monster who grows seven new heads
for each one cut off. The complete control of life is impossible
for the reason that we are part of it, and that, in the last
analysis, the system is not a thing controlled but a thing
controlling.[1]

We are therefore compelled to have faith in something
which is at once ourselves, in the most basic sense, and
not ourselves, in the sense of the ego, the remembered "I".
But this faith cannot have any tangible content, such as a
system of beliefs, for the simple reason that the fundamental Self cannot be defined.[2] Therefore it is not to be verbalized
positively as a believing in or about. It is to be expressed
negatively, as a *not* trying to control and to grasp, as a
"letting-go" and not as a "holding-to". Furthermore, such
"letting-go" faith must come about not as a positive work
to be done, but through the realization that there is really
nothing else to do, since it is actually impossible to grasp
the inmost Self.

The positive consequences of this faith in terms of love, joy,
and illumination are strictly gratuitous. They emerge unpre-
dictably and uncontrollably from the inner depths. The
"letting-go" removes the obstacle to their coming, but the
actual coming, the Second Advent, is "like a thief in the
night", and we "know not the day nor the hour". Generally
speaking, they follow immediately upon the act of release.
The apparent delay is usually due to the fact that one is trying
to force their arrival, so that the release is not actually complete.

---

[1] Gödel has now proved that no system can explain its own axioms without
self-contradiction, in an elaborate mathematico-logical verification of the point
that a knife cannot cut itself.

[2] And this, furthermore, is the proper sense of the "supernatural"—that
which transcends "nature", where nature is understood as classification, genera,
species, etc.

And the mind stops "forcing" only through the clear conviction of its uselessness.[1]

As soon as one gets used to looking at the Christian images from this outside-in point of view, it becomes obvious that, in this way, they make sense as they never did before. God returns to his temple, the heart, the centre of all things—of man, of time, of space. Heaven is no longer in the place of Hell, the "outer darkness" of the most distant spaces and far-off times, but appears in the place of the most intense reality—the *now*. Christ actually rises from the dead, and is revealed in *this* moment, and is no more locked up in the tomb of the remote past, in the dead letter of the written Gospels. The Mass is for once effectively sacrificed, for the Body of Christ, the Church, is really willing to be broken, finding no further need to hold itself together with definitions and claims. The Faith becomes actual *faith*, which is self-surrender, as distinct from all anxious clinging to dogmatic rocks and doctrinal idols. The authority of the Church becomes self-evident, which is to say that the Church actually realizes authority, so that there is no more necessity to prove it, to convince itself, by exaggerated proselytism and preposterous claims of spiritual monopoly. The dispensation of the Law, in which virtue is forced, actually gives way to the dispensation of Grace, in which virtue happily "happens", and is not grotesquely imitated.

So understood, the marvelous symbols of Christianity might still—one is tempted to say, might begin to—have a message for Western man, that anxious and restless eccentric who has "no time" because he has reduced his present to an abstract dividing line between past and future, and who confuses his very self with a past which is no more and a future which is not

[1] This is not the place to enter into a detailed account of the psychology of mystical faith and spiritual experience—a subject which I have discussed in a number of works entirely devoted to it, such as *The Meaning of Happiness* (2nd edn., Stanford, 1953), *Behold the Spirit* (New York, 1947), *The Supreme Identity* (London and New York, 1950), and *The Wisdom of Insecurity* (New York, 1951).

yet. He, too, needs to be turned outside-in, to live in the real world which he thinks is abstract, instead of in the abstract world which he takes for reality. And for this he must know that the true place of Bethlehem, Calvary and Olivet is no more in history, and that Death, the Second Advent, and Heaven are not in a time to come. His "sin", his missing of the point, can only be forgiven if he repents—turns back—from his past, as from the future which it implies, and returns again to his Creator, the present reality from which he "ex-ists". Whereupon the life which had seemed momentary would be found momentous, and that present which had seemed to be no time at all would be found to be eternity.

GLOSSARY

A

ABSOLUTION
The form of words whereby a priest or bishop absolves or frees a penitent from the penalty of everlasting damnation incurred through sin.

ACOLYTE
Originally one of the seven Holy Orders (see Chapter VI). One who serves or assists the clergy at the altar, and in the various ritual and ceremonial functions of the Church.

ADONAI
A Hebrew word meaning "the Lord", cognate to the Greek Adonis and possibly to the Egyptian Aton or Aten. When the Hebrew scriptures are read aloud, the word is always used in place of the written Tetra grammaton (q.v.) YHVH—the unutterable Name of God.

ALLELUIA
In Hebrew "Hallelujah"—"Sing praise to YHVH." An exclamation of praise, adoration and joy, constituting the eternal song of the saints and angels in heaven. Actually a "non sense" sound, expressive of a state of consciousness beyond any sense which words can express. It is not sung in the Church between Septuagesima and Good Friday inclusive, but is particularly connected with the joy of Easter. As a part of the Proper of the Mass, the Alleluia is a verse sung immediately after the Gradual (q.v.), and during the Lenten season its place is taken by the Tract.

ANAMNESIS
A Greek word signifying the "re collection" of Christ's Sacrifice, some times translated "memorial". In particular, it is that part of the Canon (q.v.) of the Mass in which the action of Christ at the Last Supper is repeated, in obedience to the commandment, "Do this in remembrance of me".

ANTIPHON
From the Greek "contrary sounding", as when a choir is divided into two parts so as to sing antiphonally, one part responding to the other through the alternating verses of a psalm or canticle. More particularly, an antiphon is a verse, changing with the season, which is sung at the beginning and at the end of psalms and canticles (q.v.).

APOCALYPSE

In Greek, the exposure of hidden things, or revelation. The opposite is "anacalypse". Thus it is the Greek title of the last book of the *New Testament*, called *Revelation* in the English Bible. This book belongs to a class of Jewish literature called "apocalyptic", books looking forward to a catastrophic intervention of God in the course of events, usually written in symbolic language so as to be understood only by those "in the know".

APOSTOLIC SUCCESSION

The tradition of faith, sacrament, and worship handed down from the original Apostles—those "sent forth" into the world by Christ himself. To be in the Apostolic Succession is to receive both the faith and order of the Church from the supposedly unbroken line of bishops descending from the Apostles themselves.

APSE

The space enclosed by the semicircular East wall of a church sanctuary, or other semicircular alcove.

ARK OF THE COVENANT

A receptacle placed in the Holy of Holies (q.v.) of the Hebrew Temple. It consisted of a box surmounted by a throne, the back and arms of which were in the form of outstretched wings. The box was said to contain the Stone Tables of the Law written by Moses, a vessel of the "bread from heaven" or *manna* found by the Israelites in the Wilderness, and the *nehushtan*, or brazen serpent. The Ark is believed to have been made under the direction of Moses himself, and to have been preserved in the Temple of Jerusalem until at least the sixth century B.C.

ATONEMENT

The reconciliation or "at-one-ment" of God and man achieved by the Sacrifice of Christ.

AVATAR

The Sanskrit word for an incarnation of Vishnu, of the Supreme Reality, in human form.

B

BAPTISM

The sacrament (q.v.) of initiation into the Christian Mystery, consisting of being immersed in water, or in having water poured upon the body, in the Name of the Holy Trinity. Its effect is spiritual regeneration, or rebirth, whereby man is "en-Christed" (christened), involving both union with Christ and the remission of sin.

BASILICA

The Greek word for the throne-room of a *basileus*, or king. Thus a cathedral-church (q.v.) patterned after such a throne-room. The word is now used as a title for certain major shrines of the Catholic Church, the first of which is St. Peter's in Rome.

BENEDICTUS

The Canticle (q.v.) of Zacharias, father of St. John the Baptist, found in *Luke* 1: 68. Its regular place in the worship of the Church is in the Office of Lauds (q.v.) and also at the Burial of the Dead. The opening words are, "Blessed (Lat., *benedictus*) be the Lord God of Israel; for he hath visited and redeemed his people". The word is also used for that part of the ordinary of the Mass which is sung immediately after the Sanctus (q.v.)—"*Benedictus qui venit*—Blessed is he that cometh in the Name of the Lord. Hosanna in the highest!"

BHAGAVAD-GITA

Sanskrit, "The Lord's Song". Perhaps the most celebrated scripture of the Hindus, being an epitome of Hindu doctrine attributed to Krishna, the great Avatar (q.v.) of Vishnu.

BREVIARY

The book of the divine office (q.v.) recited daily by all clerics of the Catholic Church, whether ordained or simply in religious orders—i.e. monks or friars below the rank of Subdeacon, commonly called lay brothers. Also used in religious orders for women. The Breviary is usually published in four volumes, one for each of the seasons.

C

CANON

The Greek word for a rule, standard or level, used ecclesiastically in the following senses: (1) Canon of the Mass. The central section of the ordinary, or unvarying part, of the Mass, sometimes called the Prayer of Consecration whereby the priest effects the transubstantiation of the

Bread and Wine. (2) Canon of Scripture. The books of the Old and New Testaments, sanctioned by the Church as the authentic Word of God. In the Roman Catholic Church this includes also the books of the *Apocrypha*, called deutero-canonical because they were admitted to the Canon at a later date. (3) The Canonical Hours. The regular Hours (q.v.) of the divine office (q.v.). (4) Canon. A cleric living under a rule, usually attached to the staff of a cathedral (q.v.).

CANTICLE

A song. The word is applied to scriptural hymns other than the psalms employed in the service of the Church. In the plural, *Canticles*, it is another name for the *Song of Songs* attributed to Solomon. The main canticles used in the Church are the *Benedicite*, or the Song of the Three Children found in the book of *Daniel*; the three Gospel Canticles—*Benedictus* (*Luke* 1: 68) sung at Lauds, *Magnificat* (*Luke* 1: 46) sung at Vespers, and *Nunc dimittis* (*Luke* 2: 29) sung at Compline; the *Venite*, which is *Psalm* 95, used as a Canticle at Lauds; and the *Te Deum*, an ancient hymn of praise, purely Christian in origin, sung on occasions of solemn thanksgiving.

CATHEDRAL

A church designated as the "seat" (Gk., *cathedra*) of a bishop, and in which is therefore to be found an episcopal throne.

CATHOLIC

The Greek term for "universal", "all-inclusive", and "complete"—literally, "according to the whole". As a matter of fact, almost all Christians claim to belong to the Catholic Church, though the term Catholic must be understood not only as the Church inclusive of all Christians, but also as the Church inclusive of all the fulness of faith, order, and worship handed down in scripture and tradition. In popular use it designates those Christians in communion with the See or Episcopal Jurisdiction of the Pope, who is the Bishop of Rome. But the designation Catholic, in its fullest sense, is also claimed by the Eastern Orthodox and the Anglican Communions.

CENSER

Also called thurible. A vessel of brass, gold, or silver, usually hung on chains, for the burning of incense. The acolyte (q.v.) who carries it is termed the Thurifer.

CEREMONY

Strictly speaking, this term should be distinguished from rite (q.v.), for ceremonial is the adornment of a ritual action by such marks of reverence as the carrying of candles, the performance of reverential gestures such as kneeling, genuflection, kissing, etc.

CHALICE

The golden or silver goblet in which the wine is consecrated at Mass. The usual form is that of a plain cup, having a stem with a boss at the centre, and a wide, heavy base. Uniform with it is the Paten or plate upon which is laid the Host (q.v.).

CHANCEL

From the Latin *cancellarium*—the screen dividing the choir and sanctuary of a church from the nave. Thus it comes to mean that part of the church which lies behind the choir-screen.

CLERGY, CLERGYMAN, CLERIC

Originally from the Gk. *clēros*, a lot, as in casting lots. Applied to the clergy as those "drawn" to perform a sacred function. Thus, through the Lat. *clericus*, we get clear, clever, or, in other words, literate. The terms date from a time when the only literate persons—clerks—were either in holy or religious orders.

COLLECT

Lat., *oratio*. The "prayer of the day" used at Mass, before the Lesson (q.v.), and at each of the Canonical Hours (q.v.). The collect changes with the feast or the season, is usually quite brief, and is always introduced with the formula: *Dominus vobiscum* (The Lord be with you), to which is answered, *Et cum spiritu tuo* (And with thy spirit), and then *Oremus* (Let us pray).

COMMON

A section of the proper or variable part of both Mass and Office used upon feasts of the saints when either the particular feast or the particular saint has no specific proper assigned. On such occasions one uses the Common (or "all-purpose") propers provided for Martyrs, Doctors, Virgins, etc., as the case may be.

COMMUNIO

That part of the proper or variable section of the Mass which is sung at the time of Communion (q.v.).

COMMUNION

(1) The reception of the Body and Blood of Christ under the forms of Bread and Wine. Communion is normally received by the faithful at Mass, and always by the celebrating priest. It may also be received outside Mass, as when the priest takes it to the bed of one sick or dying. (2) A group of Christians in Communion with one another, who, by reason of unanimity in matters of faith and order, will celebrate Mass and receive Communion together. Those outside such a Communion are, from its standpoint, ex-communicate. (3) Communion of Saints. The *koinonia* or fellowship of all members of the Body of Christ, of all realizing him as their Head or real Self.

COMPLINE
v. Hours.

COPE
v. Vesture.

CREED

Lat., *Credo*, a summary of the articles of faith. The Catholic Church has three Creeds: (1) The Nicene-Constantinopolitan, dating from the fourth century, which is sung at Mass after the Gospel for the day. (2) The Apostles' Creed, of uncertain but early date, in general a shorter form of the Nicene. Recited in the divine Office (q.v.). (3) The so-called Athanasian Creed or *Quicumque vult*, from the first words, "Whosoever would be saved", dating from the ninth century, and recited on certain occasions at Matins.

D

DEACON

From the Greek *diakono*, to minister or serve. Deacons occupy the third rank of the Holy Orders (*v.* Chap. VI) and their traditional function is to assist the priest at Mass and in other sacraments, to sing the Gospel at Mass, and to have care of the sick and needy of the Church.

E

ELEVATION

The ceremonial climax of the Mass, when, immediately after the consecration of the sacred elements, the priest genuflects and elevates first the Host (q.v.) and then the Chalice (q.v.) in the sight of the people. This act is accompanied by the solemn ringing of bells, at the altar and in the church tower, and with the offering of incense.

EMBER DAY

The Ember Days occur four times a year, being set aside as special days for the ordination of priests and deacons, and for the prayers of the people for the clergy.

EPISTLE

(1) The books of the *New Testament* which are the epistles or letters of the Apostles, such as St. Paul, St. John, and St. James, to the early congregations of the Church. (2) The portion of such an Epistle read at Mass, by the Subdeacon, immediately after the Collect (q.v.) and before the Gradual (q.v.).

EXORCISM

The casting out of devils from a person, church or house, or from any object intended for holy use.

F

FONT

Lat., *fons*, fountain. The receptacle for the baptismal waters, usually a large stone bowl mounted upon a pedestal and placed by the West door of the church. Sometimes a sunken bath or stone-lined pool.

G

GLORIA

(1) The hymn *Gloria in excelsis Deo* (Glory be to God on high) sung at Mass immediately after the Kyrie (q.v.). (2) The doxology (ascription of glory) *Gloria Patri* sung at the end of each psalm in the divine office (q.v.). "Glory be to the Father and to the Son and to the Holy Spirit. As it was in the beginning, is now, and ever shall be, unto all the ages of ages. Amen."

GOSPEL

The *god* (good) *spell* (tidings), or *ev-* (good) *-angel* (message), constituted by the life and teaching of the Christ, and recorded in the Four Gospels. More particularly, the portion of the Gospel solemnly sung by the Deacon at Mass.

GRADUAL

That section of the proper or variable part of the Mass which is sung immediately after the Lesson or Epistle (q.v.), while incense is blessed and other preparations made for the singing of the Gospel.

GREGORIAN CHANT

The traditional music of the Catholic Church, otherwise known as Plainchant. So named from the particular encouragement and advancement of its use by Pope Gregory the Great (*d.* 604) in the sixth century. A type of unharmonized, modal chanting designed to be sung unaccompanied and to follow the natural rhythm of the spoken word.

H

HOLY OF HOLIES

The inmost sanctuary of the Hebrew Temple, containing the Ark of the Covenant (q.v.). It was constructed in the form of a perfect cube, symbolizing the wholeness of God, and was entered but once a year, and by the High Priest alone.

HOLY WATER

A mixture of water and salt, both of which are solemnly exorcized and blessed for the banishment of devils and for the infusion of divine grace. Its primary use is for the rite of the Asperges, the sprinkling of the people, which occurs immediately before High Mass each Sunday. Otherwise it is placed in a stoup or small basin at the entrance of churches, and kept by the faithful in their homes. It is used on almost all occasions when objects are specially blessed for holy use. Sprinkling with holy water is usually accompanied by the recitation of the words from *Psalm* 51 (Vulg., 50) *Asperges me hyssopo,* "Thou shalt purge me with hyssop and I shall be clean; thou shalt wash me and I shall be whiter than snow".

HOST

Lat., *hostia,* victim. The round wafer of unleavened bread which is consecrated in the Mass to become the Body of Christ—the sacrificial Victim. These mass-breads are of two kinds, large and small. The large is the one elevated in the sight of the people, broken at the Fraction, and used for the Communion of the celebrating priest. The small are for the Communion of the congregation. Normally they are made with wheat-flour and water, with a little salt, and before baking are embossed with some sacred emblem, such as the crucifix or the sacred monogram IHC.

HOURS

The daily Hours of Prayer constituting the divine office (q.v.) and contained in the Breviary (q.v.). While the phrase "the Hours" often refers to those Offices named after the hours themselves—Prime, Terce, Sext, and None—the Hours may be taken to mean all eight Offices. These are: Matins (the "night-office", properly sung between midnight and 3 a.m.), Prime (between 3 and 6 a.m.) followed by Lauds, Terce (between 8 and 9 a.m.), Sext (between 11 a.m. and noon), None (between noon and 3 p.m.), Vespers (between 3 and 6 p.m.), and Compline (about 9 p.m.). In religious communities silence is observed after Compline, and continues until the end of breakfast the following day. The actual times at which the Offices are sung varies from place to place in accordance with custom and convenience.

I

ICON
Gk., *eikon*, image. Specifically a holy picture of Christ or of the saints or angels, such as are particularly venerated in the Eastern Orthodox Church. Usually an icon shows the figure of the sacred personage painted in accordance with archaic Byzantine traditions against a background of gold, representing the encompassing presence of God. In later times such icons were overlaid with sheet gold and embellished with precious stones.

ICONOGRAPHY
The science of sacred pictures and images—their execution, symbolism, and identification.

INTROIT
The words of the proper or variable part of the Mass which are sung at the beginning of the rite, before the Kyrie (q.v.), while the clergy say the prayers of Preparation and the altar is censed. The introit usually consists of a part of one of the psalms, with an antiphon (q.v.).

K

KYRIE
Gk., *kyrios*, lord. That part of the Latin Mass which is sung in Greek immediately after the Introit (q.v.). The words are *Kyrie eleison* (Lord have mercy), *Christe eleison* (Christ have mercy), *Kyrie eleison* (Lord have mercy). Each petition is repeated thrice, and addressed respectively to the Father, the Son, and the Holy Spirit.

L

LAUDS

v. Hours.

LESSON

(1) Any liturgical reading from the Scriptures. (2) The portion from one of the Epistles (q.v.) or from the *Old Testament* or *Apocrypha* sung at Mass by the Subdeacon immediately after the Collect (q.v.) for the day.

LITANY

A form of prayer consisting of short versicles and responses (q.v.) said or sung between the priest or a cantor and the congregation—e.g. the Litany of the Saints, sung on Holy Saturday, or the Litany for the Dying.

LITURGY

Gk., *leitos*, public, *ourgos*, work. (1) The entire rite (q.v.) of the Church's official and public worship, comprising the Mass, the divine office, and the administration of the Seven sacraments. (2) The Mass in particular, normally termed the Divine Liturgy in the Eastern Orthodox Church. In the Eastern Church it is customary to "make the Liturgy" rather than to "say" or "hear" Mass, reflecting the proper sense of Christian worship as an action *done* by the whole Church, as distinct from a form of words *said* by the hierarchy in the presence of the people.

M

MASS

Lat., *missa*, from the words of dismissal "*Ite missa est*", a problematic utterance meaning something like "Go, the mass is done", or "Go, it is sent forth" (Lat., *mitto*, send). Thus the Mass is the celebration of the Lord's Supper as the central act of Christian worship, on which see Chap. V. The order of Mass is as follows (see other articles in Glossary for specific terms):

Mass of the Catechumens:	*Mass of the Faithful:*
Introit	Offertory
Kyrie	Preface
Gloria	Sanctus and Benedictus

Mass of the Catechumens:	*Mass of the Faithful:*
Collect	Canon (of Consecration)
Lesson or Epistle	"Our Father"
Gradual and Alleluia (or Tract)	Fraction and Kiss of Peace
Gospel	Agnus Dei
Nicene Creed	Communion
	Post-Communion Collect
	Dismissal and Blessing

The traditional and proper celebration of Mass is in the form known as High Mass, which is sung, and requires three clerics—priest, deacon, and subdeacon—taking their appointed parts. So-called Low Mass is a mediaeval innovation wherein the Mass is said by a priest alone, so as to become a sort of private devotion for the priest. This latter custom emerged from the "chantry-system", chantries being small side-chapels provided so that every priest might say one Mass a day so as to assign the full measure of its benefits to some such cause as the repose of a particular soul in Purgatory, or the recovery of a sick person. Such treatment of the Mass arose from a quantitative philosophy of the divine Grace, and represented the decay of the liturgical or corporate nature of Christian worship.

MATINS
v. Hours.

MISSAL
The mass-book placed upon the altar for the Mass, containing all the words to be sung and said, and the rubrics describing the ritual and cere-monial actions to be done. Modern missals are actually "omnibus volumes" containing what were originally a number of separate books—the *Sanctorale* containing the parts, such as the Canon, to be said by the celebrant, the *Graduale* containing the propers or variable parts to be sung by the choir, the book of Lessons and Epistles to be sung by the sub-deacon, and the book of Gospels to be sung by the deacon.

O

OCTAVE
The week following certain feasts, consisting of eight days inclusive of the feast itself, during which the proper parts of Mass and Office appro-priate to the feast continue to be said.

OFFERTORY

(1) The opening action of the Mass of the Faithful, being the presentation of Bread and Wine at the altar. The Host is offered upon the Paten, or plate, and the Wine is offered in the Chalice, mixed with a little water specially blessed at this time, except in masses for the dead. Anciently both the Bread and the Wine were brought to the altar by the whole congregation, with other gifts. (2) The words of the proper or variable part of the Mass sung at this time by the choir.

OFFICE, THE DIVINE

The daily recitation of the Psalms by all clerics, in the form of the canonical Hours (q.v.). Probably instituted by St. Benedict in the sixth century, this custom is called the *Opus Dei*, the "work of God". Together with the Mass, the divine office constitutes the essential "prayer of the Church", showing that the Catholic philosophy of prayer is something quite other than the popular notion of the individual addressing his petitions and aspirations to God. For the Psalms are understood to be the "songs of the Holy Spirit", so that in reciting them man speaks to God with the voice of God. The point is that one cannot and does not pray as an individual, but only in so far as one is "no longer I, but Christ", as a member of the Mystical Body.

P

PASSION SUNDAY

The fifth Sunday in Lent, and the second before Easter, inaugurating the two-week season of Passiontide.

PATRISTICS

The study of the lives and writings of the Church Fathers—i.e. the great theologians and historians of the Eastern and Western Churches during the first ten centuries.

PERSON

When God is said to be three Persons and one God the English "Person" is a translation of the Greek *hypostasis*, for which we have no exact equivalent. By analogy, ice, water and steam are three hypostases of a single "substance", or, in Greek, *ousia*. In the same way, the three Persons of the Trinity are said to be "of one substance" (*homoousios*), which is God, yet nevertheless each of the three is a distinct hypostasis.

PREFACE

The Canon of the Mass (q.v.) is introduced with a recitation by the priest which is called the Preface. It is sung to a very ancient chant, and opens with the words, *Vere dignum et justum est*—"It is truly meet and just, and availing to salvation, that we should at all times and in all places give thanks unto thee, holy Lord, almighty Father, eternal God. . . .' The Proper Prefaces involve the insertion of some extra sentences into this formula at certain feasts and seasons. It ends with a reference to the praise of God by all the angelic hosts, and there follows at once the Sanctus (q.v.).

R

RESPONSE

The reply of the choir and/or congregation to a versicle (q.v.) sung by the priest or deacon, usually brief in form—e.g. V. The Lord be with you. R. And with thy spirit. V. Hearts on high! R. We lift them up to the Lord.

RESPONSORY

An antiphon (q.v.) containing repeated phrases.

RITE

Originally the Sanskrit *rita*, Lat., *ritus*. The action or deed constituting worship, together with the accompanying form of words which declare its meaning. "Rite" is thus almost equivalent to "liturgy" (q.v.). To be distinguished from ceremonial (q.v.), which is the ornamentation of ritual. Christian liturgy comprises a number of different rites, associated with the great historical centres of Christendom, such as Rome, Byzantium, Alexandria, etc.

RITUALE

A manual containing the forms of administering sacraments other than the Mass, with the exception of those administered by a bishop—which are contained in the *Pontificale*. It contains also the various forms of blessing and exorcism, as well as other devotions.

S

SACRAMENT

Gk., *mysterion*, Lat., *sacramentum*. A divinely instituted action with some material object which, though performed by the human agency of the Church, is in fact an action of God. Thus every sacrament comprises (*a*) the matter (e.g. the water in Baptism), (*b*) the form—the way in which the matter is used and the words which must accompany such use, and (*c*) the spiritual power or grace which the sacrament confers. See Chap. VI.

SANCTUS
Gk., *trisagion*. The angelic hymn, *Sanctus, sanctus, sanctus*—"Holy, holy, holy, Lord God of hosts. Heaven and earth are full of thy glory. Hosanna in the highest". In the Mass it follows the Preface and, with the addition of the Benedictus (q.v.), immediately precedes the Canon, *Te igitur*.

SARUM BREVIARY
Anciently Sarum or Salisbury was one of the great centres of the English Church, and had its own special rite or liturgy (q.v.), contained in the Sarum Missal and the Sarum Breviary. See "Breviary".

SHEKINAH
(Hebrew)—the glory or radiance of YHVH, which especially shone around the Ark in the Holy of Holies (q.v.). In later Hebrew theology the *shekinah* is substantially identical with YHVH himself.

STOLE
v. Vesture.

T

TETRAGRAMMATON
The four Hebrew letters of the Name of God, YHVH, or Jod, He, Vau, He, read in Hebrew from right to left thus: יְהוָה.

U

UPANISHADS
Ancient Hindu scriptures compiled between about 800 and 400 B.C., and containing the foundations of the central doctrines of Hindu metaphysic, known as the Vedanta—the "end" or "fulfilment" of the Veda. Veda or "the Vedas" is the divine knowledge (root, *vid*, to know) contained in the most ancient mythological and ritual texts of the Hindus, dating from at least 1500 B.C.

USE
An English synonym for Rite (q.v.).

V

VERSICLE

Literally a verse. A short exhortation or prayer uttered by the officiant at any service, to which the choir and/or congregation gives a response (q.v.). E.g. V. O God make speed to save us. R. O Lord make haste to help us.

VESPERS

v. Hours.

VESTURE

The ritual vestments of the Church are ecclesiastical adaptations of various types of secular clothing worn in the Graeco-Roman world. Thus the vestments of the priest at Mass are the alb (Gk., *chlamys*), a long robe of white linen, the amice, a white linen hood, the cincture, a linen girdle, the stole (Lat., *orarium*), a long band of silk hung around the neck which was formerly a cloth for wiping the mouth, the maniple, a short band of silk worn over the left wrist, originally a ceremonial handkerchief, and the chasuble (Lat., *casula*, "little house"), an almost circular "poncho" of silk hanging from the neck-hole to below the knees. In place of the chasuble the deacon wears the dalmatic, and the sub-deacon the tunicle, both of which are types of Byzantine tunic. At other functions than the Mass a common vestment is the cope, a large silken cloak with a formal hood worn hanging from the shoulders. The modern surplice, not unlike a night-shirt, often decked out with lace, is a barbarous vestment from Northern latitudes, originally used to cover up fur undergarments in cold weather. Silk vestments change in colour, in accordance with feasts and seasons (except in the Eastern Church). White is for feasts of Christ and the Virgin, and of all saints other than martyrs; Red is for feasts of the Holy Spirit and of martyrs; Purple is for penetential seasons—Advent and Lent; Green is for "ferial" days, when there is no special feast; Black is for Good Friday and for masses of the dead.

INDEX